WITHDRAWN

P9-DTF-085

MIDEAST BEAST

THE SCRIPTURAL CASE
FOR AN ISLAMIC ANTICHRIST

MIDEAST BEAST

NEW YORK TIMES BESTSELLER

JOEL RICHARDSON

 WND Books

MIDEAST BEAST

WND Books
Washington, D.C.

Copyright © 2012
Joel Richardson

All rights reserved. No part of this book may be reproduced in any form or by any means, electronic, mechanical, photocopying, scanning, or otherwise, without permission in writing from the publisher, except by a reviewer who may quote brief passages in a review.

Book Designed by Mark Karis

WND Books are distributed to the trade by:
Midpoint Trade Books
27 West 20th Street, Suite 1102
New York, NY 10011

WND Books are available at special discounts for bulk purchases. WND Books, Inc. also publishes books in electronic formats. For more information call (541-474-1776) or visit www.wndbooks.com.

First Edition

Hardcover ISBN: 978-1-936488-53-7
eBook ISBN: 978-1-936488-85-8

Unless otherwise indicated, Scripture quotations are from the English Standard Version. © 2001 by Crossway Bibles, a division of Good News Publishers. Scripture quotations marked NKJV are from THE NEW KING JAMES VERSION. © 1982 by Thomas Nelson, Inc. Used by permission. All rights reserved. are from Scripture quotations marked NASB are from the NEW AMERICAN STANDARD BIBLE®, © The Lockman Foundation 1960, 1962, 1963, 1968, 1971, 1972, 1973, 1975, 1977, 1995. Used by permission. Scripture quotations marked NIV are taken from the Holy Bible, New International Version®, NIV®. Copyright © 1973, 1978, 1984 by Biblica, Inc.™ Used by permission of Zondervan. All rights reserved worldwide. www.zondervan.com

Library of Congress information available

Printed in the United States of America
10 9 8 7 6 5 4 3 2

TO MY WIFE

ONLY A GREAT GOD could bless me with a woman as beautiful in every way as you. I wish I wrote about subjects more befitting to receive your dedication, but alas, you married *me*. For now, your name is honored in books about the Antichrist, but in the future, your name will be honored in the golden streets of the New Jerusalem.

TABLE OF CONTENTS

ACKNOWLEDGMENTS

I WOULD LIKE TO FIRST THANK and acknowledge my wife for her long-suffering and patient endurance during the writing of this book. Second, I would like to thank Joseph Farah. The Christian publishing industry needs more courageous forerunners like you. Credit also belongs to Johnny Walker, Ben Wallick, Daryl Surber, Dax Cabrera, Josh Godsey, Anthony Perkins, Billy Humphrey, Jamie Pridgen, Steven Ugan, and Stephen Holmes for reading through and assisting me with suggestions, comments, and such. Thank you, men.

I would like to thank Scott Watts for standing behind me as only he knows he has done these past couple of years. I'm quite sure that when I finish trimming my wife's hedgerow, much of my free time will be spent attending to some form of menial yard care on your mansion in the messianic kingdom. Looking forward to it.

Thanks to John and Lydia Harrigan for your friendship and helping me see the cross and the coming messianic kingdom with such clarity.

To all those who have supported me in prayer these past few years, thank you so much!

PREFACE

I N 2006, MY FIRST BOOK was published as *Antichrist: Islam's Awaited Messiah*, but later republished as *The Islamic Antichrist*. On the surface, the book was a comparison of Islamic and biblical eschatology (the study of the end-times), but in spirit, it was also my best attempt to blow a trumpet and sound an alarm. I am firmly convinced that Islam is the single greatest challenge that the Church will face before the return of Jesus, yet most are still either asleep or in denial. *Islamic Antichrist* was my sincere and deeply heartfelt effort to awaken the believing community from its slumber regarding the looming challenge and relevance of Islam as well as its premier role in the last days. And beyond this, the book was a call to action; to imitate Jesus, embrace the cross, and fearlessly give ourselves to the Muslim world, so as to perhaps snatch a few from the fire.

Islamic Antichrist set the basic biblical end-time narrative side by side with the Islamic vision of the end-times. The resultant picture brings to light the shocking reality that as a religious system, Islam is anti-Christ to its very core. Islam's basic doctrines represent a direct frontal attack against Christianity, declaring many of those doctrines that the Bible sets forth as holy, foundational, and essential to be the greatest abominations and blasphemies imaginable. Whereas the Christian faith is founded upon the belief that God Himself became a man in Jesus the Messiah, Islam declares in its Qur'an that anyone who believes in the Incarnation commits the worst form of blasphemy imaginable, is cursed by Allah, and will suffer "a grievous penalty" in this life and in the next. Beyond this, Islam's end-times narrative, in so many ways, is simply the biblical end-time story flipped on its head. While the whole book cannot be summarized here, just a couple of brief examples should paint a sufficient picture.

First, the biblical descriptions regarding the coming of Jesus the Jewish Messiah bear many striking resemblances to the coming Antichrist of Islam, whom Muslims refer to as the *al-maseeh al-dajjaal* (the counterfeit Messiah). Second, the Bible's Antichrist bears numerous striking commonalities with the primary messiah figure of Islam, who Muslims call the Mahdi. In other words, our Messiah is their antichrist and our Antichrist is their messiah. Even more shocking to many readers was the revelation that Islam teaches that when Jesus returns, He will come back as a Muslim prophet whose primary mission will be to abolish Christianity. It's difficult for any Bible believer to read of these things without becoming acutely aware of the satanic origins of the Islamic religion.

In 2008, I also had the opportunity to coauthor another book on the same subject with Walid Shoebat, a former operative for the Palestine Liberation Organization. This book, entitled *God's War on Terror*, is an almost encyclopedic discussion of the role of Islam in the last days, as well as a chronicle of Walid's journey from a young Palestinian Muslim with a deep hatred for the Jews, to a Christian man who spends his life standing with the Jewish people and proclaiming the truth concerning the dangers of radical Islam.

Together these two books have become the cornerstone of what has developed into a popular eschatological revolution. Today, I receive a steady stream of e-mails and reports from individuals expressing how much these books have affected them and transformed their understanding of the end-times. Students, pastors, and even reputable scholars have expressed that they have abandoned the popular notion that the Antichrist, his empire, and his religion will emerge out of Europe or a revived Roman Empire. Instead they have come to recognize the simple fact that the Bible emphatically and repeatedly points us to the Middle East as the launchpad and epicenter of the emerging empire of the Antichrist and his religion. Many testify that although they have been students of Bible prophecy for many years, never before had anything made so much sense, or the prophecies of the Bible become so clear. And even more important, some have even written to share that they've become believers or recommitted their lives to Jesus as a result of reading these books. Hallelujah!

Others, however, express that while the thesis presented in *Islamic Antichrist* and *God's War on Terror* makes a great deal of sense, they still have many unanswered questions. The purpose of this book is to set forth a scholarly, yet popularized, succinct presentation of the Islamic Antichrist theory based on the most relevant passages of Scripture. If there is even a chance that Islam is, in fact, the primary subject of the Bible's many antichristic prophecies, the possibility alone should be enough to merit serious consideration of the relevant texts.

I want to state at the outset that this book's purpose is not to debate what many might feel is irrelevant or even morbid end-time trivia. Many may ask why it even matters if the Antichrist will emerge from Europe or the Middle East, whether he will be a humanist or a Muslim. The fact of the matter is that the practical implications of the many subjects discussed in this book are profound. If, in fact, Islam is the religion of the Antichrist, the significance is earth-shattering. As much of the Church today, including large segments of the missions movement, increasingly embraces an approach toward reaching Muslims that flirts with syncretism and outright heresy (I am referring to what has become known as the "Insider Movement"), it is imperative that followers of Jesus determine exactly where they stand concerning the origins and nature of Islam. As we strive to love Muslims, must we also love Islam? Or is it possible to passionately care for Muslims, while hating Islam? Is Islam a faith system that can create a genuine relationship with God, or is it purely a soul-destroying ideology? Can one be both a Muslim and a follower of Jesus, as many evangelical missiologists claim? Are the Allah of the Qur'an and the God of the Bible one and the same? And what about Israel and the Jewish people? Fierce anti-Zionism and anti-Semitism are now spreading from the Muslim world into the Christian Church; what did the prophets say about these things? Where is a disciple of Jesus seeking to love both Muslims and Jews to stand on these matters? What about the "Arab Spring"? Does the Bible inform us as to where this sudden and drastic change in the Muslim world is heading? Further, while numerous demographic models inform us that Islam will soon emerge as the world's largest religion, many within the Christian Church believe and teach that most of the Islamic world (and Russia) will soon be destroyed in a series of prophesied battles, resulting in the religion of Islam virtually disappearing from the earth. But does the Bible really teach this? How we answer these questions and what we believe about these things will drastically affect our approach toward prayer, intercession, evangelism, and missions. These are not questions that the Church can afford to get wrong. Carefully searching the Scriptures so as to answer these questions accurately is absolutely essential. This is why this book was written. While this study will certainly answer many questions concerning the end-times, it is far from irrelevant or morbid eschatological trivia. As the Church seeks to plot its way forward into the ever-changing world, it is essential for the Church to grasp the truths brought forward in this study.

I also appeal to you to approach this book prayerfully. I have written the book prayerfully and I ask you to talk to the LORD as you read it. There are few subjects that are as serious and pressing as that discussed here. As we study the subject of the end-times, we must do so in a spirit of prayer. Across the body of Christ, throughout the earth, many believe this is the generation that will live to see Jesus' return. So then does this generation have a greater duty to become a community of prayer dedicated to loving one another? "The end of all things is near; therefore, be of sound judgment and sober spirit for the purpose of prayer. [NASB] Above all, keep loving one another earnestly, since love covers a multitude of sins" (1 Peter 4:7–8).

This very well may be the generation that has inherited both the massive opportunity and the immense responsibility that was spoken of by the prophet Daniel: "And those who are wise shall shine like the brightness of the sky above; and those who turn many to righteousness, like the stars forever and ever" (Daniel 12:3).

Daniel saw a glimpse of it—but many reading this book may very well be among those who will actually live it. I appeal to you to seize this opportunity with everything you have. The urgency of the hour demands no less.

END-TIMES SIMPLIFIED

FAR TOO MANY CHRISTIANS believe the subject of the end-times to be an insurmountable mountain far too high and complicated to climb. As a result, many simply entrust their beliefs regarding the end-times to their pastor or various "prophecy experts." Certainly the Lord has given some to function as teachers within the body of Christ to help guide fellow believers into a proper understanding of the more complicated aspects of God's Word, but in no way does this excuse any believer from responsibility to search these things out in the Bible for him- or herself. One of the best things any teacher can do is equip his or her students with the tools necessary to study and understand the Bible on their own. That is the purpose of this chapter: to equip both the student and the seasoned teacher alike with some very clear, simple, and easy-to-follow principles to simplify the Bible's message concerning the end-times and make them available to all. The false belief that the subject of the end-times is beyond the ability of the average Christian to understand must be shattered. After grasping the principles explained in this chapter, many who once felt intimidated by the subject of the end-times will be confident that eschatology is not a subject beyond their ability to understand. The following seven principles represent the approach to understanding biblical prophecy that we will take throughout the remainder of this book.

RULE #1: KEEP FIRST THINGS FIRST

Shortly after graduating from high school, just after becoming a believer, I worked as a house framer for a year. To build a house, one must begin by laying a proper and solid foundation. How and where one begins always affects the end result. This is true whether we are dealing with a house or theology. A bad or weak foundation will cause the end result to be unstable, faulty, or potentially even dangerous. In home building, if one were to begin by building the roof and then worked backward to the foundation, he would end up with some serious problems. Yet this is precisely what some actually do when they are trying to build a solid biblical eschatology; they decide that they want to understand what the Bible says about the end-times and then they turn right to the book of Revelation, the very *last* book of the Bible! Now, please don't get me wrong; the book of Revelation, is crucial to understand when studying God's plan for the ages. But it is not where we start. Revelation is predicated on a wealth of previously revealed prophetic knowledge found in numerous passages throughout the Old and New Testaments. Perhaps more than any other book in the New Testament, Revelation is jam-packed with direct quotes, allusions, and even more subtle echoes of dozens upon dozens of biblical passages.

Imagine going to a symphony. During the performance, you hear stringed instruments, drums, woodwinds, but it is not until the grand finale that all of these instruments come to one amazing crescendo. This is what Revelation is; it is the grand prophetic-symphonic crescendo composed of many other prophecies found throughout the Bible. But as beautiful as grand crescendos may be, they do come last for a reason. Before we can expect to understand what Revelation is trying to tell us, we must first understand what the passages upon which it is built are saying. The Bible is an unfolding story. And if we seek to properly understand the story the Bible is telling, we must begin at the beginning of the book, approaching the story as it was written, as it unfolds and expands. This is all just simple common sense.

So the first rule to follow when we desire to understand what the Bible says about the end-times is: Start with what comes first. We begin with the foundation—at the beginning. This couldn't be much simpler.

In terms of Bible study, this means that we begin with the Torah, the first five books of Moses, and move forward from there.

RULE #2: KEEP IT SIMPLE

Besides being the last book in the Bible, there are other reasons not to begin with the book of Revelation. Revelation is perhaps the most symbolic and apocalyptic book in the whole Bible. When we begin trying to understand what the Bible says about the end-times, we do not begin with the most allegorical passages. Neither do we start with passages that are tricky, hard to interpret, or confusing. Instead, we should begin with what is literal, direct, and easy to understand. So not only do we not start with Revelation; we also do not start with Daniel or Ezekiel. While both of these books come far before Revelation, they are also both very figurative, filled with dreams, visions, and much symbolism. So while Daniel and Ezekiel are essential to understand if we are to accurately grasp the Bible's message concerning the end-times, like Revelation, these are not the books we should begin with. There are numerous other essential passages that must be examined first. Not only are they older than Daniel and Ezekiel, but they are also clearer and easier to understand.

So our second rule is that we should begin with that which contains the least measure of confusing, questionable, debatable, or hard-to-understand elements.

RULE #3: BUILD DOCTRINE ON THE FULL COUNSEL OF SCRIPTURE

Many years ago, when I first become a believer, I lived just south of Boston. I was nineteen, and understandably, because of my conversion and radical life change, most of my friends no longer wanted to spend time with me. As if overnight, I had become an extremely vocal and evangelistic Christian. As such, I spent many Saturdays walking around Boston, seeking willing listeners with whom I could share my faith. In those days, one of Boston's largest semi-cultic groups was the Boston Church of Christ, sometimes referred to as "the Boston Movement," founded by Thomas "Kip" McKean. I used to run into disciples of this group quite often. One of the distinguishing beliefs of this group is that it is the actual act of baptism that saves a person. According to them, without water-immersion baptism, one absolutely cannot be saved. To establish this point, they would always turn to Acts 2:38, which reads, "Then Peter said to them, 'Repent, and let every one of you be baptized in the name of Jesus Christ for the remission of sins'" (NKJV). Being a zealous new believer, and a Berean as well, I began to examine the Bible to see what it said about the means whereby we are saved. I found seventy-two verses, from Genesis to Revelation, that state very clearly that it is our faith in Jesus and what He accomplished for us on the cross that saves us. What I found revealed that when we believe these things with sincere and repentant hearts, we are indeed baptized and sealed by the Holy Spirit. Acts 1:5 says, "For John truly baptized with water, but you shall be baptized with the Holy Spirit not many days from now" (NKJV). Ephesians 1:13–14 also states, "In Him you also trusted, after you heard the word of truth, the gospel of your salvation; in whom also, having believed, you were sealed with the Holy Spirit of promise, who is the guarantee of our inheritance until the redemption of the purchased possession, to the praise of His glory" (NKJV).

The promise, of course, is of the future completion of our salvation when our bodies are resurrected and glorified. Water baptism is merely on outward sign of the inward reality that has already taken place when we believed and were baptized by the Holy Spirit. So, let me ask: in light of the seventy-two verses on one hand that say that we are saved by faith, and the one verse on the other hand that is used to claim that it is the act of baptism that saves us, scripturally speaking, which position is built on a more solid footing? Obviously the weight of the Scriptures tell us that it is faith that saves us, and water baptism is the first essential act of obedience after we have come to faith.

The point in telling this story is to remind us not to develop theories, positions, or doctrines based on select, limited, or isolated passages, while ignoring the wealth of other passages that speak to any particular issue. Whatever position we arrive at, it must conform to the full counsel of Scripture. Our position must be able to bring together all of the numerous and relevant passages throughout the Bible, revealing a consistent story. It is both dangerous and irresponsible to base any doctrine or idea on one or even a few isolated passages. But when we see a theme that is repeated numerous times throughout the Bible, over and over, then we know that we are building on a foundation of consistency. So the third rule is to build on themes that are repeated and consistent. Build doctrine on the full counsel of Scripture.

RULE #4: REMEMBER, CONTEXT, CONTEXT, CONTEXT

Ask any Realtor what the key to home sales is, and he or she will say, "Location, location, location." Likewise, anyone who has spent three days in Bible school or seminary will tell you that the cardinal rule of responsibly interpreting Scripture is context, context, context. Perhaps one of the easiest mistakes to make when trying to understand Bible prophecy is failing to take into consideration the larger context of the Bible. Americans in particular are infamous for being self-centered with regard to our view of the world, and as such, it is we who are most likely to make this common error. Because of America's relative geographic isolation as well as our exalted role in the earth in recent history, we may even have some legitimate reason for our lack of awareness of the world around us. But when attempting to interpret and understand Bible prophecy, such a self-focused attitude is highly detrimental. Let me explain.

Today, the Church in the United States, and the West in general, is contending with various issues, such as moral and cultural relativism, secular humanism, Darwinism, religious pluralism, and intellectual atheism. The list could go on and on. All of these anti-Christian ideas and worldviews seem to be increasing their hold on Western culture and society. So the Western Church lives in an atmosphere where the television shows, movies, and media to which we are exposed continually send us messages that conflict with a biblical worldview. Likewise, if our children attend public school or a secular university, the teachers and students alike aggressively espouse one or all of these anti-Christian worldviews. The result is that Western believers tend to imagine that the same spirit of the age we are contending with here is also being contended with in every other part of the world. As we rightly discern the demonic powers behind many of these ideas that are daily assaulting our families and our faith, many assume that this prevailing spirit is in fact the premier spirit of the Antichrist. Many imagine the Antichrist to be a leader of a global world religion that welcomes everyone, except true Christians, of course. Because Western culture is the only world that most Westerners know, as we turn to the Bible and read the end-time prophetic passages, many make the mistake of reading their own worldview and personal experiences into its pages. The problem with this, of course, is that the Bible is and always has been a thoroughly Jerusalem-, Israel-, and Middle Eastern–centric book. As we will see, biblical prophecy tells a very Jerusalem-centered story. Jerusalem is the city around which the entire story of the return of Jesus revolves. This is the city from which Jesus will literally rule the earth after His return. This fact must not be missed.

So if one is living in Jerusalem today, while the ideas that flood Western society are present, the primary demonic spirit that is threatening to destroy the Jews and Christians, the people of God, is not religious pluralism or intellectual atheism; it is Islam, through and through. In the United States, the spirit of Islam is less significant; thus it is easier for Americans to be slow to grasp this point. But when we look to Israel, the epicenter of the geographic context of the Bible, it is easy to see that the spirit dominating the entire region is not universalism or new age religion, but Islam. Extending several hundred to thousands of miles around Jerusalem, Islam controls the Middle East, Northern Africa, Asia Minor, and Central Asia. Israel sits in the center of this ocean of hatred.

So as we approach the Bible to understand what it is saying with regard to the end-times, the fourth rule is that we must take into consideration its proper context. We must be cautious not to read a Western worldview—a *foreign* context—into the pages of this Eastern book called the Bible. We must never forget its Middle Eastern/Israel-centric context. The Bible was not written primarily for Americans or Westerners. The Bible is a Jewish book with a Middle Eastern emphasis and worldview.

RULE #5: DO NOT READ PROPHETIC LITERATURE AS IF IT IS A TECHNICAL MANUAL

This rule piggybacks on the previous rule. It says that Westerners must acknowledge that most prophecies in the Bible are written as ancient Hebrew prophetic poetry or apocalyptic literature. Western Bible students should familiarize themselves with the characteristics of these types of literature and the many literary devices they utilize. This includes things such as Hebrew idioms, hyperbole, and the dual fulfillment of so many prophetic passages. Because much of the West's cultural and intellectual roots are found in the Enlightenment, we have particular ways of thinking, reasoning, and viewing things that are often in conflict with the manner in which the Bible is written.

I was once speaking at a conference and explained that reading the Bible literally sometimes means that we do not take things in a hyper-literal fashion. Sometimes reading poetry in a hyper-literal or technically literal fashion can lead to all sorts of problems and misinterpretations. Sure enough, after I spoke, a somewhat confrontational man met me at the front of the church. "I read the Bible literally, period," he said, inferring of course, that I was encouraging a nonliteral or slightly liberal interpretive method. Feeling a bit feisty, I opened my Bible to Isaiah 60, a passage that speaks of the blessings that will come to the Jewish people during the messianic kingdom. "So you take the Bible literally, no matter what?" I asked as I handed him my Bible, pointed to verse 16, and asked him to read it aloud: "You shall drink the milk of the Gentiles, and milk the breast of kings; you shall know that I, the LORD, am your Savior and your Redeemer, the Mighty One of Jacob."

Not wanting to admit that reading this verse literally would have some rather embarrassing implications, he said that he would need to study "this one" a bit further. But I believe he understood my point. I hold to a literal interpretive method, but I read prophetic poetry as prophetic poetry, historical narrative as historical narrative, proverbs as proverbs, etc. These things all speak of very literal realities, but they represent different types of literature and use varied expressions to convey these realities, each with its own rules and characteristics. So when we are reading Hebrew apocalyptic literature or prophetic poetry, we do not read this material as if we are reading an owner's manual for a Toyota Tundra. For further exploration of this issue, I highly recommend a very simple book, *How to Read the Bible for All Its Worth*, by Gordon D. Fee and Douglas Stuart.

RULE #6: RECOGNIZE THE ULTIMATE EMPHASIS, THE BIG STORY OF BIBLICAL PROPHECY

Understanding the general nature of biblical prophecy is not nearly as difficult as many Western interpreters have sometimes made it. While nearly every prophecy has historical application in either the immediate or near future of the prophets, the ultimate burden of all biblical prophecy is the coming of the Messiah, the Day of the Lord (God's judgment on the earth), and the messianic kingdom to follow. While each prophet was most often first speaking either to the circumstances of his day and age or to events in the near future, the primary burden of the entire Bible, of every prophet and apostle, is the coming of Jesus and the establishment of His kingdom rule over the earth. As such, one can rightly say that biblical prophecy is first and foremost *Messiah-centric*. It is ultimately about Jesus.

Of course, in highlighting the Messiah-centricity of Scripture, one must acknowledge both the first and the second coming of Jesus. Modern Christians most often major in the prophecies that point to the first coming of Jesus, and minor in the prophecies that speak of His second coming. The fact of the matter, however, is that the primary emphasis of Scripture is the second coming. Far more prophecies address the second coming than the first. So the three primary emphases of biblical prophecy are:

- the immediate historical context of the prophets' era,

- the first coming of Jesus, and

- the second coming of Jesus/the Day of the Lord.

But here is the problem: One of the characteristics of Western thought is that we like to organize and classify things into neat categories. Westerners like to systematize everything, including our theology. We may even attempt to dissect the living Word of God as if it is a frog in a high school science lab. As such, when attempting to interpret the Bible, we often attempt to define each verse or passage as if it is speaking of either the historical or the future fulfillment as if it must be one or the other. But we need to understand that the Bible is an Eastern book and was not written with a Western mind-set. And so, almost as if to drive

Westerners crazy, we frequently find in the Scriptures an *intermingling* of the historical and the future into one seamless passage. Consider, for example, the following classic passage:

> For unto us a Child is born, unto us a Son is given; and the government will be upon His shoulder. And His name will be called Wonderful, Counselor, Mighty God, Everlasting Father, Prince of Peace. Of the increase of His government and peace there will be no end, upon the throne of David and over His kingdom, to order it and establish it with judgment and justice from that time forward, even forever. The zeal of the LORD of hosts will perform this. (Isaiah 9:6–7 NKJV)

This passage speaks as if the primary purpose of this Child, this Son, is to vindicate Israel over and against her enemies. Consider what the Child brings about: Israel's boundaries will be expanded; the yoke that burdens the Jewish people will be shattered; warriors' boots and blood will be things of the past. This Child will bring in everlasting peace. Yet the Child has come, but the remainder of the prophecy has not yet been fulfilled. Israel is still oppressed. Wars continue. Within this passage there is a two-thousand-year pause or gap. Yet a face-value reading of this passage gives no real indication of this. In one seamless passage, we have both the historical (the Child was born) and the future fulfillment (He will rule, shatter the rod of oppression, and bring in everlasting peace). As much as we in the West like to approach a passage and divide it up into neat categories of historical or future, oftentimes both elements are intertwined. Sometimes a passage may be partially historical with shadows of futuristic prophecies. Other times, a prophet may be speaking almost entirely of the future with only a slight shade of historical emphasis. Still other times, a passage may be entirely futuristic or historical. How then are we to understand such passages? The answer lies in understanding the big story that all of the prophets were telling and identifying the commonly repeated themes that make up this big story. Let me explain.

Most have heard the saying "Don't miss the forest for the trees." The point of the saying is to warn against becoming so caught up in the many intricacies or details (trees) of any subject that you miss the bigger picture (the forest). Perhaps nowhere is this warning more appropriate than with regard to the study of biblical prophecy. When studying the

Bible's many end-time passages, it's very easy to become so engrossed in one particular passage that the larger story is missed. I've watched both students and teachers make this mistake dozens upon dozens of times. But this error is easy to avoid. Before running with any one passage, we must first solidly grasp the larger, overarching, ultimate story being conveyed throughout the many prophecies of the Bible. Thankfully, this is not difficult. The wonderful thing about the Bible is that it tells the same story over and over again in numerous ways. Whenever a theme is important, it will be repeated multiple times throughout the Bible. When something is important from a prophetic perspective, the Bible will make that point abundantly clear by reiterating it dozens of times in a number of passages. It is through taking note of the commonly repeated themes that one is able to grasp the "big picture" of biblical prophecy.

Repeating what was said earlier, while every prophet was speaking either to the immediate circumstances of his day or the near future, the ultimate burden of all biblical prophecy is the coming of the Messiah, the Day of the Lord, and the messianic kingdom to follow. The coming of Jesus and the establishment of His kingdom is the big story that all of the prophets were telling. This is the emphasis of the entire Bible. In the next chapter, we will briefly survey some of the most important prophetic passages regarding the Day of the Lord and the return of Jesus. For the purpose of this study, we will consider the specific nations against which Jesus executes judgment when He returns. What we will see is that over and over, the same general story is being told. While numerous subthemes could be highlighted so as to expand this basic picture, the four primary themes that will emerge are clear:

- In the last days, the Antichrist, his empire, and his armies will arise from out of what today are the Muslim majority nations of the Middle East and North Africa.

- These nations will form a coalition, union, or alliance and invade the nation of Israel. Severe persecution of Jews and Christians will be a global pandemic.

- After a short but extremely terrible season of victory by the Antichrist and his armies, Jesus will return from heaven to deliver the surviving Jewish people, many of whom will have been taken captive by the conquering invaders.

- The righteous dead will awaken and, together with the living saints, be "caught up" in the air, where they will instantly receive eternal life in their glorified resurrection bodies.

- Jesus will destroy the Antichrist and his armies and establish His messianic kingdom over the earth from Jerusalem.

While there are certainly numerous other details that we could unfold, as we will see, it is these four larger themes that are repeated most frequently throughout the Prophets. When trying to understand the biblical prophets, it is through understanding the big story concerning the coming Day of the Lord and the kingdom to follow that many formerly confusing passages throughout the Prophets will suddenly make sense. While they were all speaking to the events of their day or near future, they are all ultimately telling the same big story and pointing to the same glorious future.

RULE #7: UNDERSTAND THAT WHEN GOD ALMIGHTY IS PORTRAYED AS BEING PHYSICALLY PRESENT ON THE EARTH, IT IS GOD THE SON (JESUS).

This final rule is more of an observation, but it is essential to grasp if we are to properly understand numerous passages throughout the Prophets that speak of the return of the Messiah and the Day of the Lord: when God is portrayed as being physically on the earth, it is usually either a historical, pre-incarnate appearance of God the Son or a prophetic portrayal of Jesus the Messiah at the time of His return. Many Christians miss this fact because they are confused regarding the nature of the Trinity. Often, when the individual being described is referenced as God, or with the sacred name Yahweh, most often translated as "LORD," many simply assume this is God the Father. But throughout the Bible, God the Father does not come down to the earth until the very end (Revelation 21–22).

God has appeared to men and women at various times. Consider just a couple of examples:

Then she called the name of the LORD who spoke to her, You-Are-the-God-Who-Sees; for she said, "Have I also here seen Him who sees me?" (Genesis 16:13 NKJV)

So Jacob called the name of the place Peniel: "For I have seen God face to face, and my life is preserved." (Genesis 32:30)

But despite these and other appearances of God throughout the Old Testament, the apostle John made it clear that no one has ever seen God the Father, except God the Son:

"No one has seen God at any time. The only begotten Son, who is in the bosom of the Father, He has declared Him." (John 1:18 NKJV)

"Everyone who has heard and learned from the Father comes to Me. Not that anyone has seen the Father, except He who is from God; He has seen the Father." (John 6:45–46 NKJV)

The apostle Paul also made it clear that God the Father has never been seen:

I urge you in the sight of God who gives life to all things . . . He who is the blessed and only Potentate, the King of kings and Lord of lords, who alone has immortality, dwelling in unapproachable light, whom no man has seen or can see, to whom be honor and everlasting power. Amen. (1 Timothy 6:13–16 NKJV)

Yet throughout the prophets, there are numerous passages that speak of God being present on the earth. While several passages could be cited, consider the following:

Then Moses went up, also Aaron, Nadab, and Abihu, and seventy of the elders of Israel, and they saw the God of Israel. And there was under His feet as it were a paved work of sapphire stone, and it was like the very heavens in its clarity. But on the nobles of the children of Israel He did not lay His hand. So they saw God, and they ate and drank. (Exodus 24:9–11 NKJV)

While numerous individuals and groups of people saw God histori-cally throughout the Bible, all of these passages must be understood as pre-incarnate appearances of God the Son. So also when we see God physically present in the context of future prophecy, should we understand these references to "God" or "Lord" as references to Jesus after His return. Consider for example the passage in Zechariah:

> For I will gather all the nations to battle against Jerusalem; the city shall be taken, the houses rifled, and the women ravished. Half of the city shall go into captivity, but the remnant of the people shall not be cut off from the city. Then the LORD will go forth and fight against those nations, as He fights in the day of battle. And in that day His feet will stand on the Mount of Olives. (14:2–4 NKJV)

Here Yahweh, the Lord, is seen to physically stand on the mountain. He is described as fighting against the armies of gentile nations. This is clearly a messianic prophecy concerning the day when Jesus the Messiah will stand on the Mount of Olives as He executes judgment against those nations that come against Jerusalem.

SUMMARY

In conclusion, let's summarize the rules of interpretation that we've discussed in this chapter. By following and applying these simple rules, anyone can find biblical prophecy far more approachable and easy to understand:

- **RULE #1**: Begin with what comes first, *not* what comes last.

- **RULE #2**: Begin with what is clear, direct, and easy to under-stand, not with that which is highly symbolic, allegorical, or difficult to interpret.

- **RULE #3**: Build on themes that are consistent and occur repeat-edly throughout Scripture.

- **RULE #4**: Always remember: context, context context.

- **RULE #5**: Do not approach the Bible as if it is a technical manual, but instead keep in mind its Eastern nature.

- **RULE #6**: Recognize the ultimate emphasis of biblical prophecy; that is, know the "big story."

- **RULE #7**: Recognize that when God Almighty is portrayed as being physically present on the earth, this is God the Son, either historically as the pre-incarnate Son of God or as Jesus at the time of His return.

INTRODUCTION TO THE

ISLAMIC ANTICHRIST THEORY

S WE BEGIN OUR STUDY, our purpose will be to briefly survey some of the most important prophetic passages regarding the Day of the Lord and Christ's return. The study is certainly not comprehensive. Our focus will be the specific nations emphasized as being reserved for judgment on the Day of the Lord. What we will see is the same general story repeated many times.

GENESIS 3: HE WHO WILL CRUSH THE HEAD OF THE SERPENT

Our study must begin in the third chapter of Genesis, often referred to as the "protoevangelium" by theologians, because in this very first book of the Bible, albeit in seed form, we are introduced to the wonderful news of messianic hope.

We all know the story: In the beginning, there was one word to describe the nature of God's creation: *good*. Adam and Eve were in the Garden, and things were ideal in every way. God and man were in perfect communion, dwelling together in paradise. But through their own sinful choices, in agreement with the temptation of Satan, Adam and Eve rebelled against God's commands, and humankind fell into the broken state in which we now all find ourselves. We are living far from paradise, far from unbroken communion with God, all slumping toward the day when our bodies die and decay. But this present state is not how things are supposed to be. Neither will it remain this way. After God's redemptive plan is complete, sin and death will be things of the past. By "God's redemptive plan" we are simply referring to the unfolding story of God bringing humankind back to eternal life, back to the Garden, back to paradise, and back to the place of unbroken communion and fellowship with Himself. It is the restoration and redemption of all creation, precisely what the apostle Peter meant when he spoke of "the times of restoration of all things, which God has spoken by the mouth of all His holy prophets since the world began" (Acts 3:21). This is the "big story" of the entire Bible.

And so here, in the midst of the story of Adam and Eve and Satan the serpent, in one simple verse, God gave an overview of the entirety of redemptive history: "I will put enmity between you and the woman, and between your offspring and her offspring; he shall bruise your head, and you shall bruise his heel" (Genesis 3:15).

Eve, the mother of all humanity, sinned, and God declared that from that day forward there would be hostility between herself and Satan. Beyond this, Satan's "seed," or followers, would be at enmity with the offspring of Eve, those who are not followers of Satan. But even more important, Satan's seed would be at war with the "Seed," which is the Messiah, and His followers. According to this ancient prophecy, history would be the story of the people of Satan in conflict with the people of God.

Then comes the glorious promise that although Satan would merely bruise the heel of the Messiah, in the end, the Messiah will crush the skull of Satan as well as his followers. From the very beginning of humankind's long history, God declared that Eve's "Seed," the Messiah, will make right all of the damage done on that very sad and dark day in the Garden. In a single verse, in one brief declaration, we have a synopsis of redemptive history. It is appropriate, then, that scholars James E. Smith and Walter C. Kaiser Jr. refer to this verse as "the mother prophecy."[1] It is this prophecy that gives birth to all of the other prophetic promises in Scripture regarding the Messiah. For the remainder of this chapter, we will examine several of her prophetic children. As we will see, while each passage delivers new or additional details, all are expansions of the same original story.

NUMBERS 24: THE RULER FROM ISRAEL WHO CRUSHES MOAB, EDOM, AND THE SONS OF THE EAST

Still within the Torah, we find one of the earliest and most direct messianic prophecies in the Bible. This is the story of King Balak and the prophet Balaam. Balak was the king of Moab, and Balaam was a prophet. As the scene unfolds, Balak and Balaam are standing on a high overlook, gazing down over Israel—that is, the Hebrews—as they encamp in a vast valley below. The exodus from Egypt has just occurred, and the Hebrews are making their way into the promised land. Balak however, is upset by the fact that such a vast people group is encroaching the borders of his kingdom, so he has paid Balaam to pronounce a curse on the Hebrew people. But instead, as they both stand there together, Balaam begins to prophesy under the inspiration of the Holy Spirit of God. Looking down at the Israelite camp, this is what he says:

> "And now, behold, I am going to my people. Come, I will let you know what this people will do to your people in the latter days. . . . I see him, but not now; I behold him, but not near: a star shall come out of Jacob, and a scepter shall rise out of Israel; it shall crush the forehead of Moab and break down all the sons of Sheth. Edom shall be dispossessed; Seir also, his enemies, shall be dispossessed. Israel is doing valiantly. And one from Jacob shall exercise dominion and destroy the survivors of cities!" Then he looked on Amalek and took up his discourse and said, "Amalek was the first among the nations, but its end is utter destruction." (Numbers 24:14, 17–20)

The prophecy declares what the Hebrews will do to the Moabites in the "latter days." This phrase in the Hebrew is *acharyith yawm*, literally meaning "the last days." While this phrase at times can, in a limited sense, refer to the distant future, it is most fully realized in the end of this age, the time of the Messiah. So Balaam declares that in the end-times, a ruler would arise from out of Israel. From very early on, Jewish interpreters understood this passage to be a prophecy concerning the Messiah. The first-century false messiah Simon ben Kosiba actually changed his name to Simon bar Kokhba (Simon, son of the star) in a transparent attempt to present himself as the fulfillment of this prophecy. According to the commentary of Jamieson, Fausset, and Brown, in mind here is an "eminent ruler—primarily David; but secondarily and pre-eminently, the Messiah."[2] It is certain that this passage did not find its ultimate fulfillment with King David, as long after his death the prophet Jeremiah repeated Balaam's prophecy, and still placed its fulfillment in the future (Jeremiah 48–49). It was also this prophecy, together with Micah 5 (which specifies that the Messiah would be born in Bethlehem), that led the wise men from the East to follow a star to Bethlehem, hoping to find the one "born King of the Jews" (Matthew 2:1–2). This prophecy is ultimately pointing us to Jesus the Messiah and the work He will accomplish at the time of His return.

But what does the passage say the Messiah will carry out when He returns? What did the Holy Spirit emphasize as the primary accomplishment of the Messiah on that day? Picking up and expanding on the theme in Genesis 3, "the mother prophecy," the Messiah is once again seen to "crush" the head of the seed of Satan. This time, however, Satan's seed is not quite as vague as in Genesis 3. Here the people are very clearly specified. The Messiah comes back to crush the heads of Moab, Edom, Seir, the sons of Sheth, and the Amalekites. But what do these terms mean? To whom are they referring?

The Moabites and the Edomites were a people who lived to the east of modern-day Israel in what is today the nation of Jordan. Mount Seir was a prominent mountain within the territory of Moab. Thus, the references to Moab, Edom, and Seir all point to the same general region and its people historically. Likewise, the Amalekites were a people group that lived throughout the greater region to the east of Israel. All of these peoples, throughout biblical history, carried enmity toward the Hebrews. But what about this term, the "sons of Sheth"? Scholars have debated its meaning. Some have suggested that it is a reference to Adam's son Seth and refers to all of humanity. The ancient Jewish interpretation, however, as found in the Jerusalem Targum translates it as "all the sons of the East." The Babylonian targum of Jonathan ben Uzziel goes further and explains it as a reference to "the armies of Gog who were to set themselves against Israel in battle array."[3] This understanding as a reference to the sons of the East is consistent with the other terms to which it is associated (Moab, Edom, Seir, and the Amalekites). In the end, we have a grouping of names that point us to the desert peoples that lived east of Israel. But it is not merely the geography of the peoples that is in mind here. Beyond mere geography, it is primarily their deep hatred for the Hebrew people that marks them for ultimate judgment when the Messiah returns.

Now, the question must be asked, in the ultimate fulfillment of the prophecy, where or to whom are these references pointing us? When Jesus returns, who does this passage tell us He will judge? If we take this passage at face value, would it be more reasonable and responsible to interpret these references as pointing us to the modern-day inhabitants of the lands to the east of Israel, where the Moabites, Edomites, and Amalekites once dwelled? Or is it more reasonable to hold that this prophecy is pointing us to Germany, Italy, and England, as so many teachers of prophecy today do? Wouldn't we look to the same lands and its desert peoples who are the primary torchbearers of the ancient anti-Semitic hatred of the Jewish people? The answer here should be clear.

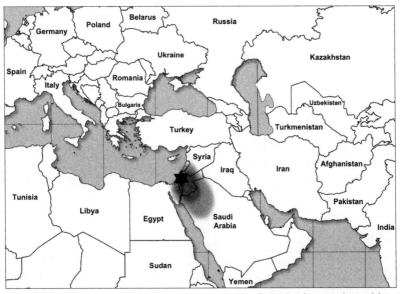

Numbers 24: Edom, Moab, Amalekites

ISAIAH 25: THE SOVEREIGN LORD WILL CRUSH MOAB

Many reading this have attended a funeral at one time or another where Revelation 21:4 was read: "[God] will wipe away every tear from their eyes. There will be no more death or mourning or crying or pain, for the old order of things has passed away" (NIV). But few are aware that the book of Revelation actually borrowed this passage directly from Isaiah 25. But in the Isaiah passage, the Lord is doing more than just wiping away tears and eliminating death. According to Isaiah 25, God will also remove the disgrace of His people Israel from the earth. What else will the Lord do at this time? Let's look at the passage.

> He will swallow up death forever; and the Lord GOD will wipe away tears from all faces, and the reproach of his people he will take away from all the earth, for the LORD has spoken. It will be said on that day, "Behold, this is our God; we have waited for him, that he might save us. This is the LORD; we have waited for him; let us be glad and rejoice in his salvation." For the hand of the LORD will rest on this mountain [Zion], and Moab shall be trampled down in his place, as straw is trampled down in a dunghill. And he will spread out his hands in the midst of it as a swimmer spreads his hands out to swim, but the LORD will lay low his pompous pride together with the skill of his hands. (vv. 8–11)

Commenting on this passage, the ancient Latin commentator Jerome wrote of the reaction of God's people: "After death has been swallowed up forever, the people of God, who had been delivered from the hand of death, shall say to the Lord, Lo, this is our God, whom unbelievers regarded as only a man."[4]

But has this time come yet? Has God already swallowed up death and wiped away all tears? Of course not. The context of this passage is the future, at the return of the Messiah. In the coming messianic age, those who enter the kingdom as unbelievers will live extraordinarily long lives (Isaiah 65:20), while those who enter as believers will have undergone the first resurrection and will possess immortal bodies: "They lived and reigned with Christ for a thousand years. . . This is the first resurrection. Blessed and holy is he who has part in the first resurrection. Over such the second death has no power, but they shall be priests of God and of Christ" (Revelation 20:4–6 NKJV).

This is the time that all of creation has been waiting and longing for. And once again, here at the end of the age, the Lord is portrayed with His hand of blessing and protection resting on the head of Zion, his people, while his foot crushes the head of Moab, his enemy. In this passage however, the Lord is not portrayed as simply crushing their skulls. He is seen with His foot on the back of the head of His enemies, crushing them facedown into a pile of dung.

Once more, we must take note that it is not a vague or universal enemy of God's people that is specified. As in Numbers 24, it is "Moab" whom Jesus the returning Messiah will judge. As one surveys a sampling of commentaries on this passage, most commentators will claim that Moab here merely represents all of Israel's last-days' enemies in a very general and vague way. But the specific usage of the term "Moab" should not be interpreted as having absolutely no purpose whatsoever. Interpreters must be cautious not to take such an extreme allegorical approach that inspired biblical terms become virtually meaningless or entirely irrelevant. But while this approach of over-allegorization is irresponsible, how much more reckless is it to read "Moab" and see Europe? Yet this is precisely what many European Antichrist teachers would have us do.

And so once again I ask, according to this passage, at the time of the Lord's return, will the primary recipients of His judgment be from Europe, or is the text once again pointing us to the anti-Semitic sons of the East? Again, common sense clearly tells us that it is the latter.

OBADIAH: JUDGMENT OF THE LORD AGAINST EDOM

The entire theme of the short prophecy of Obadiah is the ultimate victory of "the Mountain of Zion" over "the Mountain of Edom." Mountains are a commonly used biblical motif for kingdoms. While the prophecy has a significant partial-historical fulfillment in the ancient conflict between the kingdoms of Israel and Edom, its ultimate fulfillment is in the future. Pastor Chuck Smith of Calvary Chapel rightly states that the final fulfillment of this prophecy and the judgment of Edom will occur during "the day of the Lord when God blesses Israel once again when the deliverer is in Zion and the Lord reigns."[5] Likewise Dr. Tommy Ice addresses the timing of Obadiah's fulfillment: "When will Obadiah's prophecy be fulfilled? . . . The passage clearly says it will be fulfilled when 'the day of the Lord draws near on all the nations.' Such an event is clearly scheduled to occur at the same time when Isaiah, Jeremiah, Ezekiel, Amos, and others indicate that the nations will be judged at the end of the tribulation, during the campaign of Armageddon."[6]

The "Day of the Lord" context is also seen in the final verse of the prophecy, which states that in that day "the kingdom shall be the LORD's": "Saviors [or, salvation] shall go up to Mount Zion to rule Mount Esau, and the kingdom shall be the LORD's" (Obadiah 1:21).

Further evidence for an ultimate fulfillment in the Day of the Lord is seen in the fact that the text speaks of the prisoners and captives of Israel finding freedom in order to "possess" the land of Edom:

> But in Mount Zion there shall be those who escape, and it shall be holy, and the house of Jacob shall possess their own possessions. The house of Jacob shall be a fire, and the house of Joseph a flame, and the house of Esau stubble; they shall burn them and consume them, and there shall be no survivor for the house of Esau, for the LORD has spoken . . . The exiles of this host of the people of Israel shall possess the land of the Canaanites as far as Zarephath, and the exiles of Jerusalem who are in Sepharad shall possess the cities of the Negeb. (Obadiah 1:17–20)

But since Obadiah's day, Israel has never "possessed" the land of Edom at any time in history. The only option is to acknowledge that the ultimate fulfillment of this prophecy will take place in the future, under the reign of Jesus the Messiah. Having established the ultimate "Day of the Lord" context of the prophecy, then, against whom is the prophecy directed? Once more, the prophet Obadiah reiterated that which so many of the other Hebrew prophets emphasized:

> Will I not on that day, declares the LORD, destroy the wise men out of Edom, and understanding out of Mount Esau? And your mighty men shall be dismayed, O Teman, so that every man from Mount Esau will be cut off by slaughter. Because of the violence done to your brother Jacob, shame shall cover you, and you shall be cut off forever . . . For the day of the LORD is near upon all the nations. As you have done, it shall be done to you; your deeds shall return on your own head. (1:8–10, 15)

In keeping with the Israel-centricity of all biblical prophecy, once again we see the motivating factor and basis for God's judgment against Edom, Esau, and Teman is their violent treatment of Jacob/Israel. The people of Edom, it should be noted, are simply the descendants of Esau, Jacob's brother. Obadiah's use of three names—Edom, Esau, and Teman—is a typical characteristic of ancient Hebrew prophetic poetry:

employing synecdoche, synonyms, or variants of the same name for the purpose of emphasis. The ultimate and yet simple message of the prophecy is that in the context of the Day of the Lord, when He executes judgments against the nations, Edom will find its complete and final judgment.

EZEKIEL 25: JUDGMENT AGAINST ISRAEL'S SURROUNDING NEIGHBORS

In Ezekiel 25, we have yet another clear prophecy of divine judgment directed against Edom:

> Thus says the Lord GOD: Because Edom acted revengefully against the house of Judah and has grievously offended in taking vengeance on them, therefore thus says the Lord GOD, I will stretch out my hand against Edom and cut off from it man and beast. And I will make it desolate; from Teman even to Dedan [northern Saudi Arabia] they shall fall by the sword. And I will lay my vengeance upon Edom by the hand of my people Israel, and they shall do in Edom according to my anger and according to my wrath, and they shall know my vengeance, declares the Lord GOD. Thus says the Lord GOD: Because the Philistines acted revengefully and took vengeance with malice of soul to destroy in never-ending enmity, therefore thus says the Lord GOD, Behold, I will stretch out my hand against the Philistines [Palestinian territories], and I will cut off the Cherethites [Gaza] and destroy the rest of the seacoast. I will execute great vengeance on them with wrathful rebukes. Then they will know that I am the LORD, when I lay my vengeance upon them. (25:12–17)

Once more, what is the specific reason that God will judge Edom? The text is clear. It is because of how they treated "the house of Judah." They "greatly offended," and they executed vengeance against God's chosen people. For this reason, God will avenge Judah in return with "wrathful rebukes."

But is the text merely speaking of the region of modern-day Jordan? It is much more than this. In fact, included in Edom's judgment is the ancient city of Dedan, located in what is now Saudi Arabia and known as Al-ʿUla, as well as the Palestinian territories. Because the extent of the judgment includes both Teman (in modern-day Jordan) and Dedan (in north-central Saudi Arabia), we must take note that according to this text, God's judgment is directed against the entire region stretching from Jordan southward along the Red Sea well into north-central Saudi Arabia.

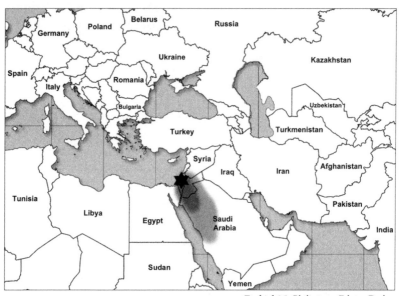

Ezekiel 25: Philistines, Edom, Dedan

EZEKIEL 30: THE DAY OF THE LORD AGAINST EGYPT, SUDAN, LIBYA, ARABIA, TURKEY, AND NORTH AFRICA

As we are beginning to see, the Lord's judgment against peoples and regions that are today Islamic is a theme that is repeated in numerous passages throughout the Scriptures. The following prophecy of Ezekiel is no exception:

> The word of the LORD came to me: "Son of man, prophesy, and say, Thus says the Lord GOD: "Wail, 'Alas for the day!' For the day is near, the day of the LORD is near; it will be a day of clouds, a time of doom for the nations. A sword shall come upon Egypt, and anguish shall be in Cush, when the slain fall in Egypt, and her wealth is carried away, and her foundations are torn down. Cush [Sudan], and Put [Libya and North Africa], and Lud [Turkey], and all Arabia, and Libya, and the people of the land that is in league, shall fall with them by the sword." (Ezekiel 30:1–5)

While these events have also seen partial fulfillment in history, the ultimate context of the passage is the Day of the Lord and Christ's return. And here, as in so many other passages, the Messiah comes to execute judgment against the enemies of His people, Israel. Included in the list of those marked for judgment are Egypt, Sudan, Libya, Turkey, Arabia, and possibly the nations of northern Africa. Once again, in the context of the Day of the Lord and Christ's return, the nations that the Scriptures identify as marked for judgment are Islamic.

ZEPHANIAH 2: THE DAY OF GOD'S ANGER AGAINST ISRAEL'S NEIGHBORS

Following in the footsteps of all of the prophets that came before him, Zephaniah prophesied that on "the day of the LORD's anger" (2:3 NKJV) Gaza, Ashkelon, Ashdod, Ekron, the Cherethites, Canaan, and the land of the Philistines will all be utterly ruined. Together, these names point us to the whole region of modern-day Israel's southwest coast, including the current Gaza Strip:

> Seek the LORD, all you humble of the land, who do his just commands; seek righteousness; seek humility; perhaps you may be hidden on the day of the anger of the LORD. For Gaza shall be deserted, and Ashkelon shall become a desolation; Ashdod's people shall be driven out at noon, and Ekron shall be uprooted. Woe to you inhabitants of the seacoast, you nation of the Cherethites! The word of the LORD is against you, O Canaan, land of the Philistines; and I will destroy you until no inhabitant is left . . . You also, O Cushites, shall be slain by my sword. And he will stretch out his hand against the north and destroy Assyria, and he will make Nineveh a desolation, a dry waste like the desert. (Zephaniah 2:3–5, 12, 13)

As Ralph L. Smith, in the *Word Biblical Commentary*, has stated, "Judgment against Judah's neighbors is the major motif of this section. Philistia in the west, Moab and Ammon on the east, Ethiopia [actually Sudan] or Egypt on the south, and Assyria to the north will all experience the judgment of Yahweh."[7]

It is imperative to note that in the midst of His judgment against Israel's enemies, the Lord will intervene on behalf of Judah, and return her captives. This is yet another important indicator that the ultimate emphasis of this prophecy is the return of the Messiah. That the inhabitants of modern-day Israel will be taken captive during the reign of the Antichrist, only to be delivered when Jesus returns, is a common theme in eschatological passages. In Luke's gospel, Jesus warns the inhabitants of Judah, in no unclear terms, that a time will come for them to flee to the mountains, lest they be taken away as prisoners:

> But when you see Jerusalem surrounded by armies, then know that its desolation has come near. Then let those who are in Judea flee to the mountains, and let those who are inside the city depart, and let not those who are out in the country enter it, for these are days of vengeance, to fulfill all that is written . . . They will fall by the edge of the sword and be led captive among all nations, and Jerusalem will be trampled underfoot by the Gentiles, until the times of the Gentiles are fulfilled. (Luke 21:20–24)

But despite Jesus' warnings, it is clear that many will not take heed and will be taken captive. In the end, He Himself will step down from heaven to deliver the prisoners from among the nations where they have been taken. Consider the following passages, in which the Lord Himself comes down from heaven to deliver Jewish prisoners from the surrounding nations:

> Therefore thus says the Lord GOD: "Now I will bring back the captives of Jacob, and have mercy on the whole house of Israel." (Ezekiel 39:25 NKJV)

> For in Mount Zion and in Jerusalem there shall be deliverance, as the LORD has said, among the remnant whom the LORD calls. For behold, in those days and at that time, when I bring back the captives of Judah and Jerusalem . . . (Joel 2:32–3:1 NKJV)

> The Spirit of the Lord GOD is upon me . . . He has sent me to bind up the brokenhearted, to proclaim liberty to the captives, and the opening of the prison to those who are bound; to proclaim the year of the LORD's favor, and the day of vengeance of our God; to comfort all who mourn; to grant to those who mourn in Zion . . . (Isaiah 61:1–3)

You will arise and have pity on Zion; it is the time to favor her; the appointed time has come . . . From heaven the LORD looked at the earth, to hear the groans of the prisoners, to set free those who were doomed to die. (Psalm 102:13, 19–20)

Because Zephaniah wrote of the Day of the Lord's anger against Israel's enemies in conjunction with the Lord's personal intervention and deliverance of the captives, we can understand the ultimate context of Zephaniah 2 to be the return of Jesus. But beyond judgment against Gaza and the Palestinians, the prophecy continues with a warning concerning the future of Moab, Ammon, the modern-day Republic of North Sudan (Cush), as well as Assyria and Nineveh:

"I have heard the taunts of Moab and the revilings of the Ammonites, how they have taunted my people and made boasts against their territory. Therefore, as I live," declares the LORD of hosts, the God of Israel, "Moab shall become like Sodom, and the Ammonites like Gomorrah, a land possessed by nettles and salt pits, and a waste forever. The remnant of my people shall plunder them, and the survivors of my nation shall possess them . . . You also, O Cushites [Sudan], shall be slain by my sword. And he will stretch out his hand against the north and destroy Assyria [Syria, Turkey, Lebanon, and Iraq], and he will make Nineveh a desolation, a dry waste like the desert." (Zephaniah 2:8–9, 12–13)

We have already discussed the location of Moab, east of Israel. Ammon was the region immediately to north of Moab, also in modern-day Jordan and Syria. During Zephaniah's day, in the sixth century BC, Assyria straddled the borders of modern-day Turkey, Syria, Lebanon, and Iraq. The ancient city of Nineveh, now called Mosul, is in northern Iraq. And so once more, in the context of the Day of the Lord and Christ's return, the nations specified for judgment are all Muslim-majority nations.

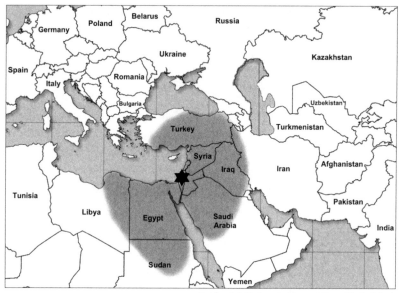

Zephaniah 2: Assyria, Egypt, Libya, Cush, Moab

JOEL 3: THE LORD'S JUDGMENT AGAINST LEBANON AND GAZA FOR DIVIDING THE LAND OF ISRAEL

In 2007, a published statement signed by more than eighty prominent evangelical Christian leaders was sent to then American president George W. Bush, titled "An Evangelical Statement on Israel/Palestine." In brief, it was an appeal to Christians and governmental leaders globally to divide the land of Israel to prevent further terrorism:

> As evangelical Christians committed to the full authority of the Scriptures, we feel compelled to make a statement together at this historic moment in the life of the Holy Land . . . In the context of our ongoing support for the security of Israel, we believe that unless the situation between Israel and Palestine improves quickly, the consequences will be devastating . . . We believe that the way forward is for the Israelis and Palestinians to negotiate a fair, two-state solution . . . We call on all evangelicals, all Christians, and everyone of good will to join us to work and pray faithfully in the coming months for a just, lasting two-state solution in the Holy Land. We call on all involved governments to work diligently toward this goal.[8]

The Statement was signed by the presidents of several well-known conservative evangelical Christian colleges and seminaries. What is so disturbing about this statement is that in the name of "justice" and "peace," it is a direct rejection of the position that Jesus will so clearly take in the timing and the context of His return. Consider the following portion from the prophecy of Joel:

> For behold, in those days and at that time, when I restore the fortunes of Judah and Jerusalem, I will gather all the nations and bring them down to the Valley of Jehoshaphat. And I will enter into judgment with them there, on behalf of my people and my heritage Israel, because they have scattered them among the nations and have divided up my land, and have cast lots for my people, and have traded a boy for a prostitute, and have sold a girl for wine and have drunk it. What are you to me, O Tyre and Sidon, and all the regions of Philistia? Are you paying me back for something? If you are paying me back, I will return your payment on your own head swiftly and speedily. (3:1–4)

In the last chapter, we specified some of the primary themes that virtually all of the prophets reiterated over and over again with regard to the Day of the Lord. This particular prophecy contains a few of the more commonly repeated themes. We have the multinational coalition of the Antichrist invading Israel and surrounding Jerusalem. We have the people of Israel being taken captive to the nations. The Lord then specifies some of the nations involved, namely Tyre, Sidon, and Philistia. These are essentially references to Lebanon and the Gaza Strip. Then there is the promise from the Lord of vengeance against the nations that have committed these sins against His people. It is difficult to deny the Day-of-the-Lord context of this passage, as well as the striking precision with which it reflects today's political atmosphere in the region. Rather than Lebanon and Gaza, one could nearly insert Hezbollah and Hamas. But despite the strong warning of this passage and the many others we have surveyed, an increasing number of evangelical Christians, including leaders who claim Scripture as their final authority, are positioning themselves not on the side of Jesus, but on the side of the nations whom Jesus will judge. When the evangelical leaders who signed the Statement on Israel/Palestine claim their motivation is to prevent further terrorism and negative views of the U.S. and Israel, it is clear that they are guided by the spirit of this world and not by the Word of God. They are guided by the fear of terrorism, not by the fear of the Lord. Although the following statement may offend some; the times in which we live demand that those who genuinely desire to follow Jesus reject the leadership of such blind guides.

ISAIAH 34: THE LORD HAS A SACRIFICE IN BOZRAH AND EDOM

The entire chapter of Isaiah 34 is a poetic portrayal of a ritual sacrifice in the land of Edom. Here, the Lord's wrath is executed against a very specific people and for very specific reasons. Let's look at the text:

> For my sword has drunk its fill in the heavens; behold, it descends for judgment upon Edom, upon the people I have devoted to destruction. The LORD has a sword; it is sated with blood; it is gorged with fat, with the blood of lambs and goats, with the fat of the kidneys of rams. For the LORD has a sacrifice in Bozrah, a great slaughter in the land of Edom . . . Their land shall drink its fill of blood, and their soil shall be gorged with fat. For the LORD has a day of vengeance, a year of recompense for the cause of Zion. And the streams of Edom shall be turned into pitch, and her soil into sulfur; her land shall become burning pitch. (vv. 5–9)

The "sword" of the Lord's wrath is against whom? Once again, it is specifically "the people" of Edom—Israel's enemies. Why is Jesus judging Edom? To uphold "the cause of Zion." The King James Version translates this Hebrew word (*riyb*) as "the controversy of Zion." It carries the connotation of a legal dispute or controversy, which is precisely what Israel finds itself embroiled in today. Whether it is from the systemically anti-Zionist and anti-Semitic Muslim nations that surround her on every side or from the left-wing anti-Zionist propagandists whose numbers are growing throughout the earth, the claim is that Israel is an illegal, unjust, apartheid state. The truth, of course, is just the opposite, and thus it is for this very reason that the Messiah comes to settle the issue once and for all. According to this passage, Jesus returns to defend Israel against the unjust assault of her enemies and to specifically execute judgment against "Edom, the people I have totally destroyed" (v. 5 NIV).

ISAIAH 63: TREADING THE WINEPRESS OF THE WRATH OF GOD ALMIGHTY IN EDOM

Revelation 19 contains the most well-known passage concerning Christ's return in the entire Bible. In this quintessentially dramatic picture, Jesus bursts forth from heaven, riding upon a white horse with "the armies of heaven" following him.

> Then I saw heaven opened, and behold, a white horse! The one sitting on it is called Faithful and True, and in righteousness he judges and makes war. His eyes are like a flame of fire, and on his head are many diadems, and he has a name written that no one knows but himself. He is clothed in a robe dipped in blood, and the name by which he is called is The Word of God. And the armies of heaven, arrayed in fine linen, white and pure, were following him on white horses. From his mouth comes a sharp sword with which to strike down the nations, and he will rule them with a rod of iron. He will tread the winepress of the fury of the wrath of God the Almighty. On his robe and on his thigh he has a name written, King of kings and Lord of lords. (vv. 11–16)

Most Christians are familiar with this passage. Yet few are aware of the meaning of Christ's blood-soaked robe. When teaching on this passage, I have made it my custom to ask the congregation where this blood came from, or to whom did it originally belong? The first and most common answer given is that this is Jesus' own blood. Many fellow congregants will shake their heads in agreement, assuming this must be a symbolic picture of the blood that Jesus shed on the cross. If this is the case, I ask, why is His robe soaked with His own blood? Quizzical looks come over the crowd. I ask for any other suggestions.

The second answer given is that Jesus' robes are soaked with the blood shed by the faithful martyrs who were killed during the great tribulation and even down throughout Church history. While the origin of these answers is understandable, the fact is that neither answer is correct. The answer is found in Isaiah 63, from which Revelation 19 is taken. Let's look at the passage:

> Who is this who comes from Edom, in crimsoned garments from Bozrah, he who is splendid in his apparel, marching in the greatness of his strength? "It is I, speaking in righteousness, mighty to save."

Why is your apparel red, and your garments like his who treads in the winepress? "I have trodden the winepress alone, and from the peoples no one was with me; I trod them in my anger and trampled them in my wrath; their lifeblood spattered on my garments, and stained all my apparel. For the day of vengeance was in my heart, and my year of redemption had come." (vv. 1–4)

In this highly dramatic passage, Isaiah the prophet is looking eastward from Jerusalem. In his mind's eye, he sees a majestic and determined figure—it is Jesus the Messiah—marching victoriously toward His throne in Jerusalem, out of Edom and Bozrah. Bozrah was the capital city of ancient Edom. Today it is called Petra.

In Revelation 19:15 we read that Jesus "will tread the winepress of the fury of the wrath of God the Almighty" where God's enemies are portrayed as being crushed like grapes. But it is in Isaiah 63 that we have the original context for this passage. And it is specifically in Edom that Jesus is seen to be crushing His enemies, actually soaking His garments with their blood. It is also essential to take note of the timing of the passage, set squarely in the midst of the Day of the Lord. The passage specifically refers to this day as the day of the Messiah's vengeance and redemption, which, having been long awaited, has finally arrived. And so once more, in the context of the return of the Messiah and the Day of the Lord, Jesus is shown judging His enemies, who are squarely placed in the land of Edom.

CONCLUSION

As we have seen, throughout the Scriptures, repeatedly and abundantly, whenever specific nations are named and highlighted for the judgment of God at the Day of the Lord, apart from the Lord's chastisement against His own people Israel, it is always pointing us to regions or nations that today are vastly dominated by Islam.

Many prophecy teachers today claim that the religion of the Antichrist will be humanism or some form of all-inclusive religious pluralism. If this is the case, then one must also believe that the overwhelming majority of Middle Eastern nations today will convert from Islam to a belief system common in the West, but embraced by very few in the Middle East. Yet not once in the entire Bible is an exclusively European nation actually named in the context of judgment on the Day of the Lord. The Bible certainly references European nations, but never in the context of His judgment. Yet this is where the majority of prophecy teachers have told us the Antichrist and his empire will emerge.

What shall we conclude from this? How do we responsibly interpret these many passages? Shall we simply ignore these references? Or should we claim that they are all to be taken allegorically, assuming that names such as Edom, Moab, Cush, Arabia, Assyria, Libya, Lydia, or Persia are meant to imply any or every nation in the world as the vague or general enemies of God and His people? This hyper-allegorical approach is actually very common when approaching these passages. As I have already stated, I find it irresponsible and not in keeping with a conservative and literal hermeneutic. Will God exclusively judge Muslim nations and bless all Western or non-Muslim nations? How do these nations relate to the coming empire of the Antichrist? The answer to these questions are essential if we are to grasp the message of the prophets. The implications and ramifications for evangelism and missions as well as the prayer focus of the Church are immense. In the next two chapters, we will attempt to answer these questions and develop a solid method of interpretation to understand these passages.

3

THE DOMINION OF THE
ANTICHRIST: ABSOLUTE
OR LIMITED?

NOW THAT WE HAVE REVIEWED a sampling of prophetic texts that specify where the emphasis of Jesus' judgment will rest when He returns, one point stands out: the overwhelming emphasis of the Lord's anger and judgment is directed toward the hostile nations that surround the nation of Israel. While many of the prophecies we examined were partially fulfilled in history, they will find their ultimate fulfillment when Jesus returns. The problem, however, is that because much of the Church believes that the coming kingdom of the Antichrist will include every single nation of the earth, no matter how specific the Scriptures are in naming the primary nations reserved for the Lord's judgments, many will simply interpret these Scriptures allegorically to simply mean every nation of the earth. Therefore, whether one views the coming kingdom of the Antichrist to be absolutely global or limited will significantly determine one's method of interpretation. Within the realm of theology, virtually every belief affects or impacts several other doctrines. As we will see, this problem of over-allegorizing large segments of the prophetic Scriptures often begins with the belief that the Antichrist's kingdom or alliance will be absolutely universal, including every last nation of the earth. It is therefore essential to determine what the Scriptures truly say about this issue. *Will* his coming kingdom literally include every single nation on Earth, or will it be limited in any way?

The belief that the Antichrist's kingdom will be absolutely global and unlimited is held by a wide range of prophecy teachers and students. Dr. Thomas Ice, for instance, says, "The Revived Roman Empire will come to power via a 10 nation confederacy . . . This will be the springboard for the Antichrist's global empire."[1]

David Reagan expresses a similar belief concerning the Antichrist's absolute authority over every government, military, and religious system in every nation of the earth, without exception: "The final Gentile empire will unite the world politically, socially, economically and spiritually. Every nation will be included."[2]

Now, let me say that I fully understand and very much sympathize with this position. I held to this view myself for many years. But as shocking as this may be to many who read this, the Bible does not predict an absolute global empire controlled by the Antichrist. While there are some verses that have led many to take such a view, there are also several other very important texts that make this an impossibility. After a thorough examination of all of the relevant passages that pertain to this issue, it will become quite clear that what the Bible predicts is a vastly powerful, yet limited empire controlled by the Antichrist. Let's consider the evidence.

THE ANTICHRIST'S EMPIRE IS PRIMARILY A TEN-NATION ALLIANCE

We begin our study by taking note of the repeated emphasis the Bible places on the Antichrist's kingdom as a ten-nation alliance. The first such passage is found in Daniel 7 and speaks of a future empire, symbolized through the motif of a "beast." This empire would follow after the Babylonian, Medo-Persian, and Grecian Empires, being a powerfully destructive force that would utterly trample the regions it conquered. It is said to have "ten horns": "After this I saw in the night visions, and behold, a fourth beast, terrifying and dreadful and exceedingly strong. It had great iron teeth; it devoured and broke in pieces and stamped what was left with its feet. It was different from all the beasts that were before it, and it had ten horns" (v. 7).

After this, an angel informed Daniel that the ten horns represent "ten kings" which would arise from this kingdom. The leader of these ten kings is the Antichrist: "As for the ten horns, out of this kingdom ten kings shall arise, and another shall arise after them; he shall be different from the former ones, and shall put down three kings. He shall speak words against the Most High, and shall wear out the saints of the Most High" (vv. 24–25).

But it is not only in the book of Daniel that we find references to this number. John the apostle also relayed the same information in the book of Revelation. In fact, between these two books, the Lord reiterated the specific number of nations that will initially comprise the Antichrist's empire eight separate times. Here are six more examples:

> And about the ten horns that were on its head, and the other horn that came up and before which three of them fell, the horn that had eyes and a mouth that spoke great things, and that seemed greater than its companions . . . (Daniel 7:20)

> And I saw a beast rising out of the sea, with ten horns and seven heads, with ten diadems on its horns and blasphemous names on its heads. (Revelation 13:1)

> And he carried me away in the Spirit into a wilderness, and I saw a woman sitting on a scarlet beast that was full of blasphemous names, and it had seven heads and ten horns. (Revelation 17:3)

> But the angel said to me, "Why do you marvel? I will tell you the mystery of the woman, and of the beast with seven heads and ten horns that carries her." (Revelation 17:7)

> And the ten horns that you saw are ten kings who have not yet received royal power, but they are to receive authority as kings for one hour, together with the beast. (Revelation 17:12)

> And the ten horns that you saw, they and the beast will hate the prostitute. They will make her desolate and naked, and devour her flesh and burn her up with fire. (Revelation 17:16)

The point in fully citing all of these passages is to demonstrate the weight of emphasis the Lord has so obviously placed on the number 10 as the number of nations that would be the willing supporters of the Antichrist. Does this mean that the Antichrist's kingdom will always include only ten nations, never to expand? Not at all. As our study continues, we will see that from this ten-nation base of the willing, the Antichrist will expand his empire through military conquest.

THE LIMITED MILITARY EXPANSION OF THE ANTICHRIST'S DOMINION

Several Bible passages very directly address the military expansion of the Antichrist's empire. That the Antichrist will conquer many nations is very clear. But what is also clear is that the Antichrist will never literally conquer or control every last nation of the earth. Let's consider the evidence.

Twice Daniel 11 says that the Antichrist will "invade many countries." Specifically, Egypt will fall to his forces. Beyond this, we are told the Antichrist will invade the land of Israel, called, "the glorious land" (v. 16). But this passage also may suggest that the Antichrist will not conquer *every* nation. In fact, it specifically says that Edom, Moab, and the leaders of Ammon will escape "his hand":

> And he shall come into countries and shall overflow and pass through.
> He shall come into the glorious land. And tens of thousands shall fall,
> but these shall be delivered out of his hand: Edom and Moab and the
> main part of the Ammonites. He shall stretch out his hand against the
> countries, and the land of Egypt shall not escape. (vv. 40–42)

It is noteworthy that when this passage speaks of the nations that fall to the Antichrist's military expansion, it says "many countries," not "every nation." And then it specifically lists three ancient kingdoms that will be "delivered out of his hand." Because of the grouping of Edom, Moab, and Ammon together, the passage seems to be referring to the modern-day Hashemite Kingdom of Jordan. And so based on this passage alone, it may be that Jordan will not come under the Antichrist's authority. It could also simply mean that Jordan will not be crushed, but will instead willingly submit to the Antichrist. But as we will see, there are certainly other nations that will not fall under his dominion.

Just a few verses later, we learn that in the midst of his campaign of conquest, the Antichrist hears of "news from the east and the north," which troubles him and throws him into a frantic state of rage and annihilation. Because the context of the whole of the passage is military conquest and war, the "news," or "rumors," as some translations word it, should also be seen in this light. It is likely that the news is a reference to a gathering military response against the Antichrist: "But news from the east and the north shall alarm him, and he shall go out with great fury to destroy and devote many to destruction. And he shall pitch his palatial tents between the sea and the glorious holy mountain. Yet he shall come to his end, with none to help him" (vv. 44–45).

Many commentators have suggested that China (to the east) and Russia (to the north) could be in mind, although we cannot know for sure. Prophecy expert and scholar John Walvoord says that the Antichrist will

> hear reports of additional armies coming from the East and the North. This apparently refers to the great army from the East described in Revelation 16:12 as "the kings from the East." Some connect this also with Rev 9:13-16 which states the army is 200 million. This will probably not only include the armies which will fight but also supporting personnel behind them. It is significant that China today boasts a militia of 200 million men.[3]

We can conclude from this text that there will be nations not in alliance or under the authority of the Antichrist. Right up until his end, the Antichrist will be at war with "many nations."

UNTIL THE END, THERE SHALL BE WAR

Daniel 9 also establishes this reality: "And the people of the prince who is to come shall destroy the city and the sanctuary. Its end shall come with a flood, and to the end there shall be war. Desolations are decreed" (v. 26).

Simply stated, a king with absolute, universal authority is not at war. The presence of wars establishes the fact that the Antichrist does not control *every* nation, but that there are resisting governments. He does not control their militaries. This is proof of the Antichrist's limited authority right up to the end. As Finis Jennings Dake accurately states, "No earthly man will become the worldwide dictator before Christ comes to reign . . . Thus the old theory of the Antichrist being a man who will miraculously bring world peace and prosperity, is unscriptural. He is a man of war from the time he comes until he is destroyed at Armageddon."[4]

But despite the fact that the Antichrist's dominion will be limited, his military apparatus will be a force to be reckoned with. In Revelation 13, we see the people of the earth asking who is able to make war against the Antichrist's empire. It will seem as if none are capable of waging a successful war against him: "And they worshiped the dragon, for he had given his authority to the beast, and they worshiped the beast, saying, "Who is like the beast, and who can fight against it?" (v. 4). (Note that if every nation were under his control, this question couldn't be asked.)

INTERPRETING HYPERBOLE IN SCRIPTURE

To accurately interpret biblical prophecy, it is essential to understand *hyperbole* and its frequent use throughout the Scriptures. Hyperbole is simply an exaggeration used to create emphasis. Hyperbole is used in everyday, casual speech. An example might be, the exclamation "Oh my gosh, boy, you weigh a ton!" when a man picks up his four-year-old grandson for the first time in a few months. Of course, the boy does not actually weigh anywhere close to two thousand pounds. The grandfather used the expression simply to convey that the boy has become quite heavy.

The Middle Eastern culture that gave birth to the Bible is particularly fond of hyperbole. And because the Bible uses the idioms common to the peoples of the region, to correctly interpret multitudes of biblical passages requires an understanding of this device.

In discussing his native Syrian culture, Abraham Mitrie Rihbany, in his classic work *The Syrian Christ*, recalls a somewhat humorous example of everyday Middle Eastern hyperbole in how a friend welcomed him to his home: "You have extremely honored me by coming into my abode. I am not worthy of it. This house is yours; you may burn it if you wish. My children are also at your disposal; I would sacrifice them all for your pleasure."[5]

When Westerners hear hyperbole used in such a way, they can easily misunderstand the speaker's intended meaning. Some may feel such comments are offensive or outright misleading. Of course this man would not have allowed his friend to burn down his house, nor was he offering his children to be sacrificed. This flamboyant language was simply a normal way in Middle Eastern culture to express great honor and welcome to Rihbany.

EXAMPLES OF HYPERBOLE IN SCRIPTURE

Now let's briefly consider just a few passages of Scripture where hyperbole is used. In pondering the difficulties of entering the Promised Land, the Hebrews expressed their dismay, not only at the size of the people in the land, but also of the walls that surrounded their cities: "Where are we going up? Our brothers have made our hearts melt, saying, 'The people are greater and taller than we. The cities are great and fortified up to heaven. And besides, we have seen the sons of the Anakim there'" (Deuteronomy 1:28).

Did the walls of the cities literally reach up to heaven? How high, exactly, is heaven? One hundred feet? Is heaven more than a thousand feet up? Of course the walls were not literally fortified "up to heaven." They were just intimidatingly high. That is all this expression means.

Here's another fun example of hyperbole: "And the king made silver and gold as common in Jerusalem as stone, and he made cedar as plentiful as the sycamore of the Shephelah" (2 Chronicles 1:15).

I cannot speak to the amount of sycamore trees in the Shephelah during Solomon's day, but having spent a substantial amount of time in Israel, I guarantee that there were gazillions of stones everywhere. To suggest that silver and gold were literally as abundant and "common" in Israel as stones is just plain silly. The point is that during Solomon's reign, wealth was abundant in Israel.

Numerous other examples could be cited. It is beyond question that the Bible frequently uses hyperbole. But even more relevant to our larger discussion, the Bible repeatedly uses hyperbole specifically with regard to the extent of various pagan empires. This is absolutely critical to note if one desires to properly interpret the passages that speak of the extent of the Antichrist's coming kingdom.

HYPERBOLE APPLIED TO KINGDOMS IN SCRIPTURE

Now, despite the fact that the passages we've examined reveal that there will be at least some nations not under the Antichrist's authority, some Bible students have looked to passages such as Daniel 7:23 as proof of his universal authority: "As for the fourth beast, there shall be a fourth kingdom on earth, which shall be different from all the kingdoms, and it shall devour the whole earth, and trample it down, and break it to pieces." These students immediately assume that the phrase "the whole earth" literally means every single nation across the globe. But there is no difficulty or contradiction with this verse and a limited dominion of the Antichrist. The phrase "the whole earth" is the Aramaic *kol 'ara'*, appropriately understood here as a large, but limited section of land. Commenting on this particular verse, Gleason L. Archer Jr., perhaps the chief apostle of the doctrine of Biblical inerrancy and a well-known translator and scholar of Biblical languages, states:

> The whole earth (*kol 'ara'*) refers, not to all known parts of the inhabited earth, but rather (as in general OT usage) to the entire territory of the Near and Middle East that in any way relates to the Holy Land. The word *'ara'* (and its Hebrew equivalent *ères*) does not necessarily mean globe in the sense of "the entire inhabited globe" but—depending on context—might mean a single country (*ères yiśrā'ēl* is "the land of Israel") or a larger geographical unit, such as "territory" or "region."[6]

Daniel 2:39 uses this exact Aramaic phrase of the Alexandrian Greek Empire: "Another kingdom inferior to you shall arise after you, and yet a third kingdom of bronze which shall rule over all the earth." Of course, no historian would ever claim that the Greek Empire ever actually ruled the entire planet. In claiming that the "whole earth" in Daniel 7:23 must literally mean the whole earth, one must ignore the meaning of the words in their original language both there and in Daniel 2:39—and Alexander the Great did *not* rule over every last nation on the earth.

Now let's consider another example of this phrase, this time translated from the Hebrew word *'erets*: "As I was considering, behold, a male goat came from the west across the face of the whole earth, without touching the ground. And the goat had a conspicuous horn between his eyes" (Daniel 8:5).

Here, the symbol of a male goat represents the Alexandrian Greek Empire, which began in Macedonia and swept all the way eastward to India. Imagine, if you can, a goat that leaps off the ground from modern-day Greece and flies through the air, all the way to India. This would no doubt be quite impressive, even for a goat! But despite the vast distances covered, the marvelous leap of the super-goat would still not qualify as having literally covered "the whole earth." Yes, Alexander conquered a vast region, but not the entire globe.

Now let's consider another classic example, this time from the gospel of Luke: "In those days a decree went out from Caesar Augustus that all the world should be registered" (Luke 2:1). Here we are told that Caesar was requiring "all the world" to be subjected to the census. But in reality, only the subjects of the Roman Empire were registered. The rest of the world would have paid absolutely no attention to this decree. Some scholars have said that verses such as this speak only of "the inhabited world." But this is not an accurate statement. When the census went forth, China was certainly inhabited by a thriving and well-organized civilization, as was the Parthian Empire, immediately to the east of the Roman Empire. So again, while the Roman Empire was massive and covered a large portion of the earth, in no way can one say that it literally included *all* the world, or even the *inhabited* or *known* world.

Another example of hyperbole is found in Daniel. Here we are told that wherever mankind, animals, or birds lived, anywhere on the earth, King Nebuchadnezzar was given dominion over them all:

> "This was the dream. Now we will tell the king its interpretation. You, O king, the king of kings, to whom the God of heaven has given the kingdom, the power, and the might, and the glory, and into whose hand he has given, wherever they dwell, the children of man, the beasts of the field, and the birds of the heavens, making you rule over them all—you are the head of gold." (2:36–38)

But once more, it doesn't take a historian to acknowledge that King Nebuchadnezzar, though he achieved an astonishing degree of dominion, never possessed global rule. Beyond the kingdoms that immediately surrounded and even competed with Nebuchadnezzar, other significant kingdoms coexisted during his reign.

After Nebuchadnezzar, Cyrus, the king of Persia used hyperbole to describe his own dominion: "Thus says Cyrus king of Persia: The LORD, the God of heaven, has given me all the kingdoms of the earth, and he has charged me to build him a house at Jerusalem, which is in Judah" (Ezra 1:2). Once more, Cyrus never possessed "all the kingdoms of the earth."

It was not a contradiction for the biblical authors at times to refer to "all the earth," "the whole world," "all nations," and similar phrases when simply some vast region was in mind. From the biblical perspective, such phrases most often spoke of the greater Middle East, the Mediterranean, and Northern Africa. When desiring to interpret the Bible properly, the Western reader must be very careful not to apply a modern, Western mind-set to the pages of this ancient Eastern book.

THE PRIMARY OBJECTION

But the most significant objection that most have with a limited reign of the Antichrist is based on Revelation 13:7–8: "Also it [the Antichrist] was allowed to make war on the saints and to conquer them. And authority was given it over every tribe and people and language and nation, and all who dwell on earth will worship it, everyone whose name has not been written before the foundation of the world in the book of life of the Lamb who was slain."

It is easy to understand how this passage could convince one to believe that the Antichrist will possess a global empire, but even the phrase "every tribe and people and language and nation, and all who dwell on earth" is immediately limited by "those whose name has not been written . . . in the book of life." Beyond this, no passage can be understood in a vacuum. And as we have already seen, the presence of wars, resisting nations, and militaries until the very end proves that the dominion of the Antichrist will not be absolutely universal. But when I have suggested this in the past, some have expressed incredulity. Yet if we consider Daniel 5:18–19, we find a nearly identical phrase: "O king, the Most High God gave Nebuchadnezzar your father kingship and greatness and glory and majesty. And because of the greatness that he gave him, all peoples, nations, and languages trembled and feared before him."

The Septuagint translation of this verse uses exactly the same words that are used in Revelation. (Daniel uses *laos*, *phulé*, and *glóssa*, whereas Revelation uses *laon*, *phylē*, *glōssa*, and *ethnos*). If we interpret Daniel's passage without acknowledging its use of hyperbole, we would be forced to conclude that King Nebuchadnezzar was literally feared by every human on the earth. But he was not even heard of by every single person in every part of the entire planet, let alone greatly feared by them. So based on our knowledge of history and common sense, we acknowledge the use of hyperbole in this passage too. Likewise, Revelation 13:7–8 does not mean every last person on the earth worships the beast, but instead, a multitude from numerous nations and people groups. Specifically, those "whose name has not been written . . . in the book of life."

Another important factor worthy of consideration is the phrase "authority was given him *over* . . ." The word for "over" in Greek is *epi*. Besides "over" it can also mean "in," "on," or "upon." As such, the English translation could just as easily read, "And authority was given him in [or among] every tribe, tongue, and nation." If Islam is the religion used by the Antichrist, which I personally believe to be the case, then it also stands to reason that the Antichrist will have followers in virtually every nation throughout the earth. While we know that he will not be given absolute authority over every government, it seems as though he will have some authority and a deep influence among the vast majority of nations throughout the earth. So while the Antichrist's dominion may not necessarily be over every last nation, it is possible that he will possess authority *within* every nation, including many that do not come under his complete governmental authority.

THE GATHERING OF ALL NATIONS AGAINST JERUSALEM

There remain a few important passages that have led many to believe that the Antichrist's dominion will be global. These passages speak of "all the nations" that will gather against Jerusalem under the leadership of the Antichrist. Let's look at the verses first, and then discuss their meanings.

> I will gather all the nations and bring them down to the Valley of Jehoshaphat. And I will enter into judgment with them there, on behalf of my people and my heritage Israel. (Joel 3:2)

> For I will gather all the nations against Jerusalem to battle, and the city shall be taken and the houses plundered and the women raped. Half of the city shall go out into exile. (Zechariah 14:2)

Now, are these references to "all the nations" actually referring to every single, solitary nation on the earth? No, further investigation leads us to recognize that the nations that surround Jerusalem, while no doubt a massive confederacy, do not include *every* nation of the earth. Instead, the fuller context of each passage actually clarifies for us exactly which nations will attack Jerusalem. In Hebrew, the phrases are *goy cabiyb* ("the surrounding nations") and *am cabiyb* ("the surrounding peoples"). Consider a fuller reading of each of these:

> Hasten and come, all you surrounding nations, and gather yourselves there. Bring down your warriors, O LORD. Let the nations stir themselves up and come up to the Valley of Jehoshaphat; for there I will sit to judge all the surrounding nations. (Joel 3:11–12)

> Behold, I am about to make Jerusalem a cup of staggering to all the surrounding peoples. The siege of Jerusalem will also be against Judah . . . On that day I will make the clans of Judah like a blazing pot in the midst of wood, like a flaming torch among sheaves. And they shall devour to the right and to the left all the surrounding peoples. (Zechariah 12:2, 6)

> For I will gather all the nations against Jerusalem to battle, and the city shall be taken and the houses plundered and the women raped. Half of the city shall go out into exile, but the rest of the people shall not be cut off from the city. . . . Even Judah will fight at Jerusalem. And the wealth of all the surrounding nations shall be collected, gold, silver, and garments in great abundance. Then everyone who survives of all the nations that have come against Jerusalem shall go up year after year to worship the King, the LORD of hosts, and to keep the Feast of Booths. (Zechariah 14:2, 14, 16)

Ezekiel could not have been clearer when he wrote of the day when the people of Israel will no longer be surrounded by people who despise them:

> Thus says the Lord GOD: "Behold, I am against you, O Sidon, and I will manifest my glory in your midst. And they shall know that I am the LORD when I execute judgments in her and manifest my holiness in her; for I will send pestilence into her, and blood into her streets; and the slain shall fall in her midst, by the sword that is against her on every side. Then they will know that I am the LORD. And for the

house of Israel there shall be no more a brier to prick or a thorn to hurt them among all their neighbors who have treated them with contempt. Then they will know that I am the Lord GOD. (Ezekiel 28:22–24)

The phrase translated here as "all their neighbors" is once again *cabiyb*, the same word used in Joel and Zechariah to speak of the surrounding nations. So first, each of these passages uses a hyperbolic statement that "all" nations will gather against Jerusalem, but then they each add clarity and specificity by narrowing down the scope of the coming invasion. The greater context of each passage points us not to every single nation throughout the earth, but instead to the surrounding nations that will attack Jerusalem. It's actually far simpler than we have often made it.

ONLY JESUS WILL POSSESS ABSOLUTE DOMINION

As we have now seen, while the Antichrist will desire to attain a universal dominion, he will simply never achieve it. There is, however, one man who will rule the entire earth. We call Him Jesus, or in His native language, Yahshua. Concerning His coming universal reign, the book of Revelation informs us that after His return, "the seventh angel blew his trumpet, and there were loud voices in heaven, saying, 'The kingdom [*basileia*] of the world [*kosmos*] has become the kingdom of our Lord and of his Christ, and he shall reign forever and ever'" (11:15).

Now, perhaps you are asking why this passage should be interpreted universally and not as an example of hyperbole. Apart from the fact that Jesus is the Creator of all things and the Antichrist is merely a demonized man, what is so fascinating is the specific use of the Greek word *kosmos*, which means "the world, universe, or circle of the earth." This passage is speaking of Jesus possessing complete and global rule. On the other hand, in every passage in Revelation that speaks of the Antichrist's reign, the words used are either *ge* or *oikoumene*, which can mean either "the whole world"/"all the inhabitants of the earth" *or* "the land"/"a fixed region." The only word that could remove all doubt regarding absolute universality is *kosmos*, and that word is only applied to the dominion of Jesus! This is good news! While the Antichrist will try to conquer the whole earth, he will never succeed, and accordingly to the Bible, will only be here briefly,

Jesus will return to rule the *entire* planet and His reign will be eternal. Hallelujah and amen!

4

FORMULATING OUR METHOD
OF INTERPRETATION

I N CHAPTER 2, we examined several passages from throughout the prophets, demonstrating the fact that repeatedly and consistently, the nations which are named as being marked for judgment after the return of the Messiah, are Middle Eastern and North African nations. It is essential that we now discuss how to properly understand these passages. How we understand the many names, peoples, and nations mentioned by the prophets will greatly influence and inform our understanding of which nations will primarily comprise the coming empire of the Antichrist. For surely, it will be the nations that follow the Antichrist in his assault against Israel that will be the most emphasized as destined for judgment when Jesus returns. Having demonstrated in the last chapter that not every nation of the earth will follow the Antichrist, the question remains as to what nations the Scriptures say will be his willing followers. We will now discuss the best and most responsible method of interpreting and understanding the many names, peoples, and nations highlighted by the prophets as being reserved for judgment on the Day of the Lord.

THE ANCESTRAL-MIGRATION-METHOD

Although a rare position, some Bible teachers have attempted to interpret the various names of those marked for judgment by the prophets by tracking down the actual blood-line descendants of these ancient people. This approach is fraught with difficulties and uncertainties. For example, among all the names and peoples marked for God's judgment, none is mentioned more than Edom and the Edomites. Yet by most historical and scholarly accounts, the Edomites as a people disappeared by the first century. Some prophecy teachers, attempting to prove otherwise, argue that there is still a watered-down measure of Edomite blood in the modern-day Palestinians, or even the Sephardic Jews of Israel. This may or may not be the case, but in light of the various conflicting claims of most historians and scholars, proving this with any certainty is nearly impossible and certainly beyond the ability of the average student of the Scriptures. Many of the other names used would also point to peoples who have migrated, intermarried, or just plain disappeared. Because thousands of years have passed since the prophecies were made, tracking down most of the civilizations mentioned by the prophets can be quite difficult, if not impossible, and the results of such efforts are rarely convincing. There are a few cases, however, where such an ancestral connection is fairly well established and agreed upon by historians. The descendants of Ishmael, for instance, we can be confident are still identifiable as the Arab peoples of the Middle East. Other examples could be cited.

AVOIDING THE HYPER-ALLEGORICAL METHOD

Recognizing the dangers and problems of the ancestral-migration-method, many conservative scholars overcompensate in the name of caution and claim that the various names and peoples mentioned by the prophets are simply references to the *general* enemies of God's people. This is the hyper-allegorical approach. This approach allegorizes the multitude of references throughout the prophets to names such as Moab, Edom, Assyria, Libya, or Lebanon to simply mean either *every* last nation on the entire earth or *any* end-time enemy of God's people, anywhere. According to this thinking, we could literally erase the words *Edom, Moab, Libya*—any of dozens of names from the text—and simply replace them with "all nations from the far corners of the earth" and it wouldn't make any difference whatsoever. In my opinion, this approach runs rough-shod over any literal, plain-sense meaning of Scripture, rendering the texts virtually meaningless. Unfortunately, as one surveys the treatment of these texts, even in most conservative commentaries, the hyper-allegorical approach is the most commonly applied method.

THE PROPHETIC-LITERAL APPROACH

As an alternative to the excesses of the ancestral-migration-method or the hyper-allegorical approach, given our spectrum of choices, I offer that the most reasonable approach is to emphasize two correlations between the ancient names and peoples and their last-days ultimate fulfillment.

The first correlation is the same general geographic location. This method identifies the location of the land or people at the time the prophecy was made, and then looks to the nation or people that inhabit this region today. Gleason L. Archer, the revered scholar of Old Testament and semitic languages, identifies the geographic-correlation-method as the best interpretive method to understand the many names found throughout the Old Testament prophecies:

> Likewise, the ancient names of countries or states occupying the region where the final conflict will be carried on are used in the prediction, though most of those political units will no longer bear these names in the last days. Thus Edom, Moab, Ammon, Assyria, and Babylon which are mentioned in eschatological passages, have long since ceased to exist as political entities, their places having been taken by later peoples occupying their territories.[1]

This method allows us to avoid arbitrarily pointing to nations that have absolutely no real connection to the people or regions named by the prophets or which may simply be the bogeyman of any particular age. It never ceases to amaze and sadden me when I read an article or book making claims that Edom refers to America or England or Germany or even the Jewish people.

The second correlation to emphasize is the persistent violent enmity toward the people and the land of Israel. Throughout the Prophets, this is the most often repeated basis for historical judgments against the enemies of God's people. It is also the most emphasized basis for the judgment of God's people on the Day of the Lord. The emphasis of the Lord's judgment against violent anti-Semitism and anti-Zionism is captured eloquently in Ezekiel 35:

> Because you cherished perpetual enmity and gave over the people of Israel to the power of the sword at the time of their calamity, at the time of their final punishment, therefore, as I live, declares the Lord GOD, I will prepare you for blood, and blood shall pursue you; because you did not hate bloodshed, therefore blood shall pursue you. I will make Mount Seir a waste and a desolation. (vv. 5–7)

By emphasizing the coupling of geography and the "perpetual enmity" against God's people, we read the many Day of the Lord prophecies as pointing to the modern-day hostile nations that share the same general location as their ancient anti-Semitic counterparts. This approach avoids the excesses of the ancestral-migration-method as well as the vagaries of over-allegorization so common among commentators. This would seem to be the most reasonable, common-sense, conservative, and literal method of interpreting the many names, people groups, and nations specified throughout the prophets as being marked for judgment in the context of the Day of the Lord.

CONCLUSION

In conclusion, then, we have articulated a solid method for interpreting and understanding the many passages we have discussed. They all point to the Middle East and North Africa as the primary recipients of God's judgment after Jesus returns. The ramifications of this, of course, are dramatic.

But in highlighting the judgments to come to the many Middle Eastern and North African nations, am I claiming that God will exclusively judge Muslim nations and bless all Western or non-Muslim nations? Absolutely not. I have no doubt that there will be numerous nations not mentioned in the Bible that will be judged by Jesus when He returns. But the purpose of our study so far is to take note of the specific nations that are—and are not—mentioned and highlighted in the Bible as being marked for God's judgment at the end of the age. Simply stated, that which the Bible emphasizes, we should also emphasize. This is responsible Biblical hermeneutics. But as we formulate our prophetic worldview, where the Bible is silent, we should likewise remain silent, or at the very least, use extreme caution. I think Pastor Chuck Smith summarizes my thoughts well: "It is amazing how much men can say whenever the Bible is silent on a subject. And it seems to just be a take-off place for guys to develop theories and to write theme papers or doctrinal dissertations on some area where the Bible is silent. But at best, when God's Word is silent, all we can do is offer conjecture, and at best, our conjecture is worthless."[2]

As we continue, we will examine what several other key texts have to say about the nations that will comprise the coming Antichrist's empire and allow our end-time worldview to be formed not by world circumstances, but by what the Bible repeatedly states in multiple ways.

5

DANIEL 2: NEBUCHADNEZZAR'S DREAM OF A METALLIC STATUE

THE EMPHASIS OF THE BOOK OF DANIEL

There can be no question that one of the most important portions of the Bible with regard to the end-times is the book of Daniel. Its primary focus and emphasis is the final conflict between the Antichrist, his followers, and the people of God who are ultimately delivered by the coming of the Messiah, referred to as "a son of man" (Dan. 7:13). Virtually every chapter in Daniel deals with some element of this final clash. Further, the book addresses the geographical location from which the Antichrist's empire will emerge, the timing of the Antichrist's emergence, the nature of the Antichrist's persecutions against God's people, the motivations of the Antichrist, and even the theology or belief system of the Antichrist. Of course, Daniel also discusses the character, perseverance, and faith of the overcomers from among God's people, as well as the Messiah's ultimate victory over the Antichrist, and the messianic kingdom that follows.

THE FOUR PILLARS OF ROMAN END-TIME THEORY

The book of Daniel contains three of the four passages that have traditionally been used to support the belief that the Antichrist will emerge from out of the geographic base of the Roman Empire. The four texts are:

1. **Daniel 2**: Nebuchadnezzar's dream of a giant metallic statue

2. **Daniel 7**: Daniel's vision of four beasts

3. **Daniel 9:26**: "the people of the prince to come"

4. **Revelation 17**: the city on seven hills

DANIEL 2: NEBUCHADNEZZAR'S DREAM OF A STATUE

Daniel 2 begins with Nebuchadnezzar, the king of the Babylonian Empire, having a dream that deeply disturbs him. According to the prophet, the king dreamt of a towering statue that was divided into five distinct sections, each composed of a different metal. Determined to understand the dream's meaning, he gathered all of his wise men, priests, and astrologers, but none were able to offer the king any understanding or comfort. Daniel however, was able to do what none of the other "wise men" could. After seeking his God in prayer, Daniel slept, and the Lord revealed Nebuchadnezzar's dream to him. This is where we begin our study of the text. Daniel told King Nebuchadnezzar exactly what he had seen in his dream:

> You saw, O king, and behold, a great image. This image, mighty and of exceeding brightness, stood before you, and its appearance was frightening. The head of this image was of fine gold, its chest and arms of silver, its middle and thighs of bronze, its legs of iron, its feet partly of iron and partly of clay. As you looked, a stone was cut out by no human hand, and it struck the image on its feet of iron and clay, and broke them in pieces. Then the iron, the clay, the bronze, the silver, and the gold, all together were broken in pieces, and became like the chaff of the summer threshing floors; and the wind carried them away, so that not a trace of them could be found. But the stone that struck the image became a great mountain and filled the whole earth. (vv. 31–35)

Daniel then explained the meaning of the four metallic sections of the statue to the king. The first section, the head of gold, represents Nebuchadnezzar's Babylonian Kingdom: "This was the dream. Now we will tell the king its interpretation. You, O king, the king of kings, to whom the God of heaven has given the kingdom, the power, and the might, and the glory . . . you are the head of gold" (vv. 36–38)

But the sections of the statue that follow represent three other kingdoms that would succeed Babylon, each possessing its former dominion. When one consults nearly any commentary on this subject, the three kingdoms to follow are understood to be Medo-Persia, Greece, and Rome. But while both Medo-Persia and Greece are later mentioned by name in Daniel (8:20–21; 10:20), the fourth empire is never named. Despite this fact, many Bible translations, so confident of the Roman identity of the fourth empire, actually add the name Rome into the subheadings. Yet as surprising as this claim may come to many, as we are about to see, the various criteria contained in the text, as well as the clear testimony of history, make it impossible to confidently identify the final kingdom as the Roman Empire. In this chapter, we will examine the evidence against the identification of the fourth empire of Daniel 2 as the Roman Empire. We will also discuss why the historical Islamic Caliphate does meet the scriptural criteria.

The Islamic Caliphate is simply the historical Islamic government or empire, which began with the Rashidun Caliphate in 632 AD, shortly after the death of Muhammad, the prophet of Islam, and culminated in the Ottoman Empire, which officially came to an end in 1923. No doubt, many who read this will find such a proposition to be highly dubious. The idea that Rome is the fourth kingdom is such a widely held position that many will not even entertain any suggestion to the contrary. This is entirely understandable. This has been the majority position throughout Church history. However, there are several significant, perhaps even fatal difficulties with this interpretation.

THE RISE OF THE FOURTH KINGDOM

The first problem with the Roman identification of the fourth kingdom is that the Roman Empire does not meet the specific criterion of Daniel 2:40. This verse, speaking of the nature of the rise of the fourth kingdom, says that when it emerged, it would crush all three of the other kingdoms: "And the fourth kingdom shall be as strong as iron . . . and like iron that crushes, that kingdom will break in pieces and crush all the others" (NKJV).

Later in Daniel 7, speaking of this same empire, we find a very similar description: "Thus he said: 'As for the fourth beast, there shall be a fourth kingdom on earth, which shall be different from all the kingdoms, and it shall devour the whole earth, and trample it down, and break it to pieces'" (v. 23).

The three other kingdoms that would be trampled and crushed, as we already know, are Babylon, Medo-Persia, and Greece. The text is clear that the fourth kingdom would "crush," or conquer, all three of these empires. The three empires never coexisted, of course, and thus we must ask what the text means when it says that the fourth empire would "crush" all of the others.

TO CONQUER GEOGRAPHICALLY

The first meaning of the word *crush* refers simply to geography. By examining the maps at the end of this chapter, it is clear that the Roman Empire only conquered roughly one-third of the regions controlled by Babylon, Medo-Persia, and Greece. About two-thirds of the regions controlled by these empires were left entirely untouched by Rome. In fact, the Roman Empire never even reached the two Persian capital cities of Ecbatana and Persepolis.

Consider the following modern equivalence: If an invading nation conquered Boston, but never came close to reaching New York or Washington, D.C., it would hardly be accurate to say that such a nation "crushed" the United States. Neither would it be correct to say that the Roman Empire crushed the entirety of the Babylonian, Medo-Persian, or Grecian empires. Yet the text is clear; to fulfill the criterion of Daniel 2:40, an empire would need to crush, not one, but all three of these. The Roman Empire simply does not fulfill this requirement.

Some have attempted to get around this problem by claiming that because the Roman Empire succeeded Greece, which succeeded Medo-Persia, which succeeded Babylon, the Roman Empire *did* crush all of the others. This view is articulated by Stephen R. Miller, professor of Old Testament and Hebrew at Mid-America Baptist Theological Seminary, in his commentary on Daniel:

The fourth empire "will crush and break all the others." This statement may be explained in that each previous empire was absorbed by its conquerer. Therefore when Rome conquered Greece, it overcame the empires previously defeated and absorbed by Greece.[1]

But while this view is common, not only is it based on faulty reasoning; it is also simply not what the text says. To show the illogical nature of this approach, let's put it in football terms: If the New England Patriots beat the Ravens, who beat the Cowboys, who beat the Colts, would this mean that the Patriots beat the Colts? Of course not. This is what the playoffs and the Super Bowl are for! But even more important, the text simply does not say that one would succeed another that would succeed another, etc. It says that the fourth kingdom would *crush* all of the others. If we are to be faithful to the text, we must adhere to what it actually states.

Although the Roman Empire did conquer portions of the land holdings of the other empires, it clearly did not conquer all of them, not even a majority of them. The Roman Empire only conquered roughly one-fifth of the land holdings of the Medo-Persian Empire, whose capital cities of Ecbatana and Persepolis forever remained hundreds of miles out of the Roman Empire's reach. If we are to be honest, to say the Roman Empire fulfilled Daniel 2:40 would be a stretch at best. On the other hand, the historical Islamic Caliphate fully, absolutely, completely conquered all the lands of the others.

TO CONQUER CULTURALLY AND RELIGIOUSLY

But what if we expand the definition of "crush" to include more than mere geography? What if the purpose of the repeated descriptions of the beast crushing and treading everything underfoot are intended to convey more than just gaining control over a geographic region? What if they also mean he crushes its culture, religion, and language? With this expanded definition in mind, what happens when we compare the Roman Empire to the Islamic Caliphate?

Commentators have applied much hype to the Roman Empire as a crushing entity, often referencing the strength of the Roman military and its great ability to crush rebellions. But is putting down rebellions sufficient to satisfy the dramatic descriptions found in Daniel's prophecy?

When we consider the nature of the Roman Empire, it was far from being a purely destructive influence to its conquered peoples. In fact, Rome is quite well-known for being a nation-building force of the ancient world. When the Roman Empire conquered a people, rather than destroying the culture, abolishing its religion, and imposing a new language, it generally tolerated these things while adding law, building roads and infrastructure, and creating order. The famous Roman roads reached every corner of the Roman Empire. These were well-built, stone-covered roads laid on solid foundations. To control their territories, the Romans needed easy access even to the most outlying provinces. Roads also caused trade to prosper, which brought with it more taxes. Eventually every town and city of the empire was connected by an elaborate system of Roman-built roads. This led to the famous phrase "All roads lead to Rome." Rome's law and the protection of its military also created a peace and stability that came to be famously known as the Pax Romana. Rather than being a crushing force, the Roman Empire was often a positive influence to its conquered peoples. John F. Walvoord, in his commentary on Daniel, recognizes this problem and wrestles with the contradiction between the destructive nature of the fourth empire as described by the text and the constructive reality of Roman rule. Walvoord believes that "there is apparently little that is constructive of this empire in spite of Roman law and Roman roads and civilization."[2]

Beyond infrastructure, while the Romans expected to receive taxes and an acknowledgment of Caesar, by ancient standards they were a very tolerant empire. During Jesus' day, the Jewish Temple stood prominently in Jerusalem under Roman authority, and the Jews practiced their religion freely. Roman law protected the Jews' right to practice their religion. While there were exceptions, such as a brief period of persecution under Emperor Caligula, throughout the majority of its reign, the Roman Empire was relatively forbearing.

When we ponder the idea of being a culturally destructive entity, it becomes apparent that this serves as a problem when associating the Roman Empire with Daniel's fourth beast. Consider, for example, the relationship of the Roman Empire to Greek culture. Rather than crushing Greek culture, much of the Roman Empire was overwhelmed by Greek ways. Under Roman hegemony, during Jesus' day, Greek was a dominant language throughout the Middle East. With regard to religion, much of the Roman culture adopted the pagan Greek pantheon of gods. While the names were changed, the basic pantheon remained the same. Zeus became Jupiter, Artemis became Diana, Aphrodite became Venus, and so forth. In considering the requisite of being a culturally destructive force, it would seem apparent that the Roman Empire was not the crushing power referenced in Daniel 2:40.

THE ISLAMIC CALIPHATE

In contrast to the Roman Empire, the Islamic Caliphate from its inception was an Arab-Islamic-supremacist force that crushed and erased the cultures and religions of the peoples it conquered. This is due to the uniquely all-encompassing ideology of Islam, which includes every facet of life. Islam has rules and commandments that pertain to far more than just theology. It also dictates law, government, language, military, and even the sexual and hygienic practices of those under its authority. The very name Islam means "submission" to the laws of Allah, the Muslims' god, as well as the practices of Muhammad, their prophet.

Islam is the epitome of a totalitarian ideology. Wherever Islam spread, it brought with it this oppressive ideology of submission. Islam conquered all the regions of the former Babylonian, Medo-Persian, and Grecian empires. It exported and imposed the Arabic language onto a vast proportion of its conquered peoples. Today, in Jordan, Iraq, Syria, Lebanon, and throughout much of North Africa, the people speak Arabic. While the Persians and the Turks have retained their own languages, their alphabets were both Arabized. Later, Mustafa Kemal Atatürk enforced a new, anglicized alphabet in Turkey. As an imperial force, Islam imposed Arab religion and culture onto all of its dominated peoples, while erasing evidence of previous religions and non-Islamic cultures.

While an entire book could be written detailing the endless examples of Arab-Islamic imperialism and supremacism, for now a few brief cases should suffice to demonstrate this point.

Today in the ancient heartland of the early church, the Christian community is a struggling minority, often fighting for its very survival. While the cities of Antioch, Alexandria, and Jerusalem were once the thriving capitals and strongholds of the Church, today the indigenous Christian communities there are a shadow of what they once were.

The calculated and deliberate Islamic program is to deny any historical Jewish connection or presence on the Temple Mount, the singularly most central and sacred location of biblical faith. Examples of Muslim "Temple Mount denial" in both popular and academic contexts are legion. The former Grand Mufti of Jerusalem, Sheikh Ikrima Sabri, has stated on many occasions that the Jewish connection to the Temple was a myth. In 1998, Sabri stated, "Moslems have no knowledge or awareness that the Temple Mount has any sanctity for Jews."[3] Similarly, the former chief justice of the Religious Court of Palestine and chairman of the Islamic-Christian Council for Jerusalem and the Holy Places, Sheikh Taysir al-Tamimi in 2009 stated, "Jews have no connection to Jerusalem . . . I don't know of any Jewish holy sites in it . . . Israel has been excavating since 1967 in search of remains of their Temple or their fictitious Jewish history."[4] And beyond the Muslim propaganda denying any Jewish historical connection to the Temple Mount, it is also well documented that the Muslim Waqf has systematically destroyed thousands of ancient Jewish artifacts unearthed from below the Temple site. In recent years, this concerted Islamic cultural vandalism has led to the formation of groups such as the "Committee for the Prevention of Destruction of Antiquities on the Temple Mount" and the "Temple Mount Antiquities Salvage Operation," which are dedicated to sifting through hundreds of truckloads of topsoil removed from the Temple Mount by the Waqf during the construction of an underground mosque in the late 1990s. Commenting on the massive quantities of precious archaeological materials being destroyed by the Waqf, world-renowned archaeologist Dr. Gavriel Barkai exclaimed, "They should be using a toothbrush, not a bulldozer . . . These are criminal acts that have no place in a cultured country!"[5]

In Istanbul sits the Hagia Sophia, once the largest Christian Church in the World. Today it is both a mosque and a museum. Immediately after Mehmet the Conquerer took Constantinople in 1453, the Hagia Sophia was transformed into a place of Muslim worship. Christian icons and symbols were destroyed or covered up. In their place are large plaques covered in gold-leaf Arabic calligraphy extolling the names of Allah,

Muhammad, and Ali. Although the Hagia Sophia is today considered a museum, Muslims are still allowed to pray there. Christians and Christian groups, on the other hand, are forbidden to openly pray in what was once the heart of Eastern Christianity. On the outside, where the cross once crowned the vast structure, there now sits a prominent crescent moon.

In central Afghanistan, for more than fifteen hundred years, sat the ancient Bamiyan Buddhas, two statues carved out of the solid sandstone cliffs. Denouncing these statues as idols, in March 2001, the Taliban leader, Mullah Mohammed Omar, had them completely destroyed with dynamite.

In recent years, the historic London Borough of Tower Hamlets, becoming the home to a growing Muslim immigrant population, has seen the systematic elimination of numerous Christian historical sites. What was once St. Mary's Churchyard, a historic monastery dating back to 1122, is now Altab Ali Park. On one corner of the park is what is known as the Shaheed Minar ("Martyr Monument"), a replica of a national monument in Dhaka, Bangladesh.

Again, such a list could literally fill volumes. Wherever Islam has spread, the conquered culture is gradually erased, the symbols and evidences of that former culture destroyed. The religion of the subjugated peoples are most particularly targeted. This is Islam's heritage, the perfect fulfillment of the criterion of Daniel 2:40. Islam is a crushing power, that "tramples the residue with its feet." While the Islamic Caliphate fulfills this biblical description to a tee, it is very difficult to force the Roman Empire into this description. The distinction between these two empires must be seriously considered as we attempt to discern the identity of the fourth empire.

THE DEMISE OF THE FOURTH KINGDOM

The second problem for the Roman identification of the fourth empire is the criterion of Daniel 2:34–35. This time, instead of the rise of the fourth kingdom, these verses speak of its demise—the day of its destruction—and the return of the Messiah and His kingdom. Christ's kingdom is described as "a rock cut out, but not with human hands." The messianic kingdom specifically destroys the final kingdom of the Antichrist. But in doing so, we see that, by virtue of the destruction of the Antichrist's kingdom, Babylon, Medo-Persia, and Greece are also all destroyed "at the same time": "While you were watching, a rock was cut out, but not by human hands. It struck the statue on its feet of iron and clay and smashed them. Then the iron, the clay, the bronze, the silver and the gold were broken to pieces at the same time and became like chaff on a threshing floor in the summer. The wind swept them away without leaving a trace" (NKJV).

Simply stated, if the Roman Empire were fully revived today to the point of its greatest extent, and Jesus returned and fully destroyed it, Babylon, Medo-Persia, and Greece would not all be destroyed "at the same time." Although a large portion of the land holdings of these empires would be destroyed, roughly two-thirds of all three empires would be left untouched.

On the other hand, if the Islamic Caliphate were fully revived today, and Jesus returned and conquered this empire, Babylon, Medo-Persia, and Greece would all be completely destroyed as well. Once again, the Islamic Caliphate fulfills the criteria and requirements of the text, while the Roman Empire does not.

CONTEXT, CONTEXT, CONTEXT

But despite the evidence that we've considered thus far, many Westerners will continue to struggle with the idea that the prophecy does not speak of the Roman Empire. Westerners fail to recognize that the Babylonian through Roman interpretation is ultimately only true through the Western perspective and lens of history. Because Western culture traces its history and much of its culture through the Roman and Greek empires, Westerners tend to naturally assume that the Bible also views history from a Western perspective. It is essential that Westerners step out of their Western-centric worldview and consider the actual context of the passage. This passage's context is a dream that was specifically given to Nebuchadnezzar, the king of the Neo-Babylonian Empire. Although the ultimate context and focus of all biblical prophecy is Jerusalem and Israel, this passage was revealed in Babylon, to a Babylonian king, concerning kingdoms that would succeed his. This is seen clearly in the text: "You, O king, are a king of kings . . . You are this head of gold. But after you shall arise another kingdom inferior to yours; then another, a third kingdom of bronze . . . And the fourth kingdom shall be as strong as iron" (Daniel 2:37–39 NKJV).

The dream was not intended to reveal the future of America or Europe. Instead, the dream was simply showing Nebuchadnezzar those kingdoms that would succeed his own. Let's briefly review the history of the region to understand why the Roman Empire was not included in Nebuchadnezzar's dream.

BABYLON'S FUTURE

Exactly as the prophecy declared, Babylon did fall to the Medo-Persian Empire. Later, the Medo-Persian Empire was also conquered by the Greek Empire under Alexander the Great. Medo-Persia and Greece were very similar in the scope and regions they controlled. They both very clearly succeeded Nebuchadnezzar. But in the midst of Alexander's conquest of the region, he died prematurely, leaving his empire to be quartered out among his generals or successors. This fourfold division of the Alexandrian Greek Empire is discussed in great detail in Daniel 8 and 11. The most significant of these divisions was the Seleucid dynasty, which came to rule over much of the Middle East, from modern-day Turkey all the way to Pakistan and Afghanistan. But eventually the Seleucid dynasty also saw its power wane, signaling the final decline of Greek Hellenistic dominion over the Middle East. It was during this period that the Parthian people came to power in the region. The Parthians were a Medo-Persian tribe from northern Iran who came to control much of the Middle East for roughly five hundred years. After the Parthian period, the Sassanids, another Persian dynasty, were able to consolidate power throughout the region, maintaining control for another four hundred years, until they were conquered by the invading Arab Muslims. Both the rulers and the subjects of the Parthians and the Sassanids viewed themselves as Medo-Persians. The period of their rule may be rightly viewed as a greatly diminished, but residual extension of life of the Persian Empire. This diminished extension is actually mentioned later in Daniel 7: "As for the rest of the beasts, their dominion was taken away, but their lives were prolonged for a season and a time" (v. 12).

Because of their Persian ethnicity and identity, the Parthians and Sassanids were not treated as distinct empires within Nebuchadnezzar's dream. It was not until the powerful and well-organized Islamic Caliphate came and absolutely conquered the entire region that the dream describes the next "kingdom." Thus the first four divisions of the statue, as we will consider in this chapter, are as follows:

1. Head of gold: Babylonian Empire

2. Chest and arms of silver: Medo-Persian Empire

3. Belly and thighs of bronze: Grecian Empire

4. Legs of iron: Islamic Caliphate

SKIPPING ROME?

In suggesting this understanding of Nebuchadnezzar's dream, I've found that most are skeptical regarding the idea that the Roman Empire is not included in the vision, yet no one has ever had any difficulty with the fact that the Parthian and Sassanid Empires are not included. This is despite the fact that the Parthian Empire ruled the region for well over a hundred years before the birth of the Roman Empire in Europe. But when we begin by acknowledging the Babylonian context of the dream, then the absence of Rome makes complete sense. As we have already seen, while the Islamic Caliphate did completely conquer the entire region of ancient Babylon, as well as all the former land holdings of Medo-Persia and Greece, the Roman Empire did not conquer all of these regions. When we compare maps of Medo-Persia or Greece to a map of the Roman Empire, it becomes quite clear that Rome's dominion was significantly farther westward. The Roman Empire does not align itself to the context of the dream and was thus not included.

EMPEROR TRAJAN'S EASTERN CAMPAIGN

For the overwhelming majority of its roughly 1500 years of existence, the Roman Empire's boundaries were firmly set roughly five hundred miles west of Babylon. There was however one very brief period when this was not the case. In AD 116, emperor Trajan set his heart on extending the Roman Empire further east. He crossed the Euphrates, sailed down the

Tigris River, and established temporary control over the ancient ruins of the cities of Babylon and Susa. But within a short span of mere months, three things happened that would force Rome to forever abandon its brief hold on Babylon. First, in Judea, a rebellion broke out among the Jews. This required a significant deployment of troops to respond to the rebellion. Second, the conquered Parthians began fighting back against the Roman incursion into their territories. And third, Trajan suffered what many historians believe was a stroke. He quickly withdrew from the region and within weeks was dead. The Romans were forced to abandon their very brief grip on Babylon and Mesopotamia. Trajan's chosen successor, Hadrian, prefect of the eastern Roman provinces, seeing the foolishness of Trajan's efforts to extend the Empire east, withdrew the Roman troops from both Babylon and Armenia and formally declared the boundaries of the Roman Empire to forever remain west beyond the Euphrates. As Historian Dean Merivale summarizes, "There was no soil beyond the Euphrates, in which Roman institutions could take root, while the expense of maintaining them would have been utterly exhausting."[6]

Because Nebuchadnezzar's dream is a Babylon-centered prophecy that deals with a span of more than twenty-six hundred years, the Roman Empire's very brief stint into Mesopotamia was simply not sufficiently significant to be included as one of the metallic divisions. The only empires that were included are the three that did in fact actually conquer and establish a substantial rule over Babylon and the greater surrounding region.

THE FEET OF MIXED IRON AND CLAY

After describing the iron legs, Daniel begins to describe the feet, which are a mixture of iron and baked clay. Although the overall emphasis of the prophecy is placed on "the fourth kingdom," the last empire before Jesus returns is technically not the legs of iron, but the feet of mixed iron and clay. Or perhaps it would be more appropriate to say that the fourth empire will consist of two phases. The key to seeing this twofold empire is in the following portion of the passage: "The head of this image was of fine gold, its chest and arms of silver, its middle and thighs of bronze, its legs of iron, its feet partly of iron and partly of clay" (Daniel 2:32–33).

A literal, word-for-word rendering of the original Aramaic text arranged in order provides us with the following breakdown of the statue:

Head: fine gold

Breast, arms: silver

Belly, thighs: brass

Legs: iron

Feet: part iron, part clay

It is quite clear that there are not merely four, but rather five distinct sections of the statue. There is a clear distinction between the legs, which are described "as strong as iron" (2:40) and the feet, which are described as "partly strong and partly brittle" (2:43). There is both a fourth and a fifth division of the image. However, because of the continuity between the legs and the feet through the element of iron, as well as the fact that nowhere does Daniel ever refer to "the fifth empire," there is also reason to believe that these last two empires are very much related and should simply be understood as phase one and phase two of the fourth empire. This twofold empire has been recognized by many modern interpreters. Of course, most of these scholars and Bible teachers have understood the fourth empire to be Rome and the fifth empire to be a revived last-days version of Rome. However, again, the Roman Empire does not sufficiently meet the criteria of the fourth-kingdom text, whereas the Islamic Caliphate fulfills all of the criteria perfectly. Thus, in my opinion, the two distinct phases of the statue would be the historical Islamic Caliphate (legs of iron) and a revived version of the Islamic Caliphate (feet of mixed iron and clay).

In summary, we conclude the empires of Nebuchadnezzar's dream should be understood as follows:

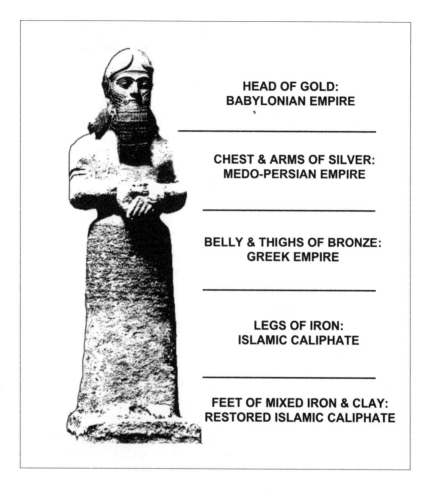

HEAD OF GOLD:
BABYLONIAN EMPIRE

CHEST & ARMS OF SILVER:
MEDO-PERSIAN EMPIRE

BELLY & THIGHS OF BRONZE:
GREEK EMPIRE

LEGS OF IRON:
ISLAMIC CALIPHATE

FEET OF MIXED IRON & CLAY:
RESTORED ISLAMIC CALIPHATE

A KINGDOM DIVIDED

In Daniel 2:41, we are told that a defining characteristic of the final kingdom is that it would be "divided": "And as you saw the feet and toes, partly of potter's clay and partly of iron, it shall be a divided kingdom."

Many commentators have tried to apply this description to the Roman Empire, pointing to the division of the Western and the Eastern Roman Empire. But this division certainly does not define the Roman Empire. The Western Roman Empire was founded in 27 BC and collapsed in AD 476. The Eastern Roman Empire was founded in AD 330 and collapsed in 1453. Thus the historical Roman Empire's "division" only lasted for roughly 140 years, less than one-tenth of its total 1,480-year existence. So while the Roman Empire certainly experienced a period of division, "divided" is not an appropriate term to define its overall existence.

On the other hand, it is a perfect term to describe the Islamic community. Shortly after Muhammad died, a division broke out between the Shi'a, (the minority sect, roughly 14 percent of all Muslims), who felt that the successorship belonged to Muhammad's relatives, and the Sunnis, (the majority sect, 86 percent of all Muslims), who felt felt the successorship belonged to Muhammad's companions, or the Sahabah. This division has defined Islam from its earliest days to modern times. For years, as the war in Iraq unfolded, we were treated to daily reports of "sectarian violence" with Sunnis killing Shi'a, and vice versa. Today this term is simply used with reference to the intra-Islamic violence that has been so common throughout Islamic history. This is further proof that the Islamic Empire meets the Daniel 2:41 standard perfectly.

Ironically, two well-known prophecy teachers, David Reagan and Jacob Prasch, have taken issue with the Islamic Antichrist theory specifically because they claim the nations that will comprise the Antichrist's kingdom must be able to attain a unity that has forever eluded the Islamic world. But this criticism has wrongly assumed that an Islamic Caliphate necessitates complete Muslim unity. Reagan has stated:

> Another problem with Muslim unity is that the whole idea is contradictory to one of the promises God made in His covenant with Ishmael (Genesis 16:10–12). In that covenant, in which God promised that the descendants of Ishmael would be greatly multiplied and would be given all the land east of Israel, God also stated that the Arab peoples would be like wild donkeys for they would always be in conflict with each other. As Jacob Prasch has pointed out in his writings on this subject, this aspect of the covenant with Ishmael has been manifested throughout history to this day through the internecine wars between the Arabs. They fought each other for centuries in pre-Islamic Arabia. Mohammed believed that he could unite them through the advocacy of a monotheistic religion, but he failed. Sunis [sic] and Shi'ites have hated and warred with each other since the 8th Century . . . Prasch sums up the problem of Arab unity by declaring, "The curse of Genesis prevents Islamic unity from developing a united empire over-running the West."[7]

There are three glaring problems with this criticism. First, Reagan and Prasch's point concerning Arab and Muslim division only validates the Islamic Antichrist theory, for as we just saw in Daniel 2:41, the final empire of the Antichrist will not be a unified entity; rather, it will be divided.

Second, the very passage that Reagan and Prasch highlight as pointing to the divided nature of the Arab world only supports the notion that the final divided empire of the Antichrist could in fact be an Arab empire. While Genesis 16:11–12 tells us that the Arab people would forever be in conflict, so also do the Scriptures tell us that the peoples who will comprise the Antichrist's empire will be divided. And even beyond this, other passages also inform us that even at the final hour, while in the land of Israel, the soldiers of the Antichrist will attack and kill *each other*:

> I will summon a sword against Gog on all my mountains, declares the Lord GOD. Every man's sword will be against his brother. (Ezekiel 38:21)

> Each will seize the hand of another, and the hand of the one will be raised against the hand of the other. (Zechariah 14:13)

And third, but perhaps most important, both Reagan and Prasch fail to recognize the historical reality of the Islamic Caliphate that existed in a stable, albeit ethnically and religiously divided condition for roughly thirteen centuries. While the Islamic world in recent decades has demonstrated the fact that it is incapable of being dominated by an outside power, whether that be Russia or the United States, for roughly thirteen hundred years, their history has demonstrated that they are entirely capable of being dominated by a Muslim power. The Turks, for instance, ruled the entire region for roughly five hundred years. This reality flows in perfect harmony with what the Bible says concerning the coming Antichrist's empire. It will not be an empire composed entirely of willing subjects or nations. The only issue around which his empire will seem to be unified is a mutual hatred of Jews and a desire to destroy Israel. In the final assessment, Reagan and Prasch's objection only serves to demonstrate how solidly grounded the Islamic Antichrist theory is with both Scripture and historical precedent.

As a final thought concerning the division of the fourth kingdom, many commentators have looked to the statue's two iron legs as pointing to the Western Roman Empire, whose capital was in Rome, and the Eastern Roman Empire, whose capital was in Constantinople. There are a few problems with this position. First, as we previously discussed, the Western Empire was founded in 27 BC and collapsed in AD 476, but the Eastern Roman Empire was founded in AD 330 and collapsed in 1453. John Walvoord agrees that it is best not to read too much into the fact that there are two legs, citing British commentator Geoffrey R. King's unique take on this fairly common interpretation:

> This is where I find I have to join issue with the commonly accepted interpretation. I have heard it said more than once or twice that the two legs of the image represent the Roman Empire, because in A.D. 364 the Roman Empire split in two. There was the Eastern Empire with its capital in Constantinople and the Western Empire with its capital in Rome. Two legs you see. All right. But wait a minute! To begin with, the division occurs before you get to the iron! The two legs begin under the the copper, unless this image was a freak . . . So you see, you cannot do anything with these two legs . . . I don't think there is any significance in the two legs at all. And of course, if you want to make two parts of the Roman Empire to be represented by the two legs, you are in a difficulty because the Western Empire only lasted for a few hundred years. The Eastern Empire lasted until 1453. You have to make this image stand on one leg most of the time![8]

THE KINGDOM WILL BE "MIXED"

Another very interesting hint regarding the ethnic base of the final phase of the fourth kingdom is found in Daniel 2:43. This particular verse is one that interpreters have wrestled to understand, largely due to its fairly enigmatic, riddle-like nature. Here it is, from two different versions:

> As you saw the iron mixed with soft clay, so they will mix with one another in marriage, but they will not hold together, just as iron does not mix with clay.

> As you saw iron mixed with ceramic clay, they will mingle with the seed of men; but they will not adhere to one another, just as iron does not mix with clay. (NKJV)

Three times, this verse uses the same word translated as "mixed," "mingle" and "mix." It is the Aramaic word, `arab. My initial reaction when I discovered this was to disregard it, considering it to be too reminiscent of "Bible code" scholarship. But this is not a case of finding a word that means something in English and something different in the original language. In Aramaic, the word for "mixed" is simply `arab. In the ancient Middle East, the Arabs were viewed as the mixed desert peoples. In Hebrew, the word is `ereb. Because the descendants of Ishmael and Esau had so intermarried among the various desert pagan tribes, they had essentially become known collectively as "the mixed ones." The first reference to the Eastern desert peoples as the "mixed ones" is found in the book of Nehemiah. After the Book of the Law had been rediscovered in the Temple, all Israel gathered together to hear the scroll read publicly: "On that day they read from the Book of Moses in the hearing of the people, and in it was found written that no Ammonite or Moabite should ever come into the assembly of God . . . So it was, when they had heard the Law, that they separated all the mixed multitude [`ereb] from Israel. (13:1–3).

After reading the Law, the Jews realized that it was forbidden for them to take wives from the mixed pagan peoples of the desert. Specifically mentioned are the Ammonites and the Moabites, who lived in what is today the Hashemite Kingdom of Jordan. Essentially, the verse is saying that when the people heard this law, they excluded from Israel all who were of "arab" descent. Again, in the ancient Near East, the words *mixed* and *"arab"* were synonymous. The very name Arab in its etymological origins refers to the mixed people that lived primarily to the east of Israel. A literal translation of Daniel 2:43, then, is "As you saw iron mixed with ceramic clay, they will be Arab; and will thus not remain united, just as iron does not mix with clay."

The riddle-like nature of this verse, seemingly pointing to the primary peoples from which the fourth empire would arise, is very reminiscent of another episode in Daniel 5, where Daniel interpreted the writing on the wall as pointing to the fall of the Babylonian Empire to the Medes and the Persians: "This is the interpretation of each word. MENE: God has numbered your kingdom, and finished it; TEKEL: You have been weighed in the balances, and found wanting; PERES: Your kingdom has been divided, and given to the Medes and Persians" (vv. 26–28).

In the Aramaic of Daniel 5:28, "divided" (*peres*) was interpreted to indicate that the "Persian" (*Paras*) peoples would conquer the Babylonian Empire. Likewise, it is not at all unreasonable to consider that in the Aramaic of Daniel 2:43, the word "mixed" (`*arab*) could also be understood to mean that the "Arab" (`*arab*) peoples would be the primary representatives of the fourth and final kingdom.

CONCLUSION

Thus far, we have surveyed several Old Testament prophetic passages concerning the return of the Messiah, and now we have examined the first supporting pillar of the European Antichrist theory. Despite the fact that most throughout Church history have interpreted the legs of iron in Daniel 2 as the Roman Empire, instead, as we have seen, a far more solid case is made for the Islamic Caliphate as the fulfillment of this passage. If the legs of iron are understood to be Rome, then this causes a significant tension with numerous other passages throughout the Prophets. But if the iron legs represent the Islamic Caliphate, then the message of Daniel 2 is seen to flow together seamlessly with all the other passages throughout the Prophets that speak of Jesus judging Muslim nations and Israel's neighbors on the Day of the Lord. As we proceed to examine the key biblical texts that speak of the coming empire of the Antichrist, we will only see this pattern continue. Despite the often complicated, puzzle-like, multi-invasion, multifaceted scenarios espoused by many prophecy teachers, what we will see is that all of the prophets told the same general story. Understanding this narrative is far easier than many have made it. While the prophets told this story through different means and through varying lenses, the same general narrative is repeated over and over again.

The contextual epicenter of Nebuchadnezzar's dream, the city of Babylon, is marked with the large, black dot. The radius of the dot extends roughly 175 miles in every direction from Babylon.

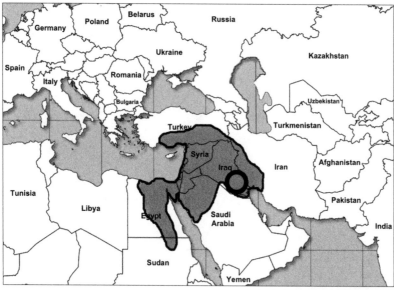

Babylonian Empire (c. 600 BC)[9]

The Medo-Persian Empire crushed the entire region of both the city and the empire of Babylon.

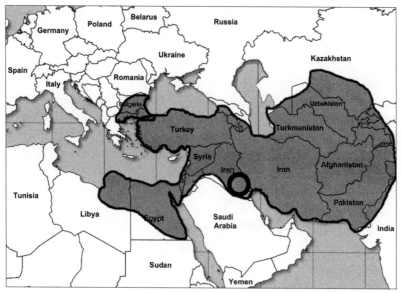

Medo-Persian Empire (c. 530)[10]

Like the Medo-Persian Empire before it, clearly the Alexandrian Greek Empire also crushed virtually the entire region of both the city and the empire of Babylon.

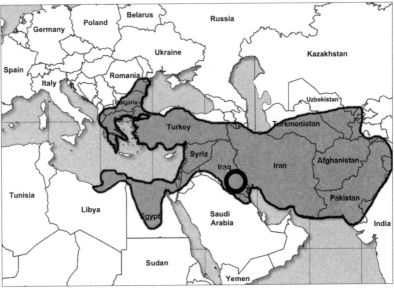

Alexandrian Greek Empire[11]

Apart from Trajan's brief excursion east in late AD 116–117, the Roman Empire remained far west of Babylon throughout the majority

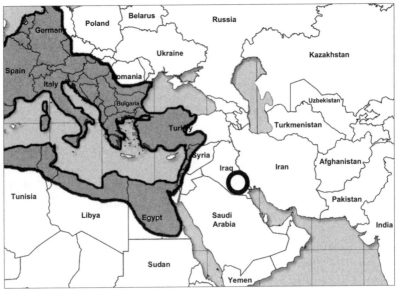

Roman Empire (c. AD 54–70)[12]

of its fifteen-hundred-year existence. It also left over two-thirds of Medo-Persia and the Greek Empires entirely untouched, failing to fulfill the scriptural requirement of crushing "all the others."

The Islamic Caliphate absolutely crushed all of the Babylonian, Medo-Persian, and Greek Empires. Beyond conquering their territories, in most cases it was also successful in imposing its own culture (Arab), religion (Islam), and language (Arabic) as well.

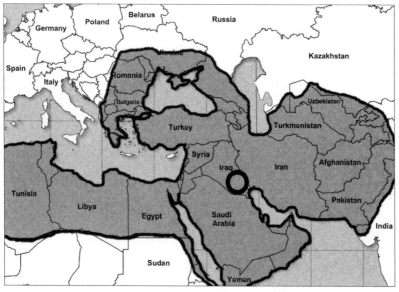

Islamic Caliphate (c. 632–1923)

Here, the land of Israel is marked with a star surrounded by the regions that have been under the control of the Islamic Caliphate. When considering the Israel-centricity of biblical prophecy, what would seem to be more relevant to Israel and God's prophetic plan: Europe or the Islamic world?

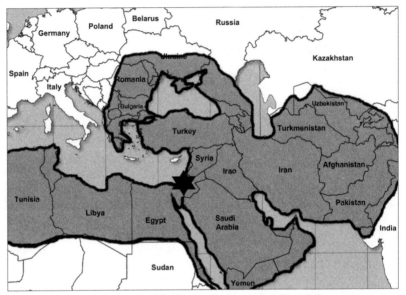

The Nation of Israel surrounded by Muslim majority nations

6

DANIEL 7: DANIEL'S VISION

OF FOUR BEASTS

IN THE LAST CHAPTER, we examined Daniel 2 and Nebuchadnezzar's dream of a metallic statue. We determined that the dream points us to a succession of four historical empires culminating with a revived version of the Islamic Caliphate. We concluded the chapter by discussing the fact that all of the prophets throughout the Bible told the same basic story. Although they all prophesied through the events and circumstances of their time, the ultimate picture they painted is the same. They often emphasized different aspects—or used different brushes, if you will—but it is still the same picture. As we examine Daniel 7, we will see this pattern continue. The same picture of four successive historical pagan empires, succeeded by one final, last-days empire, has been painted yet again. This time, however, instead of using the imagery of a metallic statue, the story is told through the symbolism of four *beasts*. Fourth-century Christian commentator Ephrem the Syrian believed that the vision we are about to discuss was simply a recapitulation of Nebuchadnezzar's dream: "The present vision of Daniel perfectly fits in with the already mentioned dream of Nebuchadnezzar, who saw a statue, and it forms a single and same prophecy with it."[1]

John Walvoord reiterates the same consensus among scholars today: "Interpreters of the book of Daniel whether liberal or conservative, generally have agreed that chapter 7 is in some sense a recapitulation of chapter

2 and cover the same four empires."[2]

While the imagery of Daniel 2 was conveyed through a dream given to Nebuchadnezzar, the imagery of Daniel 7 came through a dream given to Daniel: "In the first year of Belshazzar king of Babylon, Daniel saw a dream and visions of his head as he lay in his bed. Then he wrote down the dream and told the sum of the matter. Daniel declared, "I saw in my vision by night, and behold, the four winds of heaven were stirring up the great sea. And four great beasts came up out of the sea, different from one another" (vv. 1–3).

Though Daniel was able to interpret Nebuchadnezzar's dream, when he received his own vision, he inquired of an angel for a fuller explanation: "I approached one of those who stood there and asked him the truth concerning all this. So he told me and made known to me the interpretation of the things" (v. 16).

The angel explained, "These four great beasts are four kings who shall arise out of the earth" (v. 17).

As in the dream of Daniel 2, the kings here also represent kingdoms. Hippolytus of Rome, one of the most important Christian theologians of the third century, discussed the meaning of the prophecy: "As various beasts were shown to the blessed Daniel, and these were different from each other, we should understand that the truth of the narrative deals not with certain beasts but, under the type and image of different beasts, exhibits the kingdoms that have arisen in this world."[3]

As the four beasts are revealed, they perfectly parallel the four kingdoms in Nebuchadnezzar's dream.

A WINGED LION

The first beast "was like a lion and had eagles' wings. Then as I looked," Daniel wrote, "its wings were plucked off, and it was lifted up from the ground and made to stand on two feet like a man, and the mind of a man was given to it" (Daniel 7:4).

Many commentators view the lion as an appropriate symbol for Babylon. Nebuchadnezzar himself was referred to by the prophet Jeremiah as a "lion from the thickets of the Jordan" (Jeremiah 49:19). More than 120 lions, fashioned out of colorful glazed ceramic brick, decorated the

"Processional Way" of the ancient capital city of Babylon. The Processional Way was a walled road leading out of the city through the Ishtar Gate. Ishtar, a Mesopotamian goddess, worshipped both by the Assyrians and the Babylonians, was represented by a lion. The winged lion, then, would correspond to the head of gold in Daniel 2. The comment "and a man's heart was given to it" is often understood to refer to the humbling of King Nebuchadnezzar as recounted in Daniel 4.

A LOPSIDED BEAR

The next kingdom to emerge is portrayed through the symbolism of a lop-sided bear: "And behold, another beast, a second one, like a bear. It was raised up on one side. It had three ribs in its mouth between its teeth; and it was told, 'Arise, devour much flesh.'" (Daniel 7:5).

The lopsided bear represents the Medo-Persian Empire, of which the Persian portion was much stronger than the Median portion. Commentators both ancient and modern see the three ribs in the bear's mouth as symbolic of the three provinces of Media, Persia, and Babylon. Jerome, in the late fourth century, wrote, "Therefore the three rows in the mouth of the Persian kingdom of the Babylonians, the Medes and the Persians, all of which were reduced to a single realm."[4]

A FOUR-HEADED LEOPARD

The third beast to emerge is a four-headed leopard: "After this I looked, and behold, another, like a leopard, with four wings of a bird on its back. And the beast had four heads, and dominion was given to it" (Daniel 7:6).

Nearly as quickly as Alexander the Great conquered the Middle East, his life came to an end in 323 BC. After his death, Alexander's vast empire was divided up by his generals, friends, and family. What ensued were roughly fifty years of wars between these various successors, known as the Diadochi. By the third century, Alexander's kingdom was largely controlled by four dynasties. These four divisions were:

1. the Ptolemaic dynasty ruling over Egypt

2. the Seleucid dynasty ruling over the region extending from modern-day Turkey to Afghanistan and Pakistan

3. the Lysimachean dynasty ruling over the modern region of Bulgaria

4. the Cassandrian dynasty ruling over the region of Macedonia or modern-day Greece

A FOURTH BEAST

This fourth beast correlates with the fourth kingdom of Daniel 2. While the beast here has iron teeth, the fourth kingdom of Daniel 2 is represented by iron legs. In Daniel 2, the emphasis was on the kingdom's crushing power. Here also, the fourth kingdom is repeatedly emphasized as one that would crush, devour, and trample the people and kingdoms it conquered:

> After this I saw in the night visions, and behold, a fourth beast, terrifying and dreadful and exceedingly strong. It had great iron teeth; it devoured and broke in pieces and stamped what was left with its feet. (Daniel 7:7)

> Then I desired to know the truth about the fourth beast, which was different from all the rest, exceedingly terrifying, with its teeth of iron and claws of bronze, and which devoured and broke in pieces and stamped what was left with its feet. (v. 19)

While the overwhelming majority of interpreters throughout Church history have believed this fourth beast to represent the Roman Empire, as we discussed in the previous chapter, the Roman Empire in many ways was anything *but* a destructive empire. Instead it was rather *con*structive, often adding infrastructure, order, and law to the lands it conquered. Alternately, the empire of Islam, wherever it has spread, has most often been a destructive force to those it has conquered. As mentioned in the previous chapter, today in the ancient heartland of the early Christian Church, the small Christian communities often struggle, with many fighting for their very survival. While Antioch, Alexandria, and Jerusalem were once the thriving capitals and strongholds of the Church, today the indigenous Christian communities there are a shadow of their former glory. Alternately in the capitol city of Rome, the entire city has been "Christianized." While the Islamic Caliphate has beaten down the Christian Church, it was the Christian Church that ultimately prevailed over and conquered the Roman Empire. As we argued concerning Daniel 2, the descriptions of the fourth kingdom here fail to match up to the Roman Empire, but perfectly align with the description of the Islamic Caliphate.

THE TEN HORNS REPRESENT A REVIVAL OF THE FOURTH KINGDOM

Out of the beast grow ten horns. These ten horns represent the revived Islamic Caliphate and correlate to the feet of iron and clay in Daniel 2. Many commentators also see the ten horns as specifically correlating with the ten toes on the statue: "It devoured and broke in pieces and stamped what was left with its feet. It was different from all the beasts that were before it, and it had ten horns" (Daniel 7:7).

We are told that the ten horns represent ten kings, or kingdoms, that together, will compose the coming Antichrist's empire: "As for the ten horns, out of this kingdom ten kings shall arise" (v. 24).

THE LITTLE HORN IS THE ANTICHRIST

Then from among the ten horns, Daniel saw another horn emerge. This eleventh horn seemed to uproot three other horns and then take complete charge over all ten: "I considered the horns, and behold, there came up among them another horn, a little one, before which three of the first horns were plucked up by the roots. And behold, in this horn were eyes like the eyes of a man, and a mouth speaking great things" (Daniel 7:8).

This introduction of the "little horn" is where this vision extends beyond the information revealed in Nebuchadnezzar's dream. Whereas Daniel 2 revealed the coming four empires, this portion of Daniel's revelation introduces us to the leader of the final kingdom.

Then I desired to know the truth about the fourth beast, which was different from all the rest, exceedingly terrifying, with its teeth of iron and claws of bronze, and which devoured and broke in pieces and stamped what was left with its feet, and about the ten horns that were on its head, and the other horn that came up and before which three of them fell, the horn that had eyes and a mouth that spoke great things, and that seemed greater than its companions. As I looked, this horn made war with the saints and prevailed over them, until the Ancient of Days came, and judgment was given for the saints of the Most High, and the time came when the saints possessed the kingdom. (Daniel 7:19–22)

The "little horn" speaks pompous words and persecutes the people of God. Christians popularly call this individual the Antichrist. As has been consistent throughout the chapter, the information is reiterated:

As for the ten horns, out of this kingdom ten kings shall arise, and another shall arise after them; he shall be different from the former ones, and shall put down three kings. He shall speak words against the Most High, and shall wear out the saints of the Most High, and shall think to change the times and the law; and they shall be given into his hand for a time, times, and half a time. But the court shall sit in judgment, and his dominion shall be taken away, to be consumed and destroyed to the end. (Daniel 7:24–26)

The actions of the Antichrist that are most emphasized are his arrogant and blasphemous words against "the Most High," as well as his persecution of God's people.

After watching and pondering the destructive power of the Antichrist and his kingdom, Daniel was "greatly troubled" (NKJV): "Here is the end of the matter. As for me, Daniel, my thoughts greatly alarmed me, and my color changed, but I kept the matter in my heart" (v. 28).

Commentator Gleason Archer addresses the primary cause for Daniel's deep concern:

Of all the beasts Daniel saw, he regarded the fourth beast with the greatest curiosity and dread. (v. 19), because it resembled no animal known to the human experience. In particular he wondered about the ten horns from which the little horn emerged (v. 20) and which was allowed to overcome God's people (v. 21). Daniel perceived the sinister implications of this for the political welfare of true believers and cringed at the prospect of their being crushed by this reviler against God.[5]

This aspect of the prophecy is particularly important for us to consider. As we have previously discussed, in the larger picture, the Roman Empire of history was relatively tolerant. Of course, when the Roman legions were responding to a rebellion, they were quite brutal. It was the Roman Empire that destroyed Jerusalem and the temple in AD 70, crushing the Jewish uprising and killing or exiling multitudes in the process. But again, this was a response to a revolt initiated by the Jewish nation. So long as the provinces of Rome willingly paid taxes and acknowledged Caesar, they were not "crushed." Throughout the majority of its days under Roman hegemony, the Jewish nation did not live in an overly oppressed state and was allowed to practice Judaism freely. Likewise for the Christian community, while Rome certainly at times persecuted the early church, in the larger picture, Christianity eventually infected and conquered the Roman Empire with its message. One could rightly say that in the end, the Church gained victory over the Roman Empire. It was not the other way around. One simply cannot say that Rome crushed and devoured the Church until even the residue was trampled. Once more, while it is possible to look to periods of the Roman Empire's history to find shades of fulfillment of this prophecy, there are also significant problems with this interpretation.

On the other hand, when we consider the empire of Islam, whether we are speaking of the regions of Babylon, Medo-Persia, or Greece; the Jewish people; or the Christian Church, they all were crushed, devoured, and trampled. Even as we saw in Daniel 2, so also here the Roman Empire only aligns with the descriptions in the text with great difficulty. The Islamic Caliphate however, fits the descriptions precisely.

In conclusion, the identification and correlation of the four beasts is as follows:

Daniel 2	Daniel 7	Empire
Head of gold	Lion	Babylon
Chest and arms of silver	Bear	Medo-Persia
Belly and thighs of bronze	Leopard	Greece
Legs of iron	Fourth Beast	Islamic Caliphate
Feet of iron and clay	Ten Horns	Revived Islamic Caliphate

THE JEWISH POSITION

Despite the fact that much of the Christian Church has viewed the final kingdom of the Antichrist to be a European kingdom, many of the Jewish rabbis and sages have long understood the final, ten-horn kingdom to be an Arab or Middle Eastern kingdom. From *Ezekiel, A Commentary Anthologized from Talmudic, Midrashic and Rabbinic Sources*, we read: "The Midrash comments that these ten horns symbolize ten kings of the Fourth Kingdom, and the eleventh horn is the final king whom Israel will confront. All these kings, the Midrash stresses, are to be descendants of Esau. The implication is that the king and initiator of the campaign against Israel will be from Esau-Edom."[6]

THE EXTENSION OF LIFE EXPLAINED

Despite the relative clarity with which Daniel 7 seems to parallel Daniel 2, there are many interpreters who see these four beasts as something entirely different from the four kingdoms of Daniel 2. The basis for this tendency to separate this vision from Nebuchadnezzar's dream are the following two verses: "I looked then because of the sound of the great words that the horn was speaking. And as I looked, the beast was killed, and its body destroyed and given over to be burned with fire. As for the rest of the beasts, their dominion was taken away, but their lives were prolonged for a season and a time" (v. 11–12).

Many have understood this passage to mean that after the destruction of the final empire—the Antichrist's empire—the other three kingdoms will live on for a time. The passage is thus believed to infer that the four "beast kingdoms" are contemporaries, all existing at the same time. Some common identifications of the beasts have been the lion as America or England, the bear as Germany or Russia, the leopard as Islam, and again, the fourth beast as the Roman Empire.

The problem with this notion, of course, is that it is based on a misunderstanding of what these verses are saying. They are not saying that the other three kingdoms would be contemporaries of the final, antichristic empire. The point is to simply contrast the nature of the final empire's destruction, which will be sudden, utter, and complete, with the destruction of the previous empires, which, though conquered, often lived on to a degree in the empire that subjugated them. In other words, while the Greek Empire was conquered by the Romans, it very much lived on in the Roman Empire. As we briefly discussed in the last chapter, Greek was a common language throughout the Middle East under Roman hegemony. The Romans actually embraced the Greek pantheon of gods as their own, changing their names, but continuing to breathe life into the sails of the Greek cult. While the kingdom of the Antichrist would be destroyed by the Messiah's kingdom, the other kingdoms would not suffer such an immediate and absolute destruction. And beyond juxtaposing the complete and utter destruction of the Antichrist's empire to the previous empires, the purpose of this passage is also to contrast it with the coming messianic kingdom, which will never be destroyed:

> I saw in the night visions, and behold, with the clouds of heaven there came one like a son of man, and he came to the Ancient of Days and was presented before him. And to him was given dominion and glory and a kingdom, that all peoples, nations, and languages should serve him; his dominion is an everlasting dominion, which shall not pass away, and his kingdom one that shall not be destroyed. (Daniel 7:13–14)

The everlasting nature of the messianic kingdom is reiterated throughout the entire chapter:

But the saints of the Most High shall receive the kingdom and possess the kingdom forever, forever and ever. (Daniel 7:18)

And the kingdom and the dominion and the greatness of the kingdoms under the whole heaven shall be given to the people of the saints of the Most High; their kingdom shall be an everlasting kingdom, and all dominions shall serve and obey them. (Daniel 7:27)

This is the meaning of this passage. There is no reason to see it as proving that these other empires all coexist as contemporaries.

DANIEL 9:26: THE PEOPLE OF THE PRINCE TO COME

OVER THE PAST SEVERAL YEARS, as I have attempted to articulate and explain the scriptural basis for the Islamic Antichrist theory, I've had the opportunity to discuss these things with several prominent, internationally known prophecy teachers who espouse the European Antichrist theory. Universally the passage that every teacher has cited as the basis for rejecting the Islamic Antichrist theory is Daniel 9:26, which speaks of "the people of the prince to come." Although this is only one verse, the weight it carries in the minds of many is profound. The second reason that many will not consider the Islamic Antichrist theory is because of tradition. I actually respect the skepticism, as I am not among those who look negatively toward tradition. The job of faithful Christians is to pass on to the next generation the right doctrines and practices they received from their fathers in the faith. Tradition is intended to preserve truth and guard against creeping error. Deviating from tradition, even in small ways, should be done only after very careful and prayerful consideration, with great humility. But if, having examined a particular tradition in the right spirit, in humility and the fear of the Lord, a tradition is found to be in error, then truth must be adhered to over tradition. After having examined this passage inside and out for years, consulted the commentaries and opinions of many other faithful men, and considered all options, I can say with confidence that the traditional Roman-centric interpretation of Daniel 9:26 is in error. If you are someone, like myself, who long held to the traditional interpretation, but are passionate about truth and are willing to reconsider your previously held assumptions, then this chapter was written for you.

WHO ARE THE PEOPLE OF THE PRINCE TO COME?

As mentioned earlier, through the years, whenever I've discussed the Islamic end-time paradigm publicly, nearly across the board, I have encountered an almost reflexive reference to Daniel 9:26. In the following comment, Dr. Ron Rhodes articulates the objection as I have heard it from dozens of other students of prophecy: "The Scriptures are very clear that the Antichrist's empire is from a revived Roman Empire. When we look at Daniel in his writings, he talks very specifically about how the Antichrist would come from the people who overran Jerusalem and destroyed the Jewish Temple. That happened in 70 A.D. It wasn't the Muslims that overcame Jerusalem."[1]

I fully understand the reasoning behind this thought, as I myself held this position for many years. But it was not until I undertook to examine the passage from a historical-grammatical perspective that I found the popular position to be in error on both counts. The first error lies in a failure to examine the historical data behind the events of AD 70. The second error lies in a failure to consider the grammar, the actual Hebrew wording of the passage.

THE HISTORICAL ERROR

Here in a one-sentence prophecy found in the ninth chapter of the book of Daniel we have the single more significant source text for the Roman-Antichrist theory: "And the people of the prince who is to come shall destroy the city and the sanctuary" (v. 26).

While varying interpretations have been offered as to the exact meaning of this passage, the majority position holds that this prophecy is telling us that the specific people (or peoples) who destroyed Jerusalem and the Temple in AD 70 are the ancestors of the people who in the last days would be the primary followers of the Antichrist (the prince or ruler who is to come). So according to this position, the verse should be understood as follows: "The people—that is, the primary followers—of the prince (the Antichrist) to come in the last days, shall destroy the city (Jerusalem) and the sanctuary (the Jewish temple of the first century)."

Most believe the destruction of "the city and the sanctuary" to be a reference to the destruction that occurred in AD 70 when the Roman legions under General Titus destroyed both the Jewish capital city of Jerusalem and its Temple. As such, a large majority of prophecy teachers and students have concluded that the Roman people of AD 70 can be identified as the ancestors of the coming followers/peoples of the Antichrist. Because the soldiers were Roman citizens, many conclude that the primary followers of the Antichrist in the last days will be Europeans in general or Italians specifically. This notion, of course, is rooted in the fact that it was the Roman commanders (whose capital was in Rome, Italy) who commanded the destroying armies but also in the mistaken belief that most of the Roman soldiers were Italians or Europeans. I say "mistaken belief" because both historical testimony and the consensus of modern scholarship tell us that very few of the soldiers who destroyed the Temple and Jerusalem in AD 70 were actually Europeans. In fact, as we will see, the historical facts reveal a dramatically different picture.

RECRUITS IN THE ROMAN ARMY

A brief bit of history is in order.

Before the Roman Empire became an empire, it was called the Roman Republic. In the early days of the Republic, as it was evolving into the Empire, the majority of the soldiers/legionnaires recruited to serve in the Roman armies/legions were Italians from Rome and the nearby regions. However, as the Empire expanded quite dramatically, it became next to impossible to man the entire Empire with soldiers only from Italy. There were just not enough Italian men to spread all over the vast Roman Empire, which included all of Europe, Northern Africa, and a large swath of the Middle East. Thus, at the beginning of the first century, Emperor Augustus made a series of sweeping reforms that led to dramatic changes in the ethnic make-up of the Roman armies. After Augustus's reforms in AD 15, the only portion of the Roman army that continued to consist largely of Italians from Rome proper was the Praetorian Guard, an elite military unit whose job was to specifically guard the emperor and the tents of the generals. The remainder of the army was increasingly composed of anything but Italian soldiers. Instead, they were known as "provincials," citizens who lived in the provinces—the outer fringes of the Empire, away from the capital of Rome. The "provincialization" of the army was true for all of the Roman legions of this time period, but it was most clearly and markedly the case for the Eastern legions that were used to attack Jerusalem. Both ancient historical records and modern scholarship clearly confirm this. Let's examine some of the evidence.

FIRST WITNESS: PUBLIUS CORNELIUS TACITUS

Publius Cornelius Tacitus was both a senator and a historian of the Roman Empire who wrote extensively concerning the specific period that we are now examining. The surviving portions of his two major works—the *Annals* and the *Histories*—have become vital sources of information from this period. Speaking of the Roman attack of Jerusalem, Tacitus detailed the specific legions and the peoples that primarily composed the attacking army: "Titus Caesar . . . found in Judaea three legions, the 5th, the 10th, and the 15th . . . To these he added the 12th from Syria, and some men belonging to the 18th and 3rd, whom he had withdrawn from Alexandria. This force was accompanied . . . by a strong contingent of Arabs, who hated the Jews with the usual hatred of neighbors."[2]

There are several important bits of information that we can gain from this reference. First, we learn that the Roman legions had been stationed in Judea, Syria, and Egypt. Second, we learn that beyond the Roman legions, "a strong contingent of Arabs, who hated the Jews," accompanied the soldiers. Sad to say, little has changed since the first century regarding the general regional hatred of the Jewish people. In fact, as we will see, it was precisely this ancient hatred that was the driving factor in the unfolding of events that led to the destruction of the Temple.

SECOND WITNESS: TITUS FLAVIUS JOSEPHUS

Titus Flavius Josephus, another irreplaceable historian from this period, confirms Tacitus's report: "So Vespasian sent his son Titus [who], came by land into Syria, where he gathered together the Roman forces, with a considerable number of auxiliaries from the kings in that neighborhood."[3]

Once again, Josephus revealed that the Roman legions used to attack Jerusalem were stationed in Syria. This is where Titus gathered them together as he proceeded toward the Jewish capital. "A considerable number" of auxiliaries, or volunteers, from Syria and the surrounding regions were also gathered for the attack. Later, Josephus also detailed the specific number of Arab soldiers who joined forces with the invading armies: "Malchus also, the king of Arabia, sent a thousand horsemen, besides five thousand footmen, the greatest part of which were archers; so that the whole army, including the auxiliaries sent by the kings, as well horsemen and footmen, when all were united together, amounted to sixty thousand."[4]

While the numbers of men that composed a legion fluctuated, during this time period a legion contained approximately five thousand men. Here we see that Malchus, the king of Arabia, sent enough auxiliary/ volunteer soldiers to compose more than a full legion.

THE EASTERN LEGIONS

Now let's look at the specific legions that were used to attack the Jewish people, as well as the regions where they were stationed during the time period leading up to AD 70, when Jerusalem was destroyed. Of the six legions, all were stationed in the Middle East. Below is a list of the legions and where they were stationed before Jerusalem fell.

Legion	Region Stationed
V Macedonia	Judea
X Fretensis	Syria
XV Appoinaris	Syria
XVIII	Egypt
III Gallica	Syria
XII Fulminata	Asia Minor / Syria

All of these legions would have consisted of a majority of Eastern soldiers: Arabs, Syrians, Egyptians, etc. By AD 70 not only the Eastern provincial legions, but literally the entire army had come to be dominated by "provincials."

MODERN SCHOLARS OF ROMAN HISTORY

Modern Roman scholars across the board all thoroughly validate the claim that by the time of Jerusalem's fall, the Roman soldiers were almost exclusively non-Italian peoples. Lawrence J. F. Keppie, scholar of Roman history, confirmed this: "[After AD 68] the legions . . . consist[ed] almost exclusively of provincials."[5] In other words, after the year 68, the soldiers in the Roman legions were almost exclusively non-Italians from the provinces on the Empire's eastern perimeter. Keppie is not alone on this issue. In fact, his position is supported by the consensus of modern-day scholars of the Roman Empire. Antonio Santosuosso in *Storming the Heavens: Soldiers, Emperors, and Civilians in the Roman Empire* claims that during the first half of the first century, approximately 49 percent of the soldiers were Italians, but by AD 70 that number had fallen to around one in five. By the end of the first century, only 1 percent of the soldiers were Italians.[6] Sara Elise Phang, PhD, author of *Roman Military Service: Ideologies of Discipline in the Late Republic and Early Principate*, indicates that the number of Italians would have been even slimmer: "Recruitment underwent major shifts from Italy in the early first century A.D. to the frontier provinces in the latter first and second centuries."[7] In fact, as Phang reveals, Roman scholars are now in universal agreement that the overwhelming majority of the soldiers that attacked Jerusalem were Eastern provincial recruits:

> That Italians were increasingly replaced in the legions during this period by provincials is in itself no longer a novelty among scholars . . . In the East, that is Asia Minor, Syria and Egypt, it seems clear that local recruitment was well under way under Augustus [d. 14 A.D.], so that by his death only a very small number of legionaries derived from Italy or indeed any of the western provinces . . . Under Nero [d. 68 A.D.], when the eastern legions required supplementation . . . it was to Cappadocia and Galatia that [Rome] looked for recruits. This was doubtless stan-

dard procedure. [The] legions of the East consisted largely of "orientals" [Middle Easterners].[8]

And again Phang leaves no doubt as to the Eastern ethnic composition of the legions in AD 70:

> To the Roman public, the army of 69–70 A.D. probably seemed little different than its counterpart under Julius Caesar. The legionaries wore familiar equipment, and marched behind the silver aquila, their legions bearing names and titles which reflected their origins and the exploits of earlier days. But in reality much had changed: What had been an army of Italians was increasingly becoming an army of provincials owing no particular allegiance to, or common bond with the Senate or the urbs Roma . . . Increasingly they began to identify their interests with those of the provinces in which they were stationed . . . By A.D. 69 Gallica III, like other legions long stationed in the East, contained a very high proportion of men born in the eastern provinces."[9]

Gallica III was one of the legions that was involved in the destruction of Jerusalem.

In his book, *Soldiers, Cities, and Civilians in Roman Syria*, Nigel Pollard, PhD, professor of Roman history at Oxford University, examines in great detail specifically the ethnicity of the Roman soldiers of the eastern provinces during the first century. After reviewing the most up-to-date scholarship on the subject, Pollard details two possible positions that reveal the ethnicity of the soldiers we are attempting to identify. Both positions confirm that the overwhelming majority of the soldiers that destroyed the Temple were primarily Syrians, Arabs, and Eastern peoples.

According to Pollard, the first position holds that after the reign of Emperor Nero (AD 68), the "legionaries of provincial birth outnumbered the Italians by about four or five to one."[10] And this is with regard to the whole of the Roman Empire, not merely in the East. The second position that Pollard examines holds that the eastern legions were made up entirely and exclusively of eastern provincials: "Legions based in Cappadocia, Syria, and Egypt were made up from of recruits from Asia Minor, Syria, and Egypt."[11] Either scenario leaves us with little doubts that the overriding majority of the soldiers that attacked Jerusalem under Titus were Middle Eastern peoples and not Europeans.

CRUNCHING THE NUMBERS

But let's actually calculate what all of this information means with regard to the ethnic composition of the "Roman" armies that attacked Jerusalem. Josephus tells us that "the whole army, including the auxiliaries sent by the kings, as well horsemen and footmen, when all were united together, amounted to sixty thousand."[12] Remember that a legion contained roughly 5,000 soldiers. There were four full legions and two partial legions involved in the attack. This would mean that there were approximately 25,000 men who were full-time legionaries with the remaining 35,000 men, who were either volunteers or auxiliaries. The auxiliaries were non-Roman citizens raised up from the fringe of the provinces. Josephus confirms this when he says that the auxiliaries were "sent by the kings" from "the neighborhood" of Syria, Asia Minor, and Arabia. If Pollard's higher estimations are correct as to the five-to-one margin of the Eastern soldiers versus the Western, then this would mean that there could have been no more than 5,000 Western soldiers in the whole invading army. The remaining 55,000–56,000 were all Easterners. And this is allowing for the maximum estimates of Western soldiers. That would mean that there was no more than one Western European soldier to every eleven Middle Eastern soldiers. Eleven to one! Yet in all likelihood, the ratio was much higher.

FURTHER EVIDENCE

Concluding the discussion, Pollard also offers a very interesting piece of information: "Other evidence that Syrian legions of the Flavian period were characteristically 'Syrian' in some way comes from Tacitus' reference to Legion 3 Gallica saluting the rising sun 'according to the custom of Syria' . . . in A.D. 69."[13]

The implication is clear, of course: the soldiers of that legion were worshippers of some form of sun deity. This was typical of Middle Easterners, who throughout ancient history worshipped various astral deities. Thus, these Eastern "Roman" soldiers were in fact the physical and, to a degree, spiritual ancestors of those who today bow down to Allah, the god who is most often represented by the crescent moon.

All said, the historical evidence is overwhelming. Josephus elsewhere recorded that under Nero, several years prior to the Jewish War, in Caesarea Maritima, a coastal city in northern Israel, a conflict broke out between the Jews and the Syrians who inhabited that city. As the battle raged, the Roman soldiers stood against the Jews and assisted the Syrians because, wrote Josephus, the Roman soldiers were in fact ethnic Syrians: "The greatest part of the Roman garrison was raised out of Syria; and being thus related to the Syrian part, they were ready to assist it."[14]

CLOSING ARGUMENTS

After examining a broad sampling of evidence from both ancient historians as well as the most up-to-date modern scholarship, we may very confidently conclude that the "Roman" soldiers in the Eastern provinces that destroyed Jerusalem and the Temple were in fact Eastern peoples—the inhabitants of Asia Minor, Syria, Arabia, and Egypt. Again, they were the ancestors of the modern-day inhabitants of the Middle East. We can certainly understand how a hasty or perfunctory reading of Daniel 9:26 would lead one to conclude that the Antichrist's followers would be Europeans, but having now done due diligence, completed our homework and examined the evidence, it is clear that the reality is quite different from what has been commonly and popularly understood.

ONE FINAL OBJECTION

But old habits—and paradigms—often die hard. As such, after having brought forth this argument in our book, *God's War on Terror: Islam, Prophecy and the Bible*, my coauthor, Walid Shoebat, and I have seen our findings harshly challenged. One such critique, featured in *The Christ in Prophecy Journal*, follows:

> A good example of Shoebat's tortuous logic can be found in his attempt to explain away the meaning of Daniel 9:26. The plain sense meaning of this passage is that the Antichrist will come from the people who will destroy the Temple. Shoebat and Richardson argue that the Roman legions that carried out the destruction of Jerusalem and the Temple in 70 A.D. were composed primarily of Arabs, mainly Syrians and Turks. They therefore conclude that the Antichrist will arise from the Syrians

or Turks and will be a Muslim. This is really grasping at straws in the wind! It doesn't matter whether or not the legions were composed of Australian Aborigines, it was the Roman government that decided to destroy Jerusalem, it was the Roman government that gave the orders, and it was Roman generals who carried out the destruction. Rome was the rod of God's judgment and it is from the Roman people that the Antichrist will arise.[15]

Or reworded, this critic is willing to admit that the Roman soldiers may have been Eastern peoples, but this is irrelevant because they were under the authority of Italian commanders, who not only desired but also commanded the destruction of Jerusalem and the Temple. Thus the burden of responsibility is placed on the Roman authorities. There are two fatal problems with this argument. The first is that it fails to consider the actual grammar of the passage. Let's look at this issue first, for it is crucial.

THE GRAMMATICAL ERROR: WHAT DOES THE PROPHECY ACTUALLY STATE?

Again, briefly, the verse states: "The people of the prince who is to come shall destroy the city and the sanctuary" (Daniel 9:26).

What we need to do is zero in on the word *people*. If we look up the meaning of that word (*am*) in the Hebrew, we find that it is an ethnic denotation. It does not refer to the kingdom or empire under which the people lived, but rather the people themselves. The *Strong's Lexicon* lists the meaning of *am* as "people, nation, persons, members of one's people, compatriots, country-men, kinsman, kindred." Wilhelm Gesenius, the Hebrew lexiconographer, lists the primary meaning of the word as "single races or tribes . . . race or family . . . the kindred, relatives." We are not looking to an empire, but rather a race. Yet consistently, when writers claim that this prophecy points us to Rome or Europe, an improper understanding of the word *am* is always at the root of the error. Consider the following commentary by one prophecy blogger: "The angel Gabriel was explicit in explaining to Daniel the nationality of the coming Antichrist. This is no theory, it is currently unfulfilled prophecy. Period. Antichrist WILL COME from among the people who destroyed the city and the sanctuary in 79 AD [*sic*]. Antichrist WILL COME from the descendants of the people of Rome. Period.[16]

While complete confidence in the reliability of the Scriptures is admirable, such certainty must also be in accordance with the actual grammar of the passage. The popular position misses this most essential point. Hebrew scholar Arnold Fruchtenbaum accurately summarizes the actual meaning of this verse: "We are dealing here with a bloodline, and not a country."[17] This distinction between bloodline and country is essential and cannot be missed. If the purpose of the verse were to highlight the broader kingdom or the empire under which the people lived, it could have used the Hebrew words *mamlakah* (kingdom or empire) or *goy* (nation). But this is simply not what the verse says. Instead, it points us to the ethnic identity of the majority of the peoples who made up the Roman legions. The language of the verse does not allow us to look to the empire that had authority over the people, but rather, it would have us look at the peoples themselves who carried out the destruction. If we desire to submit to the passage, then we must draw out its true meaning (exegesis) and submit to our findings. We cannot force the passage to conform to our positions (eisegesis), despite what it actually states.

Another way to highlight the important distinction between citizenship and ethnicity is to look at the apostle Paul. Paul was a Roman citizen (his *mamlakah* was Rome) but this in no way diminishes the fact that he was ethnically a Jew (his *am* were the Jews) (Acts 21:38–39; 22:1–3).

To put it in a clearer light, imagine that I was walking down the city of some well-known American city late one evening and was robbed by three individuals. After the police arrived, they asked me if I could identify my assailants. "Of course. I got a really good look at all three of them," I state.

"Good," the officer responds. "What did they look like? What can you tell us about them?"

"Well, they were Americans," I reply.

Now, knowing that Americans come in all shapes, sizes, and ethnicities, what exactly have I told the police? Nothing. As we all know, the mere designation "American" tells us virtually nothing about one's ethnicity. One could be an Anglo-American, an Asian-American, an African-America, an Arab-American, or perhaps a hundred other types of hyphenated Americans. Likewise, the Roman Empire of the late first century was perhaps even more diverse than the United States of today.

The Roman Empire contained numerous people groups (*am*). One could be a full-fledged "Roman" citizen, yet hail from any number of people groups. One could be Germanic, Jewish, Gallic, Syrian, Arab, African, or one of a dozen other ethnicities, and still be fully "Roman." To be blunt, any claim that the mere designation "Roman" is sufficient to identify the ethnic identity of the people in Daniel 9:26 is sheer folly. This historically myopic view would be no different from claiming that the designation "American" could only mean ethnically Anglo. The popular claim that Daniel 9:26 points us solely to those from Italian or European ethnicities ignores the clear wording of the text and thus entirely distorts its meaning.

THE HISTORICAL REALITY

Returning to the *Christ in Prophecy Journal*'s argument that the ethnicity of the people is irrelevant, we find another problem. This time it concerns the historical record. Was it, in fact, the Roman government that decided to destroy the Jewish Temple? Was it really "the Roman government that gave the orders, and [the] Roman generals who carried out the destruction"? Once again, just a little bit of homework reveals just the opposite is true. Josephus's records make this all too abundantly clear:

> And now a certain person came running to Titus, and told him of this fire . . . whereupon he rose up in great haste, and, as he was, ran to the holy house, in order to have a stop put to the fire; after him followed all his commanders, and after them followed the several legions, in great astonishment; so there was a great clamor and tumult raised, as was natural upon the disorderly motion of so great an army. Then did Caesar, both by calling to the soldiers that were fighting, with a loud voice, and by giving a signal to them with his right hand, order them to quench the fire.[18]

One can almost imagine Titus, like the classic stereotype of an Italian, frantically using both his mouth and his hands to speak. But despite the great alarm of their general, despite his frantic shouting and hand waving, the soldiers did not obey Titus or any of their commanders. They were absolutely hell-bent on fighting the Jews. The following passage from Josephus's *Wars of the Jews* reveals exactly why:

Titus supposing what the fact was, that the house itself might yet be saved, he came in haste and endeavored to persuade the soldiers to quench the fire . . . yet were their passions too hard for the regards they had for Caesar, and the dread they had of him who forbade them, as was their hatred of the Jews, and a certain vehement inclination to fight them, too hard for them also . . . And thus was the holy house burnt down, without Caesar's approbation.[19]

Could the picture be any clearer? For these eastern soldiers, the temptation and the opportunity to kill Jews was simply too overwhelming. Given the choice between allegiance to their commanders or hatred of the Jews, they submitted wholeheartedly to their "vehement inclination" to kill the Jews. Restraint was impossible. And finally, the last line, "thus was the holy house burnt down, without Caesar's approbation," could not be more damning to any claim that the Roman leaders desired or commanded the destruction of the Temple. It was not per the commands of Rome that the Temple was burned; it was pure anti-Semitic hatred that burned down the Temple that day.

ISAAC AND ISHMAEL: THE ANCIENT HATRED

An ancient reality is emerging here. The specific reason the soldiers did not obey their commanders was because of the passionate hatred they possessed for the Jews. Then, as today, the various Middle Eastern peoples were largely possessed by a demonic hatred for the Jewish people. Even as hatred was the primary motivating factor behind the destruction of the Temple in AD 70, so also is hatred the overriding sentiment of the surrounding Islamic nations today toward the Jews. And hatred will no doubt be the primary driving factor when the armies of the Antichrist invade Israel. This hatred is seen perhaps most markedly in a gruesome episode recorded by Josephus. As the Roman armies surrounded Jerusalem, many of the citizens were choosing to surrender and desert the city. As they did so, many would swallow whatever gold or silver coins they possessed, hoping to be able to retrieve them after they had escaped the city with nothing else. But as they came out to surrender to the Roman soldiers as non-combatant supplicants, they met a terrible fate. The Syrian and Arab soldiers that made up the Roman armies would have none of it. Instead,

Josephus tells us that the soldiers killed those who were desiring to surrender, hoping to find any gold or silver that may have been swallowed: "The multitude of the Arabians, with the Syrians, cut up those that came as supplicants, and searched their bellies. Nor does it seem to me that any misery befell the Jews that was more terrible than this, since in one night's time about two thousand of these deserters were thus dissected."[20]

Notice again that among the various peoples that were laying siege to Jerusalem, it was the Syrians together with the Arabs that were mutilating those Jews who attempted to escape.

CONCLUSION

The overwhelming evidence from both ancient historians and modern-day scholarship points out the ethnic identity of the "Roman" peoples that destroyed Jerusalem and the Temple: they were the ancestors of the Muslim peoples that dominate the entire region today. The peoples of the Middle East will be the primary followers of the Antichrist, "the prince to come." These are the "people" of Daniel 9:26.

As we have already noted, the European Antichrist theory finds its most significant support in this one verse. And as we have now seen, the European Antichrist theory is built on a foundation of vapor. In the end, the passage that most have looked to as the strongest support for a European Antichrist in fact points to an Antichrist from the Middle East—as does every other passage throughout the Prophets.

DANIEL 8: THE LITTLE HORN

W E NOW TURN TO DANIEL 8, a chapter that begins with the rise of Medo-Persian Empire and concludes with Antiochus IV Epiphanes, the most prominent type of the Antichrist in Scripture. Daniel 8 should be understood as an expansion of the same story that unfolds in Daniel 2 and 7. In Daniel 2, we were told of the destructive and conquering Islamic Caliphate, out of which would come a revised version of the Islamic Caliphate in the last days. Daniel 7 tells the same story, but adds new information concerning the Antichrist, called "the little horn," who will arise out of the former Islamic Caliphate, initially taking control over three kingdoms, and eventually controlling ten. In Daniel 8, the story is developed and unfolded even further, informing us of many of the characteristics and actions of the coming Antichrist.

DANIEL 8

Daniel 8 recounts another of Daniel's fascinating visionary experiences. As the vision occurs, Daniel is in the city of Susa, the capital of Elam, in modern-day Iran, roughly two hundred miles to the east of Babylon. While some commentators speculate that Daniel was actually in Susa, perhaps on a diplomatic mission, the wording of the passage seems to indicate that he was there, not physically, but only in his vision: "And I saw in the vision; and when I saw, I was in Susa the capital, which is in the province of Elam. And I saw in the vision, and I was at the Ulai canal" (v. 2).

MEDO-PERSIA

The vision begins by portraying the rise to power of the Medo-Persian Empire, which would come to conquer the Babylonian Empire. In Daniel 7, the Medo-Persian Empire was portrayed as a lopsided bear. But here, Medo-Persia is portrayed as a ram with two horns, one longer than the other:

> I raised my eyes and saw, and behold, a ram standing on the bank of the canal. It had two horns, and both horns were high, but one was higher than the other, and the higher one came up last. I saw the ram charging westward and northward and southward. No beast could stand before him, and there was no one who could rescue from his power. He did as he pleased and became great. (vv. 3–4)

The uneven horns clearly correlate with the lopsided nature of the bear in Daniel 7. As John Walvoord has written, "The portrayal of the two horns representing two major aspects of the Medo-Persian Empire, that is, the Medes and the Persians, is very accurate, as the Persians coming up last and represented by the higher horn were also the more prominent and powerful."[1]

The identification of the ram as the Medo-Persian Empire is beyond question, as it is later identified as such by the angel Gabriel: "As for the ram that you saw with the two horns, these are the kings of Media and Persia" (v. 20).

After the Medo-Persian Empire rose to power, it conquered westward toward modern-day Turkey, Syria, Lebanon, and Greece; northward toward contemporary northern Iran, Chechnya, Georgia, Armenia, and Azerbaijan; and southward toward what are now Iraq, Israel, and Egypt.

THE ALEXANDRIAN GREEK EMPIRE

Next the vision foretold the transition from the Medo-Persian Empire to the Alexandrian Greek Empire. Here, in Daniel 8, the Alexandrian Greek Empire was portrayed as a shaggy goat with one large horn protruding from its head. This goat corresponds to the leopard of Daniel 7. The prominent single horn represents Alexander the Great:

> As I was considering, behold, a male goat came from the west across the face of the whole earth, without touching the ground. And the goat had a conspicuous horn between his eyes. He came to the ram with the two horns, which I had seen standing on the bank of the canal, and he ran at him in his powerful wrath. I saw him come close to the ram, and he was enraged against him and struck the ram and broke his two horns. And the ram had no power to stand before him, but he cast him down to the ground and trampled on him. And there was no one who could rescue the ram from his power. (vv. 5–7)

Alexander is seen utterly destroying the Medo-Persian ram, who is unable to offer a defense. As the passage states, "none could rescue" Medo-Persia from Alexander the Great's military power.

THE DIADOCHI

Next, Alexander's death is portrayed as the singular horn of the goat is "broken." In its place, four horns grow up, representing the four generals who succeeded Alexander. These generals are often referred to as the Diadochi (successors): "Then the goat became exceedingly great, but when he was strong, the great horn was broken, and instead of it there came up four conspicuous horns toward the four winds of heaven" (v. 8).

The four horns also correlate with the four wings of the leopard in Daniel 7. As with the Medo-Persian Empire and its representative ram, the angel Gabriel leaves no doubt as to the meaning of the goat and its horns: "And the goat is the king of Greece. And the great horn between his eyes is the first king. As for the horn that was broken, in place of which four others arose, four kingdoms shall arise from his nation, but not with his power" (vv. 21–22).

WARS OF THE DIADOCHI

Shortly after Alexander's death in 323 BC, the wars of the Diadochi commenced and intermittently raged for the next fifty years. After roughly twenty years of inter-dynastic fighting, two "kings,"or dynasties, emerged as the dominant rulers over the majority of the former Alexandrian Greek Empire. The largest of the two empires was the Seleucid Empire in the north, which ruled over the regions of modern-day Turkey, Syria, Lebanon, Iraq, Iran, Afghanistan, and Pakistan. In the south was the Ptolemaic Empire, which ruled over Egypt, Libya, and Sudan. Although time, deaths, and wars resulted in a constant shifting of the boundaries of these two empires, the general shape and regions remained relatively consistent for the next hundred years.

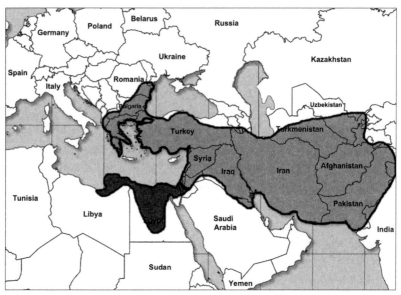

Seleucid and Ptolemaic Empires, 275 BC[2]

ANTIOCHUS IV EPIPHANES

Then, in 175 BC, Antiochus IV Epiphanes, the son of King Antiochus III, seized the throne of the Seleucid Empire. Antiochus is referred to in the text as "a little horn": "Out of one of them came a little horn, which grew exceedingly great toward the south, toward the east, and toward the glorious land" (v. 9).

Steven R. Miller, in the *New American Commentary on Daniel*, confirms the identification of the "little horn" as Antiochus IV Epiphanes: "The meaning is that from one of the divisions of the Greek Empire would emerge a king of unusual significance. Scholars agree that this little horn represents the eighth ruler of the Seleucid Greek Empire, Antiochus IV Epiphanes (175–163 B.C.)."[3]

Five years after he took control of the Seleucid Empire in 170 BC, a conflict erupted between Antiochus and King Ptolemy VI in the south. King Ptolemy was demanding the return of southern Syria. This lead Antiochus to launch a preemptive strike against Ptolemy, conquering all of Egypt except the city of Alexandria. King Ptolemy was also captured. Fearing a military response from the Romans, Antiochus allowed Ptolemy to continue reigning, but only as a puppet king. Two years later, in 168 BC, Antiochus led a second attack against the southern kingdom. While Antiochus was in Egypt, in the land of Israel, a rumor had spread that he had been killed. A rebellion followed, with the deposed high priest Jason gathering a force of one thousand soldiers and making a surprise attack on the city of Jerusalem. As Antiochus returned north, however, hearing of the rebellion, he attacked Jerusalem and executed roughly forty thousand Jews, selling as many into slavery. These events are recounted in the Apocrypha:

> When these happenings were reported to the king, he thought that Judea was in revolt. Raging like a wild animal, he set out from Egypt and took Jerusalem by storm. He ordered his soldiers to cut down without mercy those whom they met and to slay those who took refuge in their houses. There was a massacre of young and old, a killing of women and children, a slaughter of virgins and infants. In the space of three days, eighty thousand were lost, forty thousand meeting a violent death, and the same number being sold into slavery. (2 Maccabees 5:11–14)

These events led to the Maccabean revolt, which in turn caused Antiochus to respond ferociously against the Jewish people. Antiochus outlawed Judaism, abolished the Jewish daily sacrifices, and even sacrificed a pig on the altar in the Jewish Temple, spreading its juices through the Temple as a means of defilement. Beyond even this, Antiochus substituted the Jewish feasts with the drunken feast of Bacchanalia, forcing the Jews to worship Bacchus, the god of pleasure and wine. Antiochus also forbade anyone to be circumcised, or to read the Torah or any of the Hebrew Scriptures. When one mother secretly defied Antiochus and had her two boys circumcised, the king had all three of them thrown headlong together

MIDEAST BEAST

over the highest wall in Jerusalem onto the hard stone pavement below.
2 Maccabees 7:3–5 even recounts an instance where Antiochus cut out the
tongues of seven sons from the same family and then had them all roasted
alive on a large, flat iron as their mother was forced to watch. Only after
this was the mother of the boys herself finally murdered. Theodoret of
Cyr, a fifth-century bishop in the Eastern Church, also commented on
the many great offenses Antiochus committed against the Jewish temple:

> When the uprising become more serious, Antiochus arrived and put
> to death most of the devout, and he had the audacity even to enter
> the precincts of the temple; after entering he sacked the whole temple,
> appropriating to himself the treasures, all the offerings, the cups, the
> bowls and vessels, the golden table, the golden censer, the lampstands
> made of gold, and in short all the instruments of divine worship. In
> addition he built an altar to Zeus, filled the whole city with idols and
> obliged everyone to sacrifice, while he himself sacrificed a pig on the
> divine altar and named it after Zeus of Olympus.[4]

All of these atrocities are recounted as the career of the "little horn"
unfolds in Daniel's vision:

> It [the little horn, Antiochus] grew great, even to the host of heaven.
> And some of the host and some of the stars it threw down to the ground
> and trampled on them. It became great, even as great as the Prince
> of the host. And the regular burnt offering was taken away from him,
> and the place of his sanctuary was overthrown. And a host will be
> given over to it together with the regular burnt offering because of
> transgression, and it will throw truth to the ground, and it will act
> and prosper. (Daniel 8:10–12)

ANTIOCHUS AS A TYPE OF THE ANTICHRIST

Antiochus IV Epiphanes is undoubtedly one of the greatest prototypes
of the Antichrist in all of the Bible. These prophecies of Antiochus IV
Epiphanes thus have both a historical as well as a future fulfillment. The
events carried out by Antiochus as detailed in Daniel 8 will be mirrored
to a degree by the Antichrist in the last days. This view is held by a wide
range of scholars and commentators:

- John Walvoord states, "This passage, though fulfilled by Antiochus, was also typical of the description of the future role of the coming Antichrist, the man of sin, the dictator of the whole world during the last three-and-a-half years before the Second Coming."[5]

- Tim Lahaye and Ed Hindson state, "The description of Antiochus IV Epiphanes as the little horn of Daniel 8:9–13, 23–25 and the 'despicable person' in Daniel 11:21–35 marks him out as a type of the little horn (the Antichrist) . . . the similarities shared by Antiochus and the Antichrist are striking and establish a typological relationship between the two figures."[6]

- H. C. Leupold, a renowned scholar of the Old Testament, likewise sees Antiochus as a type of the Antichrist, and the prophecies of chapter 8 to have direct end-time significance: "King Antiochus is seen to be a kind of Old Testament antichrist like unto the great Antichrist; the overthrow and the defilement of the sanctuary shall correspond to the similar experiences of the great tribulation. When this is borne in mind, the chapter loses its isolation from present-day events and is seen to be typical in a very definite sense."[7]

- Gleason L. Archer notes the similarities between Antiochus in Daniel 8 and the Antichrist in Daniel 7: "It [Daniel 8] somewhat resembles it [Daniel 7] in subject matter and in manner of presentation, for it too portrays successive world empires as fierce beasts; and it culminates in a tyrant described as "a little horn.""[8]

THE END-TIMES CONTEXT

There are several very solid reasons why scholars have seen in Antiochus IV Epiphanes' actions, as recorded in Daniel 8, a clear prophetic foreshadowing of the coming Antichrist. The first, quite simply, is that the angel Gabriel directly informs Daniel of the ultimate end-time context of the vision:

And I heard a man's voice between the banks of the Ulai, and it called, "Gabriel, make this man understand the vision." So he came near where I stood. And when he came, I was frightened and fell on my face. But he said to me, "Understand, O son of man, that the vision is for the time of the end." And when he had spoken to me, I fell into a deep sleep with my face to the ground. But he touched me and made me stand up. He said, "Behold, I will make known to you what shall be at the latter end of the indignation, for it refers to the appointed time of the end." (Daniel 8:16–19)

Referring to the specific phrase "time of the end" (Hebrew: *èt-qetz*), Lahaye and Hindson speak of its ultimate end-time meaning:

> The term "time of the end" (Hebrew, *èt-qetz*) in Daniel (8:17, 19; 11:35; 124, 6, 9, 13), as in the rest of the Old Testament, is distinct from the term "latter days" (Hebrew, *acharit hayamim*) (2:28; 10:14). Both are eschatological expressions, but only èt-qetz refers exclusively to the final eschatological period or event . . . The focus on the "end-time" and the "final period of the indignation" reveals that the events pertaining to Antiochus' persecution of the Jewish people and desecration of the Temple—and therefore against God, "the Prince of prince"—would have their ultimate fulfillment with the antitype, the Antichrist during the Tribulation . . . Antiochus did many of the things the future Antichrist would do, and in this way established a prophetic pattern for what is to come.[9]

SIMILARITIES BETWEEN ANTIOCHUS AND THE ANTICHRIST

But beyond the fact that the angel Gabriel directly states that the ultimate context of the vision is the end-times, scholars have also noted numerous similarities between Antiochus and the coming Antichrist, further establishing the ultimate end-time context of this vision. Consider the following striking similarities:

1. Both Antiochus and the Antichrist are referred to using the symbolism of a "little horn." While the Antichrist is referred to as "another horn, a little one" (Daniel 7:8), Antiochus is referred to as simply "a little horn" (Daniel 8:9).

2. Both Antiochus and the Antichrist are great persecutors of God's people. While the Antichrist "shall persecute the saints of the Most High" who "shall be given into his hand" (Daniel 7:25), it said of Antiochus that he would "destroy fearfully, and shall prosper and thrive; he shall destroy the mighty, and also the holy people" (Daniel 8:24).

3. Both Antiochus and the Antichrist are pictured as "stern faced" (8:23) or having an "imposing look" (7:20). As Miller comments, "Both of these descriptions imply cruelty and harshness."[10]

4. Both Antiochus and the Antichrist exalt themselves. While Antichrist "shall speak pompous words against the Most High" (Daniel 7:25), it was said of Antiochus, "He shall exalt himself in his heart . . . He shall even rise against the Prince of princes" (Daniel 8:25).

5. Both Antiochus and the Antichrist have great power, which comes directly from Satan. Of the Antichrist, it is said that "the coming of the lawless one is according to the working of Satan, with all power, signs, and lying wonders" (2 Thessalonians 2:9). It is specifically said that Satan, the dragon, will give his "authority to the beast" (Revelation 13:4), and the Antichrist "shall act against the strongest fortresses with a foreign god" (Daniel 11:39). Concerning Antiochus, it was said, "His power shall be mighty, but not by his own power" (Daniel 8:24).

6. Both Antiochus and the Antichrist would be destroyers of men. Of the Antichrist it is said that he will "cause as many as would not worship the image of the beast to be killed" (Revelation 13:15). The apostle John, in a vision, saw "unclean spirits like frogs coming out of the mouth of the dragon, out of the mouth of the beast, which go out to the kings of the earth and of the whole world, to gather them to the battle of that great day of God Almighty" (Revelation 13:13–14). Of Antiochus it was said, "He shall destroy the mighty" (Daniel 8:24).

7. Both Antiochus and the Antichrist are master deceivers. Of the Antichrist it is said that his career will be defined by "all power, signs, and lying wonders" (2 Thessalonians 2:9). During the reign of the Antichrist, "those who dwell on the earth" will be deceived by false "signs" (Revelation 13:14). Of Antiochus it was said that he "understands sinister schemes" (Daniel 8:23), and "through his cunning He shall cause deceit to prosper under his rule" (Daniel 8:25).

8. Both Antiochus and the Antichrist are defined as proud and arrogant. The Antichrist will have "a mouth speaking pompous words," specifically "against the Most High" (Daniel 7:8, 11, 25). Of Antiochus it is said, "And he shall exalt himself in his heart" (Daniel 8:25).

9. Both Antiochus and the Antichrist would use a false peace to achieve their aims. While the Antichrist will enter into a false peace agreement with Israel (Daniel 9:26), of Antiochus it was written that he would "come in peaceably, and obtain the kingdom by flatteries" (Daniel 11:21, 24), and, "he will destroy many by peace" (Daniel 8:25).

Other similarities between Antiochus IV Epiphanes and the Antichrist could certainly be highlighted, and various commentators have done so. But despite the obvious prophetic foreshadowing of the Antichrist in Antiochus, and despite the stated end-time context of the passage, many scholars and prophecy teachers have wrestled to reconcile the "little horn" of Daniel 8 with the "little horn" of Daniel 7. Their difficulty arises because of the common but false assumption that the little horn/ Antichrist of Daniel 7 emerges from out of the Roman Empire, whereas the little horn of Daniel 8 emerges out of the Middle East. Steven Miller wrestled with this seeming contradiction in his commentary on Daniel: "The double fulfillment view in which both Antiochus and Antichrist are prophesied has difficulties. For example, Antichrist comes from Rome, not Greece as does Antiochus."[11]

But while Miller finds a difficulty here, this problem is entirely resolved by recognizing that Daniel 2 and 7 do not point to the Roman Empire, but to the Islamic Caliphate. The region of the Islamic Caliphate and the consolidated Seleucid-Ptolemaic Empire of Antiochus IV Epiphanes are the same. When one understands that both chapters refer to the Islamic Caliphate, then all of Daniel's visions flow together smoothly and the historical difficulties of interpreters are resolved. Whether Daniel 2, 7, or 8, all three prophetic passages point to the final Antichristic kingdom arising from out of the Middle East.

DANIEL 10–11: THE KING

OF THE NORTH

AS WE HAVE SEEN THUS FAR throughout the book of Daniel, while every prophecy speaks of the coming Antichrist and his kingdom, each successive prophecy builds on the last, all flowing together, but adding new, important information in each passage. Even as Daniel 2 (Nebuchadnezzar's statue) was almost perfectly paralleled by Daniel 7 (the four beasts), so also does Daniel 11 as a prophecy almost perfectly parallel Daniel 8. Both prophecies trace the fall of the Medo-Persian Empire to the Alexandrian Greek Empire, its subsequent division to the four Diadochi, and the rise of Antiochus IV Epiphanes, the prophetic prototype of the Antichrist.

DANIEL 10: THE ANGELIC MESSENGER

The vision of Daniel 11 actually begins in Daniel 10, where we are told of Daniel's encounter with an angelic being. Then in chapter 11, the vision is explained. The revelation begins when Daniel first meets the angel:

> Now on the twenty-fourth day of the first month, as I was by the side of the great river, that is, the Tigris, I lifted my eyes and looked, and behold, a certain man clothed in linen, whose waist was girded with gold of Uphaz! His body was like beryl, his face like the appearance of lightning, his eyes like torches of fire, his arms and feet like burnished

bronze in color, and the sound of his words like the voice of a multitude. And I, Daniel, alone saw the vision. (Daniel 10:4–7)

In verse 14, the angel reveals to Daniel the ultimate end-time context of the vision: "O Daniel, man greatly beloved, understand the words that I speak to you, and stand upright, for I have now been sent to you . . . Now I have come to make you understand what will happen to your people in the latter days, for the vision refers to many days yet to come." This point is essential. Like Daniel 8, the prophecy has both historical and end-time meaning. Virtually all futurist commentators acknowledge the dual-layered interpretation:

- Jerome commented that the ultimate meaning of the prophecy pertains to "what is going to happen to the people of Israel, not in the near future but in the last days, that is, at the end of the world."[1]

- Gleason L. Archer stated, "The angel begins to explain to Daniel the destiny of the Hebrew people up to the last days . . . The vision goes beyond his age to the final period in world history before the Son of Man comes in great power to establish the Kingdom of God on earth."[2]

- LaHaye and Hindson have written, "The prophecies of chapters 11 will deal with near-future events (those fulfilled historically) . . . and far-future events (those fulfilled eschatologically)—the rise of the little horn from the fourth kingdom, the Antichrist."[3]

- John Walvoord wrote, "The expression in the latter days is an important chronological term related to the prophetic program which is unfolded in the book of Daniel . . . extending and climaxing in the second coming of Jesus Christ to earth."[4]

- Steven R. Miller says, "'In the future' is a translation of the Hebrew *béahârît hayyāmîm*, usually rendered 'in the latter days.' Normally the phrase describes events that will occur just prior to and including the coming of the kingdom of God upon the earth . . . The climax of the historical preview provided by the angel is the future kingdom of God."[5]

Having explained the ultimate meaning and purpose of the vision to Daniel, the angel next begins to explain the events concerning the immediate future of the Medo-Persian Empire and its fall to Alexander the Great: "And now I will tell you the truth: Behold, three more kings will arise in Persia, and the fourth shall be far richer than them all . . . Then a mighty king shall arise, who shall rule with great dominion, and do according to his will" (Daniel 11:2–3).

As we previously saw in Daniel 8, Alexander's premature death would result in his empire being broken up among his four successors: "And when he has arisen, his kingdom shall be broken up and divided toward the four winds of heaven, but not among his posterity nor according to his dominion with which he ruled; for his kingdom shall be uprooted, even for others besides these" (v. 4).

What follows in verses 5–20 is the very detailed playing out of the historical clashes between the two most significant dynasties of Alexander's former Empire: the Seleucid Empire in the North and the Ptolemaic Dynasty in the South. Of verses 5–20, Old Testament scholar John C. Whitcomb says, "This remarkably detailed prophecy of the 150-year struggle between the various inheritors of Alexander's kingdom concentrates on Ptolemy I Soter (323–283 B.C.) and his successors in Egypt (i.e., the Kings of the South) and Seleucus I Nicator (312–281) and his successors in Syria (i.e., the Kings of the North)."[6]

Then in verses 21–35, we are told of the career of Antiochus IV Epiphanes, the "little horn" of Daniel 8, the eighth ruler of the northern Seleucid Empire: "And in his place shall arise a vile person, to whom they will not give the honor of royalty; but he shall come in peaceably, and seize the kingdom by intrigue" (v. 21).

The ongoing historical clash between the Seleucid Empire in the north and the Ptolemaic Empire in the south continues to be a major emphasis of the unfolding story: "He shall stir up his power and his courage against the king of the South with a great army. And the king of the South shall be stirred up to battle with a very great and mighty army; but he shall not stand, for they shall devise plans against him" (v. 25).

Verses 33–35 concludes the discussion of Antiochus with some exhortations to the Jewish people under Antiochus's persecution. They powerfully foreshadow the perseverance that will be required in the last days.

THE ANTICHRIST

The discussion concerning the clash between the Seleucids led by Antiochus and the Ptolemaic Empire in the south ends with verse 35. While some scholars disagree with this view, conservative futurist scholars generally accept that verses 35 and 36 mark the transition between Antiochus and his last days antitype, the Antichrist:

- Jerome, speaking in the fourth century of the Jewish and Christian interpretation of this passage, wrote, "The Jews believe that this passage has reference to the Antichrist . . . we too understand this passage to be a reference to the Antichrist."[7]

- John Walvoord wrote of the break from the historical to the end-time, "Beginning in verse 36, a sharp break in the prophecy may be observed, introduced by the expression the time of the end in verse 35. Up to this point, the prophecy dealing with the Persian and Grecian Empires has been fulfilled minutely and with amazing precision. Beginning with verse 36 however, an entirely different situation obtains."[8]

- Robert D. Culver, former professor of Old Testament and Hebrew at Grace Theological Seminary, in his *Daniel and the Latter Days*, discusses the transition from Antiochus to Antichrist in verse 36: "My own opinion (following the majority of recent Premillennial commentators) is that the prediction relates to Antiochus from verse 21 to verse 35, but that beginning with 36, Antichrist, by the designation of 'the king who shall do according to his will,' is the theme of the prophecy, to the close of chapter 11. With the view mentioned above, that Antiochus is described in verses 21–35, and that the history detailed is typical of Antichrist's future career . . ."[9]

- Dr. Thomas Ice also confirms the wide acceptance of this view: "Virtually all futurists believe that Daniel 11:1–35 was fulfilled in the past, primarily during the second century B.C. The king of the North and South in verses 1–35 clearly refer to the "conflict between the Ptolemies and the Seleucids."[10]

So scholars are in general agreement that between verses 35 and 36, a shift from the type (Antiochus) to the anti-type (Antichrist) takes place. Here, we see that Antichrist will do as he pleases, or according to his own will. As we saw in Daniel 8, he is self-exalting and arrogant. He will speak blasphemies against virtually every god, and most specifically, against Yahweh, the one true God (though in the verses that follow, we will see that there is one particular god that he does honor). And lastly, we see that he will prosper in all that he does until "the indignation is finished" when Jesus returns to bring his blasphemies to a swift end: "Then the king will do as he pleases, and he will exalt and magnify himself above every god and will speak monstrous things against the God of gods; and he will prosper until the indignation is finished, for that which is decreed will be done" (v. 36).

Verses 37–39 contain essential information concerning the Antichrist's character and belief system. We will delay the discussion of these verses for now and use the next chapter to discuss this issue in detail. For now, we will focus on verse 40 to the conclusion of the prophecy. Verse 40 tells us that the context of this final portion of the prophecy is the end-times: "At the end-time the king of the South will collide with him, and the king of the North will storm against him with chariots, with horsemen and with many ships; and he will enter countries, overflow them and pass through."

Though commentators are unified regarding the identity of the king of the North (the Seleucid kings) in the six earlier references, they are divided on the identity of the king of the North in verse 40. Some, like myself, think it is clear that the king of the North is the Antichrist. Others, however, believe he is an enemy of the Antichrist and an ally of the king of the South.

THE HISTORICAL VIEW: THE KING OF THE NORTH AS ANTICHRIST

Among those who identify the king of the North with the Antichrist include commentators from both the early church and modern times. I refer to this as the *historical view*:

- Hippolytus, a disciple of Ireneaus, in his second-century *Treatise on Christ and Antichrist*, identified the king of the North with the Antichrist.[11]

- Lactantius, in the third century, stated, "A king shall arise out of Syria, born from an evil spirit, the overthrower and destroyer of the human race, who shall destroy that which is left by the former evil, together with himself . . . he will attempt to destroy the temple of God and persecute the righteous people."[12]

• Theodoret of Cyr, in the fourth century, also identified the Antichrist as the king of the North: "The king of the south will wage war against this one, who is called the king of the north . . . Antiochus, who happened to be a type of the Antichrist, also was called the king of the north. When the king of the south engages him in fight, he will march out against him with a multitude and with strong forces both on land and on sea and acquire the victory."[13]

• Gleason L. Archer, after considering the alternative position, wrote, "It seems much simpler and more convincing, however, to take the 'king of the North' in this verse to be none other than the latter-day little horn, the Antichrist.[14]

• G. H. Lang, whose commentary on Daniel received the highest praise and endorsement in the foreword by F. F. Bruce, said, "As Antichrist is to rise from the Syrian area the prophecy naturally takes us to that country (the king of the north) and to its rival, Egypt (the king of the south). At the time of Daniel, and long after, Syria (the term now limited to the small country north of Palestine) and what is now termed Assyria were one kingdom of Syria, ruling for a time to the frontiers of India."[15]

• Edward J. Young, former professor of Old Testament at Westminster Theological Seminary, wrote, "The battles between the South and the North evidently point forward to this great battle in the end of the age. The two opponents are the Antichrist and the king of the South who begins the battle by pushing against him."[16]

• Steven R. Miller concurs: "It seems clear from the description of the 'king of the North' that he is none other than the Antichrist."[17]

• British minister and author Geoffrey R. King wrote, "I think he must be the King of the North, the Assyrian . . . He is the equivalent of the Beast of Revelation.[18]

• German theologian and Hebraist C. F. Keil argues that "in vv. 40–43 we do not read of a war of the hostile king (the Antichrist) against the king of the south and the king of the north."[19]

- Britt Gillette, a popular prophecy blogger, says, "Daniel Chapter 11 . . . clearly links the Antichrist to the Northern Kingdom of the divided Greek Empire. This kingdom was ruled by one of Alexander's generals, Seleucus, who ruled the areas of Syria, Mesopotamia, and Persia. Therefore, it is reasonable to assume that the Antichrist will in some way be linked to this geographic area of the Middle East."[20]

THE POPULAR VIEW: THREE KINGS

In contrast to the historical view, many today take the position that the passage describes three separate kings, and that the king of the North is an enemy of the Antichrist.

- Leon Wood, in his commentary on Daniel, acknowledged the debate among scholars and concluded that the king of the North is not the Antichrist, but instead a Russian leader.[21]

- Tim Lahaye and Ed Hindson, in their *Popular Bible Prophecy Commentary*, wrote, "The Antichrist's campaign will ultimately center on Israel (Daniel 11:41), but he will have to overcome a two-pronged attack by both the king of the South and the king of the North (verses 40–44) before he can achieve his objective (verse 45). Apparently, these two kings/nations will form an alliance against the Antichrist and will launch a joint attack against him."[22]

- John C. Whitcomb, says, "The king of the south must therefore be a yet future Egyptian monarch, judging from the previous use of the term in this chapter and also the clear statements of 11:42–43. Presumably in alliance with a king of the north (such as Russia today?), the eschatological Egyptian ruler will launch a diversionary thrust and will 'collide with him,' that is, with 'the king who will do as he pleases' (the Antichrist)."[23]

- Robert Culver wrote, "Up to that point, the immediate portion of the chapter is dealing with the king of the south (Egypt), the king (Antiochus) of the north (Syria), and their conflicts one with another, and with Israel. Here, however, the willful king is a third party, in conflict with both kings."[24]

PROBLEMS WITH THE POPULAR VIEW

According to the popular view, Daniel 11:36–45 describes three kings: (1) the Antichrist, (2) the king of the North, and (3) the king of the South. The king of the North and South are viewed as allies together against the Antichrist. Not only is this view in conflict with the opinions of the early church, but it is also in conflict with the clear flow and greater context of the passage. Throughout both Daniel 8 and 11, Antiochus IV Epiphanes is clearly a type of the Antichrist. All scholars agree with this. But as the final historical king of the Seleucid Empire, Antiochus was also the last king of the North. When scholars look at numerous characteristics, descriptions, actions, and titles of Antiochus IV Epiphanes as recorded throughout Daniel 8 and 11, they ascribe them all to Antichrist. These include descriptions of Antiochus as:

- the little horn (Daniel 7:8; 8:9)

- a destroyer and persecutor of God's people (Daniel 7:25; 8:24; Revelation 13:13–15)

- one who receives his power from Satan (Daniel 8:24; 11:39; 2 Thessalonians 2:9; Revelation 13:4)

- a blasphemer (Daniel 8:25; 7:8, 11, 25)

- arrogant and self-exalting (Daniel 7:8, 11, 25, 8:25)

- a vile person (Daniel 11:21)

- a desecrator of the Jewish Temple

- stern faced, of fierce countenance (Daniel 7:20; 8:23)

- a manipulator who uses deception to gain power (Daniel 8:23, 25; 2 Thessalonians 2:9; Revelation 13:14)

- one who uses false peace to attain victory (Daniel 8:25; 11:21, 24)

All of these are acknowledged as describing both Antiochus IV Epiphanes and the Antichrist. But concerning his title as king of the North, ruler of the Seleucid Empire, the popular view suddenly divorces the Antichrist from this title. The bizarre result is that Antiochus IV Epiphanes is viewed as both a type of the Antichrist *and* of the Antichrist's greatest enemy. But how can he be both? This simply doesn't make any sense. Beyond this, the kings of the North and South, who are enemies throughout the historical portion of the prophecy, are suddenly cast as allies together against the Antichrist. As Lahaye and Hindson have stated, "these two kings/nations will form an alliance against the Antichrist and will launch a joint attack against him."[25] Even J. Paul Tanner, an advocate for the popular three-king theory, admits the problematic and contradictory nature of this position: "One possible weakness of this view is the slight inconsistency with the earlier portion of the chapter. The three-king theory seems to suggest that the 'king of the North' and the 'king of the South' side together in their hostility against the antichrist, whereas the earlier part of the chapter depicted the two kings in conflict with one another."[26]

Tanner is absolutely correct, and his honesty is refreshing. This view literally twists the historical type (enemies) into its precise opposite (allies). Where is the justification for such a complete 180-degree turnaround? Despite its widespread popularity, this position is both inconsistent and lacking in any clear sense. It should be rejected by careful students of the Scriptures. But what is the basis for this position? How do so many otherwise excellent interpreters arrive at this conclusion? The answer is simple. Because most interpreters come to the passage with the false presumption of a Roman or European Antichrist, when Daniel 11 reveals the Antichrist to hail from the region of Turkey, Syria, and Iraq (the Seleucid Empire), they are unable to reconcile all the texts, and thus force an unnatural reading of the prophecy. As such, Leon Wood wrote, "The designation 'king of the north' is not an appropriate indication of the Antichrist, because his country, Rome, is not north of Palestine. A Russian ruler fits well, however, since Russia is directly north, with Moscow being on an almost direct north-south line with Jerusalem."[27]

While the entirety of Daniel 11 speaks of a Middle Eastern empire, suddenly, without any justification apart from the vague direction of "North," Wood, Whitcomb, and numerous others opt instead to see a

Russian military force. This is a classic example of pure speculative exegesis. Here we can see how the false presumption of a Roman Antichrist leads to compounding errors, tainting one's interpretation of this passage and several others. Instead, in keeping with the clearest and simplest understanding of the text, in agreement with the early church as well as the overwhelming Middle Eastern emphasis of all previous prophetic passages, we conclude that the title *king of the North* is used to describe the Antichrist. This title is used seven times in Daniel 11 (vv. 6, 7, 8, 11, 13, 15, 40). The first six times, it refers to the various kings of the Seleucid Empire. But in verse 40, the Antichrist, as the last-days Antiochus IV Epiphanes, is also referred to as the king of the North who will rule over a last-days version of the Seleucid Empire. This position is reasonable, simple, and clear, resolving the difficulties, contradictions, and tensions that have plagued many interpreters for years.

THE INVADER FROM THE NORTH

Moving back to the text, next we are told that the Antichrist will invade Israel, referred to as "the Beautiful Land" (NASB) as well as many other countries, but Edom, Moab, and the sons of Ammon will be spared from his conquests. The grouping of these three ancient nations and their fairly direct correlation to modern-day Jordan has led many commentators to believe that the contemporary Hashemite Kingdom of Jordan will not fall to the Antichrist's conquests: "He will also enter the Beautiful Land, and many countries will fall; but these will be rescued out of his hand: Edom, Moab and the foremost of the sons of Ammon" (Daniel 11:41 NASB).

After entering Israel, the Antichrist will conquer the three nations of Egypt, Libya, and Cush, which correlate with the modern Islamic Republic of North Sudan. "Then he will stretch out his hand against other countries, and the land of Egypt will not escape. But he will gain control over the hidden treasures of gold and silver and over all the precious things of Egypt; and Libyans and Cush [North Sudan] will follow at his heels" (vv. 42–43).

The Ancient Christians believed that the three nations of Egypt, Libya, and Sudan here correspond to the three horns that would first be uprooted by the Antichrist according to Daniel 7:8. Hippolytus, in his *Treatise on Christ and the Antichrist*, wrote, "And under this was signified none other than Antichrist . . . He says three horns are plucked up by the root by him, viz., the three kings of Egypt, and Libya, and Ethiopia [Cush-Sudan], whom he cuts off in the array of battle."[28]

Jerome also saw these same three nations as the three horns to first fall to the Antichrist: "We explain the final chapter of this vision as relating to the Antichrist and stating that during his war against the Egyptians, Libyans and Ethiopians [Cush–Sudan], in which he shall smash three of the ten horns . . .[29]

Then, sometime in the midst of the Antichrist's conquests, "rumors" from both the North and the East upset him greatly. Exactly what these rumors are, we can only speculate. But we would assume that they refer to the movements of large armies, perhaps from Russia in the North and China in the East: "But rumors from the East and from the North will disturb him, and he will go forth with great wrath to destroy and annihilate many" (Daniel 11:44).

Finally, the Antichrist is portrayed as "pitching his royal tents" in the land of Israel, where he is simply described as coming "to his end": "He will pitch the tents of his royal pavilion between the seas and the beautiful Holy Mountain; yet he will come to his end, and no one will help him" (v. 45).

PROPHETIC FUTURE IMPLICATIONS

In Daniel 8, Antiochus IV Epiphanes is a type of the Antichrist with regard to his character and actions against the people and the land of Israel. Here in Daniel 11, Antiochus is once again treated as a type of the Antichrist. This time it is with regard to the wars in which he will engage and the region from which he will emerge. As we have seen, this was the view of the early Christians. The implications of this prophecy with regard to the so-called Arab Spring are profound. In the days and years ahead, we should expect to see the emergence of a northern leader from the general region of Turkey, Syria, or Iraq; that is, the Seleucid Empire. Another southern leader will emerge in Egypt. The southern leader will clash with the northern leader in what will lead to a large-scale military confrontation. Egypt will fall to the northern leader. Libya and Sudan (Cush) will then submit to the northern leader. After this, seven other nations from

the region will willingly throw their support behind the northern leader/
Antichrist and his emerging empire. This revived empire is that which
was prophesied in Daniel 2 as the feet of iron and clay, in Daniel 7 as the
ten horns. This will be the final, Antichristic empire that will crush the
people of God throughout the region and in much of the earth before
being completely destroyed by Jesus the Messiah.

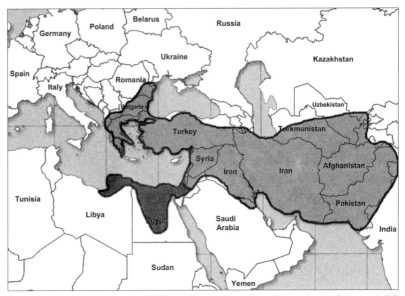

Seleucid Kingdom in the North and the Ptolemaic Kingdom in the South (c. 275 BC)[30]

1 0

DANIEL 11: THE THEOLOGY OF THE ANTICHRIST: WILL HE CLAIM TO BE GOD?

IN THE PREVIOUS CHAPTER, we examined the portion of Daniel 11 that highlighted the region from which the Antichrist would emerge as well as his prophetic title, "the king of the North." Now we must return to verses 36–39 to understand what the passage says concerning the Antichrist's religion or theology. In the last chapter, we discussed verse 36, which portrays the Antichrist as a self-willed, self-exalting one who exalts himself above every god, and most specifically, blasphemes Yahweh, the one true God. However, in the verses that follow, while it will become clear that the Antichrist does blaspheme the God of the Bible and rejects virtually every other god, there is one particular god that the Antichrist does honor: "He will show no regard for the god of his fathers or for the desire of women, nor will he show regard for any other god; for he will magnify himself above them all. But instead he will honor a god of fortresses, a god whom his fathers did not know; he will honor him with gold, silver, costly stones and treasures" (Daniel 11:37–38 NKJV).

Contained here are some very important statements concerning the religious views of the Antichrist. This passage has led some Christians to make dogmatic declarations concerning the Antichrist's beliefs, based on an isolated portion of this passage, while ignoring other portions. For instance, I have heard it quoted, "He will show no regard for any other god" to support the claim that the Antichrist will be an atheist. Others have quoted, "He will show no regard for . . . the desire of women" as proof that he will be homosexual. Still others have quoted, "He will show no regard for the god of his fathers" as proof that he will be a Jew who converted to another religion or simply rejects Judaism. But to understand the full picture painted here requires a holistic analysis of the passage. I personally believe these verses contain a fourfold statement of the Antichrist's faith. The first three elements are negative, defining that which the Antichrist rejects and denies. The fourth component reveals that which the Antichrist affirms:

- The Antichrist rejects "the God of his fathers."

- The Antichrist rejects "the desire of women."

- The Antichrist rejects "every other god."

- The Antichrist affirms and honors "a god of forces."

Let's analyze what each of these statements refer to.

THE GOD OF HIS FATHERS

The first divine entity the Antichrist rejects is "the God of his fathers." Many students of biblical prophecy have read this phrase to mean that the Antichrist will simply reject the religion of his youth, the religion of his father or grandfather. Others have argued that the specific Hebrew word here for "God" could just as easily be used for a pagan "god" or "gods." But neither of these suggestions is in keeping with the consistent and repeated meaning of the Hebrew phrase (*elohim ab*). This phrase is used frequently throughout the Scriptures. Every time it is used, it is a reference to the Lord (Yahweh). This has led many scholars to conclude that the Antichrist would be Jewish. As A. C. Gaebelein stated, "The King Antichrist shall not regard the God of his fathers. Here his Jewish descent becomes evident. It is a Jewish phrase 'the Gods of his fathers.'"[1]

Thus, because the reference is to the Lord, the God of Abraham, Isaac, and Jacob, Gaebelein and other scholars believe that the Antichrist could only be a Jew who has rejected his ancestral religion. I believe Gaebelein is correct that *elohim ab* is a reference to the God of the Jews, but this doesn't necessarily prove the Antichrist will be Jewish. The problem with this reasoning is found in a popular children's church song: "Father Abraham had man sons, many sons had father Abraham." In other words, simply because the Antichrist rejects the God of his father Abraham, in no way does this prove that he is a Jew. He could just as easily be an Ishmaelite, an Edomite, or a descendant of any number of relatives of Abraham's sons that fill much of the Middle East and are dispersed throughout the earth today. We should be very careful using this passage to limit the ethnicity of the Antichrist in an overly rigid manner. The simple point here is that the Antichrist will "show no regard" for the Lord God of the patriarchs. In fact, although many Church fathers and modern-day commentators have claimed that the Antichrist will be Jewish, the biblical pattern proves otherwise. Every type or foreshadow of the Antichrist throughout Scripture has been a non-Jewish, Gentile leader. Pharaoh, Sennacherib (the Assyrian), Nebuchadnezzar (the king of Babylon), or Antiochus IV Epiphanes, these were all non-Jewish pagan world leaders. As such, I believe it is far likelier then that the Antichrist will also be a non-Jewish world leader who rejects the God of Abraham, Isaac, and Jacob. While Muslim apologists will claim the Allah of Islam is, in fact, one and the same as the God of Abraham, this is merely Islamic propaganda. The Allah of Islam has far more in common with Sin, the moon god whom Abraham left behind in the desert, than with the Father God of the Bible.

THE DESIRE OF WOMEN

Second, the Antichrist rejects "the desire of women." This phrase has also been interpreted in numerous ways.

Some interpret this as an indictor that the Antichrist will be a homosexual. Nathan Jones of Lamb and Lion Ministries, for example, takes this passage to mean that the Antichrist might be gay, and thus could not be a Muslim: "If the Antichrist is supposedly not into women and could be gay, the Muslims would want him dead, right?"[2] Pastor John Hagee was also excoriated by the liberal media for similarly stating that the Antichrist will be "a blasphemer and a homosexual."[3]

Others have seen in this verse a reference to some Roman goddess.

But this opinion is grounded in the liberal view that the passage is not speaking of the end-time Antichrist, but rather a historical figure.

Still others see this phrase as a messianic reference to Jesus the Messiah. This view is held by a cross-section of scholars:

- Arno C. Gaebelein said, "Still more interesting is the phrase 'he shall not regard the desire of women.' The Lord Jesus Christ is in view here."[4]

- John Walvoord likewise stated, "Although Daniel is not specific, a plausible explanation of this passage, in light of Daniel's Jewish background, is that this expression, the desire of women, is the natural desire of Jewish women to become the mother of the promised Messiah, the seed of the woman promised in Genesis 3:15."[5]

- Stephen R. Miller wrote, "'The one desired by women' allude[s] to Christ because Jewish women desired to be the mother of the Messiah, and the context of the verse seems to support this interpretation."[6]

- Phillip Mauro, a preterist expositor of the early twentieth century, wrote, "The words, 'nor the desire of women,' are very significant. There can be scarcely any doubt that they refer to Christ, and that Daniel would so understand them."[7]

In other words, "the desire of women" is a Hebraic phrase referencing the Messiah. This phrase would have been understood by its original hearers as such. Ultimately this desire of Jewish women was realized and fulfilled in Mary, who rejoiced in being chosen as the blessed one and cried out, "My soul magnifies the Lord, and my spirit has rejoiced in God my Savior. For He has regarded the lowly state of His maidservant; for behold, henceforth all generations will call me blessed" (Luke 1:46–48).

THE FATHER AND THE SON

Thus far, we see that the Antichrist rejects (1) the Lord (Yahweh), the God of the Bible; and (2) Jesus the Messiah. This twofold rejection should simply be seen as a denunciation of God the Father and God the Son. Support for this view is found in the New Testament. In 1 John 2:22–23, the apostle John was specifically discussing the theology or belief system of the Antichrist. Consider his emphasis on the Antichrist's denial of the Father and the Son: "Who is a liar but he who denies that Jesus is the Christ? He is antichrist who denies the Father and the Son. Whoever denies the Son does not have the Father either; he who acknowledges the Son has the Father also."

But where did John receive this information? Because John's Scriptures consisted of the Old Testament, the primary text he would have looked to for understanding concerning the Antichrist's theology would have been Daniel 11:36–39. It is likely that this is the very text from which John derived his comments concerning the twofold denial of the Antichrist. This denial of both the Father and Son is a repeated theme among other antichristic passages as well. In Psalm 2, which repeats the common motif of the end-time gathering of the nations, specifies exactly who the gentile nations gather against: the Lord and his Messiah:

> Why do the nations rage, and the people plot a vain thing? The kings of the earth take their stand and the rulers gather together against the LORD and against his Anointed One, saying, "Let us break Their bonds in pieces and cast away their cords from us." The One enthroned in heaven laughs; the Lord scoffs at them. Then he rebukes them in his anger and terrifies them in his wrath, saying, "I have installed my King on Zion, my holy hill. (vv. 1–4)

Elsewhere Jesus also, speaking of the time when the saints would be killed because of their faith in Him, explained: "Whoever kills you will think that he offers God service. And these things they will do to you because they have not known the Father nor Me" (John 16:2–3).

This is a fascinating passage. Although its initial context is the persecution of the early messianic community by the non-messianic Jewish community, Jesus then extends the meaning to a time when those who killed the believers would actually believe themselves to be serving God. This is a difficulty for those who see humanism as the final "religion" of the Antichrist. If humanists were in mind here, then Jesus would have said that these men would think killing was *justifiable*, not that they believed their murders pleased a god in whom they do not believe. Clearly, what is meant here is a future when the members of an actual religion would kill followers of Jesus and believe that such acts pleased their god. One religion in the world today stands out as a likely candidate to fulfill this prophecy on a global scale. In fact, in many parts of the world today, Christians are already killed regularly by Muslims who believe that such acts are pleasing to their god, Allah.

EVERY OTHER GOD

Third, beyond rejecting the Father and the Son, the Antichrist rejects every other god globally. But we must be careful not to read this in an absolute sense, for as we are about to see, there is one exception to the Antichrist's disregard for all gods—a god whom he, in fact, greatly honors.

A GOD OF WAR

Finally, in Daniel 11:38, we come to that which the Antichrist *affirms*: "He shall honor the god of fortresses instead of these. A god whom his fathers did not know he shall honor with gold and silver, with precious stones and costly gifts." The King James Version translates it as "the God of forces." But what does this mean?

John Walvoord wrote, "The sole confidence of the final world ruler is in military power, personified as a 'god of war.'"[8] Scholars' and commentators' opinions have been quite conflicting here. Some see a specific god here and have attempted to identify him with certain gods of history. Hebrew scholar Wilhelm Gesenius, for instance, sees here a reference to Jupiter Capitolinus. Others have seen a reference to Mars, the god of war. Sill others have attempted to cast this "god" as no god at all, but rather, a reference to the Antichrist's commitment to military conquest. Lahaye and Hindson, for instance stated, "This king is a pagan who reveres only military might."[9] Commenting on this passage, Walvoord also said the Antichrist "is a complete materialist."[10]

But seeing the Antichrist as an atheistic materialist solely bent on conquest is simply not the natural reading of the passage. This essential point must not be missed. If the Antichrist is to be an atheist, dedicated to conquest, believing in no other power than himself, then the addition of the word "god" here only serves to confuse the actual meaning of the passage. So also does the fact that the Antichrist offers gifts of "gold, silver, costly stones and treasures" as traditional worshippers do. This god is also specifically designated as "a foreign god" further pointing to a specific god worshipped by an unnamed "foreign" people. He does not worship the God of the Jews. After considering all of the evidence, the most natural reading of the text is to see the Antichrist as a worshipper of a specific god of war. The history of the Middle East, of course, is filled with the worship of astral-and-war deities. Thus, we see that the Antichrist, while rejecting God the Father, God the Son, and all of the other various gods throughout the earth, does worship a god of war.

When the full picture is considered, it is fair to say that this description could certainly be applied to a Muslim. Islamic doctrine rejects Yahweh in exchange for the Allah of the Qur'an. Islam denies Jesus as the Son of God and rejects the gods of every other religion. And certainly the Allah of Islam could be understood as the god of war, or jihad. If Islam is the religion of the Antichrist, then the phrase "a god whom his fathers did not know," could easily be understood as a reference to Allah, the moon-and-war god of Arabia.

Finally we are told that with the assistance of this "foreign god," the Antichrist will attack the most formidable of fortresses and reward those who support his efforts: "He shall deal with the strongest fortresses with the help of a foreign god. Those who acknowledge him he shall load with honor. He shall make them rulers over many and shall divide the land for a price" (Daniel 11:39). Exactly what entity Daniel had in mind as the "strongest fortresses" we can only speculate. If we are among those who live to see the day of the Antichrist, then this will become clear.

WILL THE ANTICHRIST CLAIM TO BE GOD?

Having discussed the theology of the Antichrist, it is important that we now turn to a very important and related discussion. Over the past several years, the most significant objection that has been raised to the Islamic Antichrist theory has been that the Antichrist will claim to be God, and Muslims would never follow such a man. In *Islamic Antichrist*, I acknowledged this difficulty, and discussed two factors that could resolve this issue. The first was the powerfully seductive and deceptive sway of the False

Prophet of Revelation 13. This wonder-working assistant to the Antichrist is predicted to carry out powerful pseudo-miracles to fool the peoples of the earth: "And he deceives those who dwell on the earth by those signs which he was granted to do" (Revelation 13:14 NKJV).

The second factor I suggested was the timing of the Antichrist's demand to be worshipped. This would be literally years after he had established a significant global following, allegiance, and identity as the awaited messianic figure of the Islamic world known as the Mahdi. This scenario may very well be the case, but there are other possibilities as well. While it is clear that the Antichrist will be a shameless self-promoter and will demand absolute allegiance, subservience, and submission, there is also the possibility that he will stop just shy of actually proclaiming himself to be God Almighty. But to truly understand what the Bible says about his religious beliefs, we must consult all of the relevant texts. Three passages have led most to believe that the Antichrist will actually proclaim himself to be God. The first passage, which we examined earlier, is Daniel 11:36: "He shall exalt himself and magnify himself above every god, and shall speak astonishing things against the God of gods." But as we have already discussed, this statement cannot be divorced from the fuller context of the passage that shows that the Antichrist does, in fact, honor and make offerings to a god of war. While we must be careful in ruling anything out, it is difficult to see the Antichrist both honoring his god and also proclaiming himself to be a god.

ANTICHRIST SITS IN THE TEMPLE OF GOD

The second passage looked to as proof that the Antichrist will proclaim himself to be God is in Paul's second epistle to the Thessalonians: "Let no one deceive you by any means; for that Day will not come unless the falling away comes first, and the man of sin is revealed, the son of perdition, who opposes and exalts himself above all that is called God or that is worshiped, so that he sits as God in the temple of God, showing himself that he is God" (2:3–4 NKJV).

This passage is consistent with several other passages in the book of Daniel. Clearly, the Antichrist will be an arrogant, self-exalting individual who will openly blaspheme the Lord and all that is sacred. We also see that he will actually sit in the Temple of God. But what exactly does the text mean when it says that the Antichrist will show himself as God? Will he claim to be Yahweh, the God of the Jewish people? It does not appear so. On the contrary, the Antichrist will

- "speak blasphemies against the God of gods" (Daniel 11:36)

- "speak pompous words against the Most High" (Daniel 7:25)

- verbally blaspheme God, His name, and His Temple (Revelation 13:6)

Taken together, this is sufficient proof that the Antichrist will not claim to be Yahweh, the God of biblical faith. It appears as though the Antichrist's sitting in the Temple is an act of defiance, derision, and superiority over the God of the Temple. Does the Antichrist then claim to be some *other* god? I am also skeptical of this notion, for as we have already seen, the Antichrist worships a god of forces or war. As I said, it seems unlikely that the Antichrist would both *worship* a god of war and also claim to *be* a god.

How then can it be said that the Antichrist shows "himself to be God," as the text states? This question is answered by highlighting the fact that in Hebraic or biblical thought, the Temple was viewed as the earthly location from which the governmental authority of God was extended to the earth. In other words, the Temple is God's seat. This concept is seen throughout the Scriptures. Ezekiel, for instance, had a vision in which God spoke to Him from a future Temple and declared it to be his throne: "While the man was standing beside me, I heard one speaking to me out of the temple, and he said to me, 'Son of man, this is the place of my throne and the place of the soles of my feet, where I will dwell in the midst of the people of Israel forever'" (Ezekiel 43:6–7).

Speaking of the kingdom of the Messiah, Jeremiah the prophet also referred to the Temple as the throne of God: "At that time Jerusalem shall be called the throne of the LORD, and all nations shall gather to it, to the presence of the LORD in Jerusalem, and they shall no more stubbornly follow their own evil heart" (Jeremiah 3:17). Jesus Himself also referred to the Temple as the place where His throne will one day remain: "When the Son of Man comes in his glory, and all the angels with him, then he will sit on his glorious throne" (Matthew 25:31).

In understanding how God views the Temple, we can understand that when the Antichrist sits in God's seat, he is declaring himself to be equal to or greater than God. But this does not necessarily mean that he will verbally declare himself to be God or even *a* god.

The third passage some use to support the notion that the Antichrist will declare himself to be God is Revelation 13. Here, we are told that Satan, the dragon, will authorize the beast (the Antichrist and his kingdom) to receive worship: "And they worshiped the dragon, for he had given his authority to the beast, and they worshiped the beast, saying, 'Who is like the beast, and who can fight against it?' . . . and all who dwell on earth will worship it, everyone whose name has not been written before the foundation of the world in the book of life of the Lamb who was slain" (vv. 4, 8).

Behind the Antichrist will be Satan the dragon, who clearly desires to be worshipped (see Matthew 4:8–10). Later, we are told that the Antichrist's assistant, "the false prophet" will set up an image, and all who will not worship the beast will be killed: "And it was allowed to give breath to the image of the beast, so that the image of the beast might even speak and might cause those who would not worship the image of the beast to be slain" (Revelation 13:15).

Most reason that because the beast receives worship, he must be viewed as a god. But this is not necessarily so. The word used here for "worship" is the Greek *proskyneō*, which can mean any of the following:

- to kiss the hand, as a token of reverence,

- to fall upon the knees and touch the ground with the forehead as an expression of profound reverence,

- to kneel or prostrate oneself to pay homage (to one) or make obeisance, whether to express respect or to make a request, or

- to pay homage to men and beings of superior rank.

So while *proskyneō* most often refers to "worship," as to God or to a god, it does not exclusively mean this. The *Theological Dictionary of the New Testament* defines the Jewish understanding of *proskyneō* as: "the term for various words meaning 'to bow,' 'to kiss,' 'to serve,' and 'to worship.' . . . Most of the instances relate to veneration of the God of Israel or false gods. [But it] may also be directed to angels, to the righteous, to rulers, [and] to the prophets."[11]

There are several passages in the New Testament in which *proskyneō* is used, where actual worship is not intended, but simply great honor, respect, or subservience. Consider, for example, a parable told by Jesus of a servant and his master. In this story, "the servant therefore fell down before him, saying, 'Master, have patience with me, and I will pay you all'" (Matthew 18:26). Clearly, the servant did not worship his master as if he were God. He simply bowed before him in an act of subservience and appeal. But the word used for this act is *proskyneō*, the same word used with reference to that which is offered to the beast (the Antichrist and his empire).

Another example of *proskyneō* used in a way that clearly does not mean actual worship is in Revelation 3: "Behold, I will make those of the synagogue of Satan who say that they are Jews and are not, but lie—behold, I will make them come and bow down before your feet and they will learn that I have loved you" (v. 9). Here Jesus was speaking to the church of Philadelphia concerning a particular group who was persecuting the believers. Jesus promised that He would cause these false Jews to come and *proskyneō* before the believers in an act of repentance. Jesus was not stating that one group of people would worship another group of people.

In summary, then, in light of the range of meaning of *proskyneō*, we must be cautious in declaring dogmatically that the Antichrist will be worshipped as God or a god. These verses in Revelation 13 that state that the Antichrist will receive worship could simply indicate that the people of the earth will display utter submission to him and his empire. With this in mind, consider the fact that Islamic theology teaches that every Muslim is obligated to make a pledge of allegiance, known as the *bay'ah*, to any sitting caliph (leader of the Islamic world), the refusal of which is punishable by death. One Islamic author describes the *bay'ah* thus: "Bay'ah means taking an oath of loyalty. Whoever makes bay'ah agrees to submit his entire life to the leader . . . He will not act against the leader in agreed matters, and will be loyal to him in every action, regardless of his personal likes or dislikes."[12]

In another Islamic tradition concerning obedience to Muhammad and the caliph, it is written: "Muhammad said: Those who obey me obey Allah, the Almighty. Those who disobey me disobey Allah, the Almighty. Those who obey my leader obey me and those who disobey my leader disobey me."[13]

If the Antichrist were simply a Muslim caliph who mocked the God of the Jews, demanding absolute obedience from his followers, while also demanding that everyone worship the Allah of Islam, in no way would this conflict with any of the relevant texts that describe the Antichrist's actions, words, and demands. He would receive absolute subservience, while Satan, the dragon, bearing the title of Allah, would receive worship.

CONCLUSION

The popular belief that the Antichrist will verbally declare himself to be God and demand worship from the whole world is problematic regardless of which position one takes. It is difficult to imagine a humanistic, materialistic, atheistic Antichrist mocking God and rejecting all other gods on one hand, but claiming to *be* God on the other. This would be an oxymoron. An atheist or a humanist would cease being an atheist or a humanist if he declared himself to actually be God. Likewise, if one believes the Antichrist to be some type of universalist, religious pluralist, let's-all-get-along-ist, this is also difficult, as the Antichrist is said not only to mock the God of the Bible, but also lacks regard for any other god. Universalists give credence and validity to every god. Religious pluralists give equal credence—not equal disrespect—to all gods. But despite the challenge presented by virtually every position one might consider, curiously, it has been the Islamic Antichrist theory that has seen the most skepticism in recent years. In considering this reality, I have often felt as though it is far easier for people to believe that the Bible predicts something that only exists in their imaginations than to believe it predicts something that is *right in front of* them.

In the end, regardless of what position one takes, we must ask ourselves, if the Antichrist is not a Muslim, how will he cajole the 1.6 billion (and growing) Muslims of the earth to follow him? Many have claimed that Muslims will no longer exist by this time. But no scenario or mechanism has been set forth that could satisfactorily explain such a massive global demographic earthquake. As we have seen, the Antichrist's empire will come from the Middle East and North Africa, nations in which Muslims are the vast majority. How could a humanistic or universalist religious pluralist Antichrist sway the world's increasingly radicalizing Muslim population to follow him? Those who reject the Islamic Antichrist theory must be able to adequately answer this. For now, we can only speculate on these matters. As in all things, God knows best.

DANIEL 12: SEALED UNTIL THE END-TIMES

EFORE WE CONCLUDE our study of Daniel, there is one more very important passage that needs to be considered. As Daniel comes to its conclusion, its angelic narrator makes it abundantly clear that the ultimate context of the passage is the end-times: "At that time . . . there shall be a time of trouble, such as never has been since there was a nation till that time . . . and many of those who sleep in the dust of the earth shall awake, some to everlasting life, and some to shame and everlasting contempt" (12:1–2).

When the angel says that these things will take place at the time when "those who sleep in the dust of the earth shall awake," it is clear that he is referring to the time of the resurrection of the dead. Obviously this has not yet happened. There can be no question that these revelations are not merely historical. Then comes the verse that we must consider. The angel tells Daniel that the revelations are to be "sealed up": "But you, Daniel, shut up the words and seal the book, until the time of the end. Many shall run to and fro, and knowledge shall increase" (v. 4).

This a hard pill for Daniel to swallow. He has had a series of revelations that pertain to the future, and he is naturally wanting to better understand the meaning of the prophesies. As such, he further inquires of the angel. But Daniel is told once again that the words have been sealed and shut up until the last days, and the vision is not for him to understand;

rather, it is for the final generation: "I heard, but I did not understand. Then I said, 'O my lord, what shall be the outcome of these things?' He said, 'Go your way, Daniel, for the words are shut up and sealed until the time of the end. Many shall purify themselves and make themselves white and be refined, but the wicked shall act wickedly. And none of the wicked shall understand, but those who are wise shall understand'" (vv. 9–10).

There are two positions that scholars and commentators have been unable to agree on as to the meaning of this passage. Some claim that the prophecy is not "shut up" or "sealed," but only *preserved* or kept safe for everyone. Others claim that in Daniel's day, the book would be sealed, but understanding would gradually become more and more available to those believers who diligently and collectively study the book, though it would not ultimately be fully understood until the actual end-times.

Now, clearly, the most widely held, most traditional view of Daniel's prophecy is the Roman perspective, viewing much of the book as speaking of a coming Roman Antichrist. As early as the fourth and fifth centuries, Jerome provided strong evidence that the Roman perspective on Daniel's prophecy was the most widely held view of the day: "We should therefore concur with the traditional interpretation of all the commentators of the Christian Church, that at the end of the world, when the Roman Empire is to be destroyed, there shall be ten kings who will partition the Roman world amongst themselves."[1]

A thousand years later, nothing seems to have changed. During the Protestant Reformation, Martin Luther affirmed the nearly universal opinion of the Church on the Roman perspective of Daniel's prophecies when he said, "In this interpretation and opinion, all the world are agreed, and history and abundantly establish it."[2]

Because the Roman perspective of Daniel's prophecy as it is held by most today has remained relatively unchanged from Jerome's perspective as far back as the fifth century, it therefore becomes necessary for those who hold this view to reinterpret "sealing" to mean something other than sealing. Ed Hindson and Tim Lahaye, for example, have written, "Daniel is instructed to 'conceal these words and seal up the book until the end of time'. . . The terms 'conceal' (Hebrew, satam) and 'seal' (Hebrew, *chatam*) do not mean Daniel is to conceal these prophecies . . . Rather, because the prophecy is now complete, he is to 'keep it intact' and 'carefully preserve' the prophecies for future generations of his people."[3]

Likewise, Thomas Ice follows Stephen Miller, who argues that the "sealing" is merely a reference to the revelation being "preserved." Miller articulated this view in his commentary on Daniel:

> In the ancient Near East the custom was to "seal" an important document by impressing upon it the identifying marks of the parties involved and the recording scribe. A sealed text was not to be tampered with or changed. Then the original document was duplicated and placed ("closed up") in a safe place where it could be preserved. An excellent illustration of this process is recorded in the Book of Jeremiah: "So I [Jeremiah] bought the field at Anathoth from my cousin Hanamel and weighed out for him seventeen shekels of silver. I signed and sealed (hâtâm) the deed, had it witnessed, and weighed out the silver on the scales. I took the deed of purchase—the sealed copy containing the terms and conditions, as well as the unsealed copy—and I gave this deed to Baruch son of Neriah [the scribe]" (Jer. 32:9–12). The sealing of Jeremiah's property deed was not done to "hide" the contents or to keep them "secret" but to preserve the document. As a matter of fact, Jeremiah performed this transaction in the presence of his cousin "and of the witnesses who had signed the deed and of all the Jews sitting in the courtyard of the guard" (Jer. 32:12). There also was an "unsealed copy" of the deed that presumably was open for inspection. Gabriel therefore was instructing Daniel to preserve "the words of the scroll," not merely this final vision but the whole book for those who will live at "the time of the end" when the message will be needed.[4]

While this is an interesting bit of historical information, this position doesn't do the actual wording of the passage justice at all. Nowhere in Daniel's prophecy is there any reference to two copies—a sealed copy and an unsealed copy. Further, the angel stated, "Many shall run to and fro, and knowledge shall increase." This phrase has popularly been understood as speaking of an increase of transportation and the ease of access to information in the last days. But virtually all scholars disavow this view, seeing it instead as a reference to the gradual opening up of the prophecy by the diligent. The running to and fro involves searching the book through and through, scrutinizing it over and over until at last, at the end of the age, the book is finally unsealed and fully understood by the believing community. When Daniel asks for understanding, the angel says that this is not possible, because the revelation is hidden—*wa·hă·tōm*—and sealed—*se·tōm*. Period. *Wa·hă·tōm* means "to stop up, shut up, keep close, or secret." This word was used when Joseph's brothers were about to kill him, but instead chose to sell him to some Ishmaelites on their way to Egypt. Judah then asked, "What profit is it if we kill our brother and conceal his blood? (Genesis 37:26). Certainly no one will argue that Joseph's brother's were thinking about "preserving" his blood. Clearly, they were thinking about killing him and hiding the matter. *Se·tōm* means "to seal, seal up, affix a seal, lock up." This word is used when one seals a scroll or letter with wax. While the use of these two words make the meaning of the angel's words abundantly clear, because of its problematic nature for the traditional view, many commentators have felt the need to alter the clear meaning of the passage. But we cannot alter the meaning of the words, nor the clear and plain-sense reading of the passage, simply because it does not support our position. Thankfully, many other teachers and scholars reject the reinterpretation of this passage:

- Chuck Smith says, "The book was to be sealed unto the time of the end. In other words, 'Daniel, you're not gonna understand this; it will be understood in the time of the end.'"[5]

- John Walvoord wrote, "In verse 9, Daniel is once again informed that the revelation given to him will not be fully understood until the time of the end . . . The primary purpose of the revelation, however, was to inform those who would live in the time of the end. The confirming interpretation of history and prophecy fulfilled would be necessary before the final prophecies could be understood."[6]

- Matthew Henry wrote, "He must not expect that what had been said to him would be fully understood till it was accomplished: The words are closed up and sealed, are involved in perplexities, and are likely to be so, till the time of the end, till the end of these things; nay, till the end of all things. Daniel was ordered to seal the book to the time of the end."[7]

- G. H. Lang said, "The prophecies of Daniel were to be 'sealed,' that is, to remain a closed book, but little understood, 'even to the time of the end.'"[8]

- David Guzik wrote, "For the words are closed up and sealed till the time of the end: Daniel must make a mental departure from his questioning, because the revealing of these things will not come till the time of the end. Until then, there is a sense in which these prophecies are closed up and sealed."[9]

- Rabbi David ibn Zimra, also known as Mezudath David, commented, "Until the time of redemption, many will run to and fro; i.e., they will speculate on the meaning of the various prophecies calculating the end, but they will not understand it until the end, when everyone's eyes will be opened to understand the hints."[10]

Before concluding, let me say a few things about the value of tradition. From a Christian perspective, the purpose of tradition is to faithfully pass on "the faith that was once for all delivered to the saints" (Jude 1:3). It is tradition that when used properly will preserve both orthodoxy (right belief) and orthopraxy (right practice) throughout the generations. So although frequently impugned in today's postmodern society, tradition should be greatly valued by all Christian believers. As such, among the various factors that should inform our own personal doctrinal positions is the collective voice of those faithful men who have gone before us. That said, we should never take deviating from tradition lightly. In this particular case however, because the angel clearly said that the book would not be fully opened up and understood until the end-times, we have a solid basis for actually holding the traditional position suspect and giving far greater credence than normal to contrarian views. Of course, the Middle Eastern or Islamic-centered interpretation of Daniel's prophecy has always been a minority position, though today it is quickly gaining a wide acceptance among the believing community. While various early Jewish and Christian scholars and commentators throughout history have seen many passages as pointing to the Islamic world, never in history has the Islamic Antichrist theory been as systematically developed and as thoroughly articulated as now. I would suggest the reason for this is simply because the Middle Eastern or Islamic interpretation of Daniel as presented through the past several chapters makes sense logically, historically, and most important, scripturally. Beyond this, as a contrarian view, it does not require us to reinterpret the clear meaning of the angel's words. And so, if, in fact, the

Middle Eastern or Islamic perspective on Daniel's prophecies is accurate, then it also stands to reason that the "last days" as described throughout Daniel are now drawing near. As the angel informed Daniel, the book is now being unsealed and opened up to the believing community. How well we will heed its words is yet to be seen.

REVELATION 12, 13, 17:
THE WOMAN, THE MAN-CHILD,
AND THE BEAST

HAVING CONCLUDED OUR STUDY OF DANIEL, we will now turn our attention to a few important chapters in the book of Revelation. As we will see, the story being told in Revelation is simply one more retelling of the same story told throughout the Prophets. For our purposes, we will begin in Revelation 12 and 13. Of course, like the rest of Revelation, this story is told using a strong dose of symbolism, but don't let this scare you. Once the symbolism is unraveled, the message will become quite clear.

REVELATION 12: THE WOMAN AND HER CHILD

The passage begins with a sun-clothed woman who is not only pregnant, but also in labor: "And a great sign appeared in heaven: a woman clothed with the sun, with the moon under her feet, and on her head a crown of twelve stars. She was pregnant and was crying out in birth pains and the agony of giving birth" (vv. 1–2).

A basic principle that must always be remembered when interpreting the book of Revelation is that, unlike any other book in the Bible, it is thoroughly founded upon the multitude of prophetic passages found throughout the Old Testament. As discussed earlier, Revelation is essentially the prophetic symphony, the grand crescendo and conclusion of the whole Bible, drawing upon the myriad of passages, poems, prophecies and revelations that precede it. By understanding this principle, identifying the woman is actually quite easy. The first key to unlocking her identity is found in Genesis. It is there in Joseph's dream that we find the symbolism of the sun, the moon, and the twelve stars (eleven without Joseph) mirrored:

> Then he dreamed another dream and told it to his brothers and said, "Behold, I have dreamed another dream. Behold, the sun, the moon, and eleven stars were bowing down to me." But when he told it to his father and to his brothers, his father rebuked him and said to him, "What is this dream that you have dreamed? Shall I and your mother and your brothers indeed come to bow ourselves to the ground before you?" And his brothers were jealous of him, but his father kept the saying in mind. (Genesis 37:9–11)

So by understanding the story of Joseph's dream, we can identify the woman as representing Israel.

THE MAN-CHILD

Returning to Revelation 12, the male child the woman is about to deliver, of course, is Jesus the Messiah. He is the one upon whom the entire Bible is focused. He is the Redeemer. Through this child, God will bring complete redemption to the world and restore the paradise lost, back in the garden. But as we are all aware, God and His people also have an adversary. Satan has always desired to thwart God's plan of redemption for creation. Going all the way back to Genesis 3, the conflict between Satan (the serpent) and Jesus (the seed of woman) has been in play. In the end, Jesus the Messiah will utterly crush the head of the ancient serpent, as well as his children, or seed (see John 8:44). So while it is true to say that the entire Bible is Jesus-centric, the larger story being told is about Jesus defeating death and Satan. As such, so often when we find prophecies concerning the Messiah, Satan is lurking close by within the text. This passage is no different. Thus, in the very next verse, we are introduced to the next major character of the story: Satan the dragon.

SATAN THE DRAGON: THE ADVERSARY OF THE WOMAN AND HER CHILD

Simply stated, whatever God loves, Satan hates. Whatever God desires to redeem, Satan wants to corrupt and devour. As the story unfolds, Satan is portrayed as a dragon with seven heads and ten horns. He is perched before the woman, hoping to consume the child as soon as He is born: "And another sign appeared in heaven: behold, a great red dragon, with seven heads and ten horns, and on his heads seven diadems. His tail swept down a third of the stars of heaven and cast them to the earth. And the dragon stood before the woman who was about to give birth, so that when she bore her child he might devour it" (Revelation 12:3–4).

But the male-child Messiah was born: "She gave birth to a male child, one who is to rule all the nations with a rod of iron . . ." And despite Satan's efforts (through Herod) to kill Jesus as a mere baby, the Lord spoke to Joseph in a dream and told him to flee to Egypt with his family: ". . . but her child was caught up to God and to his throne" (Revelation 12:5).

And thus Jesus matured to adulthood, and by His own will, chose to lay down His life on the cross. Of course, His story didn't end there. Three days later, He arose from the dead and ascended into heaven, where He now resides at the right hand of the Father.

After this, we are introduced to the next major character in the story: the Beast.

THE BEAST

As the story unfolds, a beast enters the picture. And he looks bizarrely similar to the dragon, Satan: "And I saw a beast rising out of the sea, with ten horns and seven heads, with ten diadems on its horns and blasphemous names on its heads. And the beast that I saw was like a leopard; its feet were like a bear's, and its mouth was like a lion's mouth. And to it the dragon gave his power and his throne and great authority" (Revelation 13:1–2).

Later, in Revelation 17:3, we are also told that the beast is bright red. In appearance, the beast seems to be a virtual mirror image of Satan, the dragon, both in color and in the number of heads and crowns. And beyond this, Satan actually confers his power, throne, and "great authority" to the beast. Simply stated, this is Satan's beast. Even as God the Father sent forth His Son into the world as a perfect reflection of Himself, the beast is the very embodiment of Satan in the earth. We will discuss the deeper relevance of this as we conclude this segment of our study, but first, we need to understand the meanings of four symbols in this passage to make these verses become clear.

BEAST = KINGDOM OR EMPIRE

First, understand that this symbol of a "beast" represents a kingdom or an empire. The basis for this interpretation is found in Daniel 7, where Daniel saw four beasts, each one also arising from out of the sea. When the prophet Daniel asked an angel the meaning of the beasts, the angel initially explained that the four beasts were four "kings," but as he continued, what unfolded was that these kings were each representatives of their kingdoms (v. 23). And so here, in Revelation as in Daniel 7, this beast represents a kingdom or an empire.

SEA = GENTILE PEOPLES

Second, we need to understand the meaning of the sea from which the beast emerges. This symbol is defined quite clearly in Revelation 17, where an angel explains to the apostle John that the sea represents *human beings*: "And the angel said to me, 'The waters that you saw, where the prostitute is seated, are peoples and multitudes and nations and languages'" (Revelation 17:15).

But beyond merely referring to humanity, according to the prophet Isaiah, the seas specifically represent gentile peoples and nations: "Then you shall see and be radiant; your heart shall thrill and exult, because the abundance of the sea shall be turned to you, the wealth of the nations shall come to you" (Isaiah 60:5).

So as we begin interpreting the symbolism, we start with a beast representing a satanically empowered kingdom or empire that arises from out of the sea of gentile nations.

SEVEN HEADS = SEVEN HISTORICAL EMPIRES

But what do the beast's seven heads mean? Thankfully, this symbol is also specifically addressed in Revelation 17, where the same beast is again pictured:

> I saw . . . a scarlet beast that was full of blasphemous names, and it had seven heads and ten horns . . . But the angel said to me, "Why do you marvel? I will tell you the mystery . . . of the beast with seven heads and ten horns that carries her . . . The seven heads are seven mountains . . . They are also seven kings, five of whom have fallen, one is, the other has not yet come. (vv. 3, 7–10).

These "mountains," though, are not just landmasses. As commentator Robert Thomas has stated, "The seven heads and mountains . . . are seven successive empires, with seven kings of v. 10 as heads and personifications of these empires."[1]

The symbol of a mountain is commonly used throughout the Scriptures to refer to a kingdom (e.g., Psalms 30:7; 68:15–16; Isaiah 2:2; 41:15; Jeremiah 51:25; Daniel 2:35; Habakkuk 3:6, 10; Zechariah 4:17). The book of the prophet Obadiah, for instance, is entirely a prophecy concerning "the Mountain of Edom" in conflict with "Mount Zion." The prophecy, of course, is not literally speaking of a conflict between two mountains; rather, two kingdoms: the kingdom of Moab versus the kingdom of Israel. Likewise, here in Revelation 17, these mountains refer not to literal mountains but to seven historical empires.

Once it is understood that the mountains are kingdoms, the remainder of the verse is easy to understand: "The seven heads are seven mountains [kingdoms] . . . They are also seven kings." Simply put: kings and kingdoms go together, but mountains and kings have no natural correspondence. A literal mountain cannot also be a king, but a king can represent his kingdom.

The point of this passage, then, is to show that Satan's primary method of coming against God, His people, and His purposes on Earth, has always been pagan imperialism. It is through a series of pagan world empires that Satan has waged his war against God and His people throughout the ages. This has been true from the earliest days of the Hebrew people, and it is still true today. The seven-headed beast is the personification of Satan's activity on Earth. As the Church represents the body of Christ, the beast represents the body of Satan. This is why Satan the dragon is seen giving the beast his throne, power, and authority.

ROME: THE CITY ON SEVEN MOUNTAINS?

Historically, some have seen this passage as referring to Rome, but further examination reveals this position to be problematic, and thus most modern interpreters have rejected this idea: John Walvoord, for instance, notes that the ancient city of Rome sat on seven "hills." The word used in this passage is not the Greek word for hills (*bounos*), but for mountains (*oros*). If Rome were the subject of this passage, the author would have used the word for hills. And even beyond this, we need to remember that this is an end-times passage. It is not speaking of an ancient reality. The city of Rome today sits on ten hills, not seven mountains. Despite the popularity of this interpretation throughout the years, the idea that this passage is speaking about the city of Rome is untenable.

So the seven "heads" represent seven historical kingdoms. As the passage says, "five have been, one is, and the other has not yet come." While the satanic beast is primarily a symbol representing the final antichristic empire, it is also the final manifestation, the culmination of a series of seven satanically empowered kingdoms. But which kingdoms specifically are we talking about? At the time that John penned the book of Revelation, five of the kingdoms were past ("five have been"), but the sixth kingdom was presently in power ("one is"). This kingdom, of course, was the Roman Empire, the sixth "head" of the beast. But which five regional empires preceded the Roman Empire? These are the empires that Satan has specifically empowered down through history in an attempt to destroy the Jewish people and thus thwart God's grand redemptive plan. Throughout the Bible, we have the record of a series of assaults leveled against Israel, the Jewish people, and the young Christian movement, by six successive and powerful Middle Eastern empires:

1. Egypt

2. Assyria

3. Babylon

4. Medo-Persia

5. Greece

6. Rome

But the passage does not conclude with the sixth empire. After Rome, another satanic empire would emerge. When we consider which empire followed the pattern of powerful, pagan, anti-Yahwistic, anti-Semitic, anti-Zionist, and eventually anti-Christian empires that controlled the greater biblical world—the region surrounding the land of Israel—only one empire consistently meets all the criteria and follows the pattern of those that preceded it.

THE SEVENTH KINGDOM: THE ISLAMIC EMPIRE

Following on the heels of the long, slow decline of the Western Roman Empire in the seventh century, the Islamic Empire burst forth out of Arabia and quickly came to dominate the entire region. Eventually this empire dealt the fatal blow to the Eastern (Byzantine) Roman Empire as well, when in 1453, Mehmet the Conqueror subjugated Constantinople for Islam and renamed it Istanbul. Continuing the pattern of the previous beast empires, the Islamic Empire has been the frequent vehicle of an anti-Yahwistic, anti-Semitic, anti-Zionist, and anti-Christian spirit. In fact, it is entirely fair to say that the Islamic Empire embodies these traits far more than any previous empire throughout world history. The Qur'an, the most sacred text of the Islamic religion, has actually canonized and sacralized these characteristics, specifically naming Jews and Christians within its pages and singling them out as gross blasphemers (Christians) and history's greatest rebels and enemies of God (Jews).

REVELATION 13, 17: THE LAST BEAST EMPIRE

As we have seen thus far in our study, the identification of Islam as the final beast empire of world history is substantiated time and time again throughout the Scriptures, quite literally in every significant prophetic passage of the Bible. Even verses that have traditionally been looked to as proof texts for a Roman Antichrist, upon reexamination, actually point to a Middle Eastern Antichrist. Thus it is no surprise that when we come to Revelation 13, the symbolic picture of Satan's kingdom, it is revealed to possess a body that is part leopard, part lion, and part bear: "And the beast that I saw was like a leopard; its feet were like a bear's, and its mouth was like a lion's mouth" (v. 2).

As we have already seen, in Daniel 7 these same three animals represent the three empires of Babylon, Medo-Persia, and Greece. The fourth beast of Daniel's vision is the same beast we are considering here. This one is a combination of the lion (Babylon), bear (Medo-Persia), and leopard (Greece). Following the Greek Empire, the only empires to have emerged in that part of the world were the Parthian Empire, the Sassanid Empire, the Roman Empire, and the Islamic Caliphate. No other cohesive empires have arisen in this region that we might consider as candidates for the role of the dreadful fourth beast empire.

The Parthians and Sassanids, as we previously discussed, should be viewed simply as a living extension of the Persian Empire. They were not uniquely possessed by the telltale anti-Semitic or anti-Christian spirit of the six previous beast empires. The Parthians and Sassanids never attempted to destroy the Jewish people, as each previous satanic empire has done. Neither did they ever directly control Jerusalem or the land of Israel.

If we were to combine the geographic "bodies" of Greece, Babylon, and Medo-Persia, what empire would we have? Would it look like the Roman Empire or the Islamic Empire? The answer is obvious to anyone with an understanding of the geography of the region.

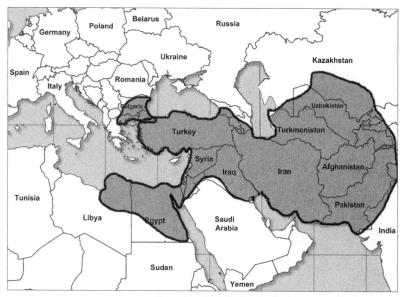

A combined Babylonian, Medo-Persian, and Grecian empire

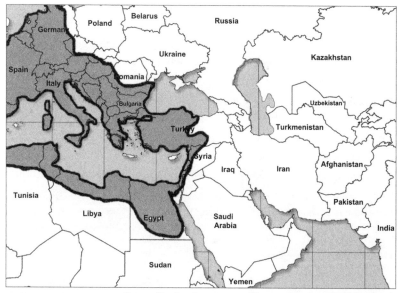

Roman Empire: does not resemble a combination of Babylon (lion),
Medo-Persia (bear), and Greece (leopard)

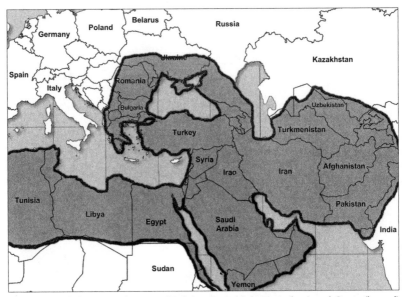

Islamic Caliphate: a combination of Babylon (lion), Medo-Persia (bear), and Greece (leopard)

The Roman Empire, with its uniquely Western/European orientation, simply doesn't come close to lining up with the geography of a Babylonian-Persian-Greek empire. As we have seen, for the overwhelming majority of its existence, the Roman Empire's borders remained roughly five hundred miles west of Babylon. The Islamic Empire, however, as we saw, "crushed" all of these regions in an unqualified and absolute manner. The Islamic Caliphate has come to dominate all of the land holdings of all three of these previous empires and far more. So once again, when considering a combination Greek, Babylonian, and Medo-Persian Empire, the Roman Empire doesn't come close to fulfilling this description, but the Islamic Caliphate fulfills it perfectly.

THE FATAL HEAD WOUND

According to Revelation 13, the final beast empire suffers what appears to be a fatal wound. The seventh empire would seemingly pass away, but then to the shock and horror of much of the world, it would experience a revival and return to life: "One of its heads seemed to have a mortal wound, but its mortal wound was healed, and the whole earth marveled as they followed the beast" (v. 3).

The prophecy concerning the healing of the fatal head wound is also repeated later in Revelation 17, where the seventh head of the beast is seen resurrecting:

> The beast that you saw was, and is not, and is about to rise from the bottomless pit and go to destruction. And the dwellers on earth whose names have not been written in the book of life from the foundation of the world will marvel to see the beast, because it was and is not and is to come . . . As for the beast that was and is not, it is an eighth but it belongs to the seven, and it goes to destruction. (vv. 8, 11)

In the last days, those who dwell on the earth will be amazed when they witness the rebirth of an empire. The Islamic Caliphate has experienced a temporary or apparent death and will revive as the eighth and final empire. The final satanic kingdom is simply a revived version of the Islamic Caliphate. Those who are living in the last days will stand in awe when they see the Islamic Caliphate that once ruled the Middle East return to life.

Some have argued that the revived beast will be one of the previous empires, such as the Assyrian Empire. But we must remember that the story told in Revelation 17 is simply a retelling of the story told in Daniel 2 and 7 (as well as 8, 9, and 11). In Daniel 2, the final, antichristic empire is represented by the statue's feet, which proceed forth out of the previous empire, symbolized by the two iron legs, which, as we have already seen, refer to the historical Islamic Caliphate. In Daniel 7, the same story is retold using the symbolism of four beasts. There, the final manifestation of the satanic empire is symbolized by ten horns that spring forth from out of the fourth beast, which again is the historical Islamic Caliphate. And thus, after having examined the various relevant passages, we may identify the following historical succession of eight satanically empowered empires:

1. Egyptian Empire

2. Assyrian Empire

3. Babylonian Empire

4. Medo-Persian Empire

5. Grecian Empire

6. Roman Empire

7. Islamic Caliphate

8. Revived Islamic Caliphate

What adds so much weight to the notion that the final two empires are in fact Islamic empires is the historical reality concerning the downfall of the Islamic Caliphate. Shortly after Muhammad, the founder and prophet of Islam, died, his companions and family took up the role of leading the Muslims. Muhammad's close friend and father-in-law, Abu Bakr, became the first caliph. The period of rule under Abu Bakr and the next three caliphs is known as the Rashidun Caliphate. Following the Rashidun was the Umayyad Caliphate, then the Abbasid Caliphate, and eventually the dominion of much of the Muslim world fell to the Ottomans. When we generically refer to the "Islamic Empire," or the "Islamic Caliphate," we are including the various aforementioned dynasties, which together ruled the Islamic world for more than thirteen hundred years. But this pan-millennial Muslim government was, in fact, beheaded in 1924 when Turkish secular reformer Mustafa Kemal Atatürk abolished the universal Islamic government known as the *caliphate* and the office of the universal Islamic leader known as the *caliph*. The formerly unified empire was fractured into modern nation-states. Today, as the Western powers vacate the Middle East, the power of the Ottomans is regenerating. The head wound is being healed, and the Islamic Empire is reviving. But that is the subject for another book . . .

ROMAN EMPIRE VERSUS ISLAMIC EMPIRE

If one holds to the Roman Antichrist theory, Revelation 17 presents a significant difficulty. This is seen in Reagan's explanation of verses 10–11:

> In this passage the Apostle John is told that there are seven kings or empires to be considered in world history and that "five have fallen, one is, the other has not yet come; and when he comes, it must remain for a little while. And the beast which was and is not, is himself also an eighth, and is one of the seven, and he goes to destruction." At that point in history, the five fallen would have been Egypt, Assyria, Babylon, Medo-Persia, and Greece. The one existing would have been the Roman. The one to come would be the revival of the Roman, out of which the eighth and final empire, the worldwide kingdom of the Antichrist would arise.[2]

I fully agree with Reagan's identification of both the five fallen empires and the sixth empire. But with his seventh empire, which he identifies as the revived Roman Empire, I disagree. I believe the Islamic Caliphate is represented here. In fact, as we just discussed, if we do *not* include the Islamic Caliphate in the sequence, then it is impossible to reconcile this passage with the previous revelations of Daniel 2 and 7. This appears to be Reagan's attempt to make it all fit together, for after the seventh head, he inserts "the eighth and final empire, the worldwide kingdom of the Antichrist." But where is this empire in Daniel 2 and 7? According to Reagan's scenario, the iron legs in Daniel 2 represent the historical Roman Empire. Out of this empire come the feet, and then apparently out of the feet, another, "worldwide empire." But there is no room for such a scenario in the text. Likewise, according to Reagan, the fourth beast of Daniel 7 represents the historical Roman Empire. Out of this empire emerges ten horns, correlating with a revived Roman Empire. But then, somehow, yet another kingdom, a "worldwide kingdom" emerges out of the horns. Again this is simply not what the text states. The Roman Antichrist theory forces one to insert a third empire where one simply does not exist.

On the other hand, when we understand that the various prophecies are all pointing us to the historical Islamic Caliphate, whether it be the seventh head of Revelation 17, the legs of iron of Daniel 2, or the fourth beast of Daniel 7, then all of the passages flow together perfectly. The historical Islamic Caliphate is the seventh head of the beast, and the revived Islamic Caliphate—the kingdom of the Antichrist—will be the eighth. It's very simple.

Some will ask why, if the Roman Empire was not included in Daniel 2 or 7, it is included in the list of empires in Revelation 17. The answer is simply because, while Revelation 17 presents us with a comprehensive list, detailing the full pan-biblical view of all of history's satanic, pagan beast empires, Daniel 2 and 7 do not list every one of Satan's empires. Neither chapter includes the Egyptian, Assyrian, or Roman empires. As we have seen, these passages simply speak of the empires that would rise after Nebuchadnezzar in Babylon, and the Roman Empirewas not included among these. It is not until we come to Revelation 12, 13, and 17 that the full, pan-historical list of Satanic empires is given.

Empire	Daniel 2	Daniel 7	Revelation 17
Egyptian	*not included*	*not included*	1st head
Assyrian	*not included*	*not included*	2nd head
Babylonian	Head of gold	Lion	3rd head
Medo-Persian	Chest and arms of silver	Leopard	4th head
Grecian	Belly and thighs of bronze	Bear	5th head
Roman	*not included*	*not included*	6th head
Islamic	Legs of iron	Fourth Beast	7th Head: Combination Lion, Leopard & Bear
Antichristic	Feet of Iron and Clay	Ten horns grow out of the Fourth Beast	Eighth King: Healed 7th head
Messianic	The Rock		

In conclusion, once again, the Roman Antichrist theory seems to have several problems aligning with the requirements of the text. And once more, the identification of the Islamic Caliphate, whether portrayed as a composite of the lion (Babylon), bear (Medo-Persia), and leopard (Greece) or as the seventh head of the seven-headed beast, flows smoothly with all of the previous prophetic passages. And so, from Genesis to Revelation, we can see that the same picture is being painted, in multiple different ways, using various imagery and language, over and over again.

13

EZEKIEL 38–39:
GOG OF MAGOG: PART I

O NE OF THE MOST frequently discussed and highly debated
passages of biblical prophecy is Ezekiel 38 and 39, most often
referred to as "the Battle of Gog of Magog." This passage
describes an evil last-days leader called "Gog," and his massive coalition of
nations, who together invade the land of Israel, only to be supernaturally
decimated. Unfortunately, besides being one of the most highly influential
prophecies of Scripture, it is also one of the most greatly misunderstood.
It is imperative, therefore, that careful students of the Bible study this
passage diligently so as to rightfully discern its true meaning and message.

THE POPULAR VIEW

In modern times, the most popularly held interpretation of this passage
is that Gog and the Antichrist are two distinct individuals. This view
holds that Gog's invasion of Israel comes some years prior to the invasion
of Israel by the Antichrist. According to this perspective, the Antichrist
emerges from Europe sometime after Gog and his armies are destroyed.
This view is well articulated by John Walvoord, who also holds the equally
popular position that Ezekiel's invading armies will be led by Russia:
"With Russia out of the way, the head of the revived Roman Empire, in
control of the Mediterranean area at the time, will be able to proclaim

himself as a dictator of the whole world."[1]

Grant Jeffrey, another well-known prophecy teacher, holds to a similar vision:

> When this Russian-Arab alliance attacks Israel, the prophet declared that God will intervene with supernatural earthquakes, hail, and pestilence to defeat the combined forces of Russian and Arab armies . . . These awesome prophetic events concerning the defeat of Russia will prepare the way for the fulfillment of the prophecies of the rise of Antichrist to rule the earth and his seven-year treaty with Israel. This treaty with the Antichrist will commence a seven-year countdown to the return of the Messiah at the Battle of Armageddon.[2]

According to this narrative, many also believe that after the destruction of Gog and his armies, Islam as a religion will virtually dry up and cease being a major world religion. Prophecy teacher David Reagan even believes that the battle described in Ezekiel 38 and 39 will conclude with "the annihilation of nearly all the armies of the Muslim nations of the Middle East": "The war of Psalm 83 followed by the war of Ezekiel 38 will result in the annihilation of nearly all the armies of the Muslim nations of the Middle East . . . Thus, if the Antichrist is a Muslim who is going to rule a Muslim empire in the Middle East during the Tribulation, then he is going to rule over an empire that has been reduced to ashes!"[3]

Mark Hitchcock says, "The elimination of this Russian-Islamic alliance and all their troops will pave the way for the Antichrist to posture himself to take over the world . . . I've often wondered if the Antichrist might even take credit for the destruction of Gog's army by claiming he has a secret weapon of mass destruction."[4]

Likewise, Nathan Jones states, "Islam is just another system that will be wiped out before the Antichrist instills his system."

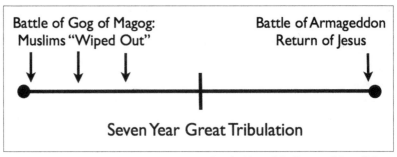

Popular View of the Timing of Gog of Magog

How and why do these teachers arrive at this position? The answer is found in two presuppositions brought to the text by those who hold to the Roman-Antichrist theory. The first presumption is that the Antichrist and his armies will come from Europe. Because Gog's forces are clearly not European, it is deduced that Gog must be someone different from the Antichrist. The second presumption is that the Antichrist will be either a humanist or a universalist who will demand to be worshipped as God or a god. Surely, it is reasoned, the Muslims of the earth would never support such a man. For those who hold this position, then, it became necessary to find some mechanism to eliminate the 1.59 billion Muslims of the earth from their eschatological narrative, paving the way for the Antichrist to bring all religions willingly together under his control. It is in Ezekiel 38–39 that Roman-Antichrist theorists find their imaginary mechanism to remove Muslims from the picture. As such, many teach that as a result of the massive casualties suffered at the Battle of Gog of Magog, Islam will either cease to be a relevant force on Earth, or will disappear altogether, thus paving the way for the coming forth of the European, humanist, or universalist Antichrist. And so the popular interpretation of Ezekiel 38–39 was born not so much out of a careful exegesis of the text, but rather, out of a need to make it fit into a previously held and well-developed eschatological narrative.

IMPLICATIONS OF THE POPULAR VIEW

It must be made clear that the aforementioned narrative is not a fringe view. Because of the popular interpretation of Ezekiel 38–39, multitudes of Christians actually believe that before Jesus returns, more than a billion and a half Muslims will either be "wiped out,"[6] will suffer "annihilation,"[7] will be "reduced to ashes,"[8] or will convert to another belief system. Most think that Russia will be decimated as well. In contrast to virtually all demographic models that indicate that within a few short decades, Islam will emerge as the world's largest religion, this radically opposite view is astounding. But what if this scenario is nothing more than a fantasy born from the misinterpretation of a few key eschatological passages? Today, large segments of the Church have embraced a view concerning Islam's future that is not only bogus, but is also highly fatalistic. The potentially devastating implications of this view for evangelism, missions, and inter-cession are alarming. As I wrote this book, a few highly respected scholars suggested to me that the debate between the Roman Antichrist and the Islamic Antichrist positions are irrelevant. I fundamentally disagree. Popular views of biblical prophecy genuinely impact the practices of large numbers of Christians. Islam's looming emergence as the world's largest religion and the Church's greatest challenge globally is poles apart from its disappearance from the earth. There is simply no middle ground between these views. This is not an issue the Church can afford to get so funda-mentally wrong. While it is imperative that students of the Scriptures diligently apply themselves to rightfully understanding the prophetic texts of the Bible, this is most particularly true with regard to Ezekiel 38–39.

THE JEWISH POSITION

In contrast to the popular Christian position, the Jewish rabbinic view identifies Gog as the final enemy of God's people. Further, he and his armies are the same invaders described by all the other prophets. In *Eze-kiel, a Commentary Anthologized from Talmudic, Midrashic and Rabbinic Sources*, we are told: "The final war when Gog will actually break into Jerusalem, is described in Zechariah 14. References to the wars of Gog and Magog abound in Scripture, overtly in the prophets . . . The longest, most detailed, and most specific accounts are contained in the books of Ezekiel, Zechariah, Joel, and Daniel."[9]

While the Jews refer to the final evil dictator as Gog, the New Testa-ment calls him by such titles as the Antichrist (1 John 2:22), the son of destruction (2 Thessalonians 2:3), the lawless one (2 Thessalonians 2:8), the Beast (Revelation 11:7), and other titles. Likewise, in the Talmud, we read:

> Behold a king shall go up from the land of Magog at the end of the days. He shall assemble kings wearing crowns and lieutenants wearing armor, and all the nations shall obey him. They shall array battle in the land of Israel against the children of the Dispersion, but the Lord shall be ready for them by burning the breath of life out of them with the flame of fire that issues from beneath the throne of glory. Their dead bodies shall fall upon the mountains of the land of Israel, and the wild beasts of the field and the birds of heaven shall come and consume

them. After that, all the dead of Israel shall be resurrected, and shall enjoy the good things which were secretly set aside for them from the beginning, and they shall receive the reward of their labor.[10]

And again: "At the end, the very end of days, Gog and Magog and their armies shall go up against Jerusalem, but they shall fall by the hand of the King Messiah. For seven full years the children of Israel shall use their weapons of war for kindling, without having to go into the forest to cut down the trees."[11]

GOG AS ANTICHRIST

With all of this in mind, we will now seek to show that Gog is the Antichrist, and the nations of Gog's alliance will be among the primary followers of the Antichrist. We will show that the invasion of Ezekiel 38–39 is simply one more retelling of the same story that all of the prophets told. While numerous additional details could be added, this basic story is summarized as follows:

- A group of nations led by Gog/Antichrist attack Israel and persecute Christians globally.

- As a result, over a period of three and a half years, the nation of Israel experiences one final, utter devastation with many being taken captive.

- Through the Messiah, the Lord intervenes to rescue the survivors and deliver the captives.

- The gentile nations turn to the Lord.

- Israel returns to the Lord forever.

- The Messiah rules from Jerusalem.

As we will see, the story told by Ezekiel is the same story told by every other prophet throughout the Bible. While using different symbolism and emphasizing different aspects of this story, all of the prophets are pointing to the same series of events.

Many who espouse the popular view see it as a very succinct series of events. This view is well articulated by Bible teacher Mark Hitchcock in *The Coming Islamic Invasion of Israel*: "Ezekiel 38–39 describes what we might call the 'One-Day War'—or even the 'One Hour-War'—because God will quickly and completely annihilate the Islamic invaders from the face of the earth by supernatural means."[12]

Thus, among interpreters who hold this view, there is an attempt to locate the timing of the battle at some very narrow location on the end-time timeline. Author Ron Rhodes, in his book *Northern Storm Rising*, lists what he sees as the only six options:

- Before the rapture and the tribulation.

- After the rapture but before the tribulation.

- In the first half or middle of the tribulation.

- At the end of the tribulation.

- At the beginning of the millennium.

- At the end of the millennium.[13]

But this view, which attempts to limit Ezekiel's prophecy to only one of these very narrow time periods, fails to recognize a very common characteristic of biblical prophecies: they often speak of a broad series of events in a very succinct and limited manner.[14] A perfect example of this is seen in Revelation 12:5, which describes the woman Zion, who gives birth to Jesus, the man-child: "She gave birth to a male child [Jesus], one who is to rule all the nations with a rod of iron, but her child was caught up to God and to his throne."

If we were to read this one verse as if it were a comprehensive description, we would be forced to believe that Jesus would be caught up to the throne of God almost immediately after his birth. What the passage makes no mention of is the thirty-three years of Jesus' earthly life that came between His birth and His ascension. But while the passage doesn't discuss, or even mention, those three-plus decades, in no way does it preclude them. With the advantage of hindsight, we know that Jesus lived on the earth for thirty-three years. Similar patterns can be observed in numerous messianic prophecies. Another such example is in Isaiah:

> There shall come forth a shoot from the stump of Jesse, and a branch from his roots shall bear fruit. And the Spirit of the LORD shall rest upon him, the Spirit of wisdom and understanding, the Spirit of counsel and might, the Spirit of knowledge and the fear of the LORD. And his delight shall be in the fear of the LORD. He shall not judge by what his eyes see, or decide disputes by what his ears hear, but with righteousness he shall judge the poor, and decide with equity for the meek of the earth; and he shall strike the earth with the rod of his mouth, and with the breath of his lips he shall kill the wicked. Righteousness shall be the belt of his waist, and faithfulness the belt of his loins. The wolf shall dwell with the lamb, and the leopard shall lie down with the young goat, and the calf and the lion and the fattened calf together; and a little child shall lead them. (11:1–7)

According to this passage, the acts of the Messiah flow seamlessly from His coming forth as the shoot of Jesse, to striking the earth and slaying the wicked. Nowhere in the text do we find any hint of a two-thousand-year gap between Jesus' initial coming and His return for ultimate victory. Obviously, numerous details are not included in this sweepingly broad prophetic overview of the Messiah's ministry. Again, many similar examples could be cited, because this is a frequently followed pattern of prophetic passages throughout the Scriptures.

This same principle is at work in Ezekiel 38–39. While numerous details are not mentioned in the passage, in no way does this mean that it is merely a simple, succinct "One Hour-War." To read this prophecy as such is to misunderstand this very common characteristic of biblical prophecy. This prophecy should not be seen as a singular, narrow, and brief event, nor should this passage be viewed as containing a comprehensive description of all the details that this episode will bring with it. Rather, it is a very general prophetic/poetic summarization of the final seven-year period leading up to the return of Jesus, as viewed from Ezekiel's particular perspective. The broad perspective of the passage is seen in that it begins with a description of God drawing Gog out to come against Israel, and it culminates with the Messiah's return and the establishment of the messianic kingdom. As direct results of the destruction of Gog and his armies:

- God's name will never again be blasphemed.

- The surviving nations will come to a saving knowledge of God.

- The captives of Israel will be delivered.

- God will pour out His Spirit on Israel.

- The survivors of Israel will come to know the Lord forevermore.

- Israel will dwell securely in their land forever.

- The Lord Himself will reside in the land of Israel.

Because these are descriptions that can only be applied to the time of the return of Jesus and the establishment of His messianic kingdom, it is impossible that Gog and his armies are anything other than the Antichrist and his armies. This, then, will be our first order, to consider several timing texts that show that the passage concludes with the Messiah's return and reign.

GOD'S NAME IS NO LONGER BLASPHEMED

Several times in the book of Daniel, we are told that throughout his career, the Antichrist will repeatedly blaspheme the Lord. In Daniel 11:36, we see that the Antichrist will "exalt himself" and "speak astonishing things against the God of gods." In Daniel 7:25, we are told that the Antichrist will blaspheme "the Most High." But consider this fact: beyond being a blasphemer himself, the Antichrist will also gather a global following of those who no doubt will imitate his example. The global religious movement inspired and led by the Antichrist will be the greatest and most significant movement of blasphemy that the world has ever known. Yet in Ezekiel we read that after the defeat of Gog and his armies, God's name will never again be blasphemed: "So I will show my greatness and my holiness and make myself known in the eyes of many nations. Then they will know that I am the LORD . . . And my holy name I will make known in the midst of my people Israel, and I will not let my holy name be profaned anymore." (38:23; 39:7)

This represents a major, if not insurmountable, problem for those who believe that Gog's defeat precedes the coming of the Antichrist. How can it be said that God's name will never again be blasphemed, immediately prior to the emergence of history's most prominent blasphemer, who will openly curse God for three and a half years? This is simply impossible. The only way this passage can be reconciled with the greater context of end-time prophecy is if we understand Gog to be the Antichrist. When Gog is destroyed, along with his armies, only then will the mouths of the blasphemers forever be shut.

THE GENTILES COME TO KNOW GOD

Isaiah the prophet informs us that after the return of Jesus, the "knowledge of God" will fill the whole earth: "They shall not hurt or destroy in all my holy mountain; for the earth shall be full of the knowledge of the LORD as the waters cover the sea" (Isaiah 11:9). As a result, during Jesus' millennial reign, even the gentile nations will worship the God of Israel: "All the ends of the earth shall remember and turn to the LORD, and all the families of the nations shall worship before you" (Psalm 22:27).

Isaiah also describes the children from among Israel's former enemies coming to her to express repentance and worship: "The sons of those who afflicted you shall come bending low to you, and all who despised you shall bow down at your feet; they shall call you the City of the LORD, the Zion of the Holy One of Israel" (Isaiah 60:14).

In keeping with this theme found throughout the Scriptures, we see that after God judges Gog and his armies, all nations come to know the Lord: "I will send fire on Magog and on those who dwell securely in the coastlands, and they shall know that I am the LORD . . . And the nations shall know that I am the LORD, the Holy One in Israel" (Ezekiel 39:6–7).

Once again, this passage is a significant difficulty for those who would place these events several years prior to the return of Jesus. Some have attempted to diminish the significance of this statement, treating it as a shallow intellectual acknowledgment of the God of Israel. But this doesn't do justice to the statement. How can it be said that the nations come to know and acknowledge that the Lord God, the Holy One in Israel, is the one true God, at a time just before they all come together to blaspheme His name, invade His land, and attack His people? Once again, this simply doesn't make any sense. As commentator Ralph Alexander says, "Ezekiel 39:7, 22 declare that the Lord's name will never be profaned again—a fact that is hardly possible with the tribulation forthcoming. Moreover, the concept of the nations 'knowing the Lord' by recognizing his sovereignty fits best at the time of the second coming rather than before the tribulation."[15]

Other commentators agree. James Burton Coffman wrote: "This also fits into the Final Judgment scene . . . Thirty seconds after the onset of the Eternal Judgment Day, there will remain no more in the whole world, either an agnostic or an infidel."[16]

The only way to do this passage justice is to view it as a reference to the nations actually coming to know and worship God, precisely as described by Isaiah when the whole earth is full of the knowledge—or more appropriately, the knowing—of God. And this simply does not happen until after Jesus returns.

THE JEWISH CAPTIVES ARE DELIVERED

Among the many terrible calamities that will befall the Jewish people during their coming subjugation by the Antichrist and his armies is that many will be taken as captives by the surrounding nations. The Lord, through the prophet Amos, speaking of this day, said, "For behold, I will command, and shake the house of Israel among all the nations as one shakes with a sieve, but no pebble shall fall to the earth" (Amos 9:9). Jesus also spoke quite directly concerning the many Jewish captives who will be taken to the surrounding nations during the onslaught of the Antichrist: "They will fall by the edge of the sword and be led captive among all nations, and Jerusalem will be trampled underfoot by the Gentiles, until the times of the Gentiles are fulfilled" (Luke 21:24).

But while several passages speak of this great calamity, others emphasize the deliverance of the captives by the hand of the Lord, through the

Messiah. King David prophesied concerning the deliverance of the Jewish captives and the glorious days that would follow:

> You will arise and have pity on Zion; it is the time to favor her; the appointed time has come . . . Nations will fear the name of the LORD, and all the kings of the earth will fear your glory. For the LORD builds up Zion; he appears in his glory; that he looked down from his holy height; from heaven the LORD looked at the earth, to hear the groans of the prisoners, to set free those who were doomed to die, that they may declare in Zion the name of the LORD, and in Jerusalem his praise, when peoples gather together, and kingdoms, to worship the LORD. (Psalm 102:13–16, 19–21)

Isaiah also connected the deliverance of the Jewish captives to the day of the Lord's vengeance: "The Spirit of the Lord GOD is upon me, because the LORD has anointed me to bring good news to the poor; he has sent me to bind up the brokenhearted, to proclaim liberty to the captives, and the opening of the prison to those who are bound; to proclaim the year of the LORD's favor, and the day of vengeance of our God" (Isaiah 61:1–3).

Zechariah connected the deliverance of the captives to the age of the Messiah's rule: "His rule shall be from sea to sea, and from the River to the ends of the earth. As for you also, because of the blood of my covenant with you, I will set your prisoners free from the waterless pit. Return to your stronghold, O prisoners of hope; today I declare that I will restore to you double" (Zechariah 9:10–12).

Joel also prophesied concerning these things: "For behold, in those days and at that time, when I bring back the captives of Judah and Jerusalem . . ." (Joel 3:1 NKJV).

Zephaniah spoke similarly: "For the LORD their God will intervene for them, and return their captives" (Zephaniah 2:7).

The testimonies of all these prophets harmonize precisely with what Ezekiel describes will take place specifically as a result of the destruction of Gog and his armies:

> Therefore thus says the Lord GOD: "Now I will bring back the captives of Jacob, and have mercy on the whole house of Israel; and I will be jealous for My holy name—after they have borne their shame, and all their unfaithfulness in which they were unfaithful to Me, when they

dwelt safely in their own land and no one made them afraid. When I
have brought them back from the peoples and gathered them out of their
enemies' lands, and I am hallowed in them in the sight of many nations,
then they shall know that I am the LORD their God, who sent them into
captivity among the nations, but also brought them back to their land,
and left none of them captive any longer." (Ezekiel 39:25–28 NKJV)

A few points must be emphasized. First, the captives of Israel are
delivered specifically and as a direct result of the destruction of Gog and
His armies. But this is not merely a general deliverance; rather, the passage states that none of the captives will remain captive "any longer." It
is a complete and final deliverance that can only be associated with the
messianic age. By placing this event several years before the coming of the
Antichrist, as the popular position does, it becomes highly contradictory
to many other passages which inform us that the armies of the Antichrist
will take many Jewish people captive (e.g., Luke 21:24). The only way this
portion of the prophecy can be reconciled with all of the other prophets
is if Gog and the Antichrist are one and the same.

ISRAEL KNOWS THE LORD FOREVERMORE

Even as the gentile nations will come to know and follow the Lord during
the messianic kingdom, survivors from Israel will also come to know Him.
The theme of the remnant, or the survivors of Israel all coming to know
the Lord after a mighty deliverance, is commonly repeated throughout
the prophets. Isaiah spoke of these things: "In that day the remnant of
Israel and the survivors of the house of Jacob . . . will lean on the LORD,
the Holy One of Israel, in truth" (Isaiah 10:20).

Elsewhere, Isaiah spoke similarly to King Hezekiah: "And the surviving
remnant of the house of Judah shall again take root downward and bear fruit
upward. For out of Jerusalem shall go a remnant, and out of Mount Zion
a band of survivors. The zeal of the LORD will do this" (2 Kings 19:30–31).

The prophet Joel also spoke of this day: "And it shall come to pass that
everyone who calls on the name of the LORD shall be saved. For in Mount
Zion and in Jerusalem there shall be those who escape, as the LORD has said,
and among the survivors shall be those whom the LORD calls" (Joel 2:32).

Micah also wrote: "I will make the remnant, and those who were cast off, a strong nation; and the LORD will reign over them in Mount Zion from this time forth and forevermore" (Micah 4:7).

Speaking of this remnant, Jeremiah prophesied concerning the day when they would all come to "know the LORD": "And no longer shall each one teach his neighbor and each his brother, saying, 'Know the LORD,' for they shall all know me, from the least of them to the greatest, declares the LORD. For I will forgive their iniquity, and I will remember their sin no more" (Jeremiah 31:34).

Later, picking up on that which the prophets before him spoke, the apostle Paul addressed the day when the surviving remnant of Israel would come to a saving knowledge of God: "And Isaiah cries out concerning Israel: 'Though the number of the sons of Israel be as the sand of the sea, only a remnant of them will be saved, for the Lord will carry out his sentence upon the earth fully and without delay'" (Romans 9:27–28).

And finally, the apostle John reflects the prophet Jeremiah in speaking about what it means to "know" God: "And this is eternal life, that they know you the only true God, and Jesus Christ whom you have sent" (John 17:3).

But it is in Ezekiel where the two themes of the surviving remnant and their coming to "know" God are fully brought together. In this passage, we are told that after Gog's armies are destroyed, all of surviving Israel will truly come to know Him from that point on: "The house of Israel shall know that I am the LORD their God, from that day forward" (39:22).

It couldn't be any clearer. This is not merely a revival wherein many Jews become more devout; rather, the whole house of Israel comes to *know* "the LORD their God." This powerful national salvation was described in detail earlier in Ezekiel 20. In this passage, the Lord connects the following essential details:

- The Lord becomes King over Israel.
- The Lord enters into judgment with Israel.
- The Lord enters into an eternal covenant with Israel.
- The rebels are "purged" from Israel.
- The Lord removes the scattered Jews from among the nations.
- All of Israel comes to know the Lord.

Consider the following passage, and as you do, ask yourself how this could be referring to anything other than the fullness of Israel's national salvation. Yet it is precisely what Ezekiel describes as taking place as a result of Gog and his armies being annihilated:

> As I live, declares the Lord GOD, surely with a mighty hand and an outstretched arm and with wrath poured out I will be king over you. I will bring you out from the peoples and gather you out of the countries where you are scattered, with a mighty hand and an outstretched arm, and with wrath poured out . . . . I will enter into judgment with you face to face . . . I will bring you into the bond of the covenant. I will purge out the rebels from among you, and those who transgress against me . . . Then you will know that I am the LORD . . . For on my holy mountain, the mountain height of Israel, declares the Lord GOD, there all the house of Israel, all of them, shall serve me in the land. There I will accept them . . . And you shall know that I am the LORD, when I bring you into the land of Israel, the country that I swore to give to your fathers. (Ezekiel 20:33–42)

ISRAEL DWELLS SECURELY IN THEIR LAND

As a result of Israel repenting of their disobedience, and their coming to know Him, every last Jew will dwell securely in the land forevermore: "They shall forget their shame and all the treachery they have practiced against me, when they dwell securely in their land with none to make them afraid . . . I will leave none of them remaining among the nations anymore" (Ezekiel 39:26, 28).

Of this passage, C. F. Keil has written, "From that time forth the people of God will no more have to fear a foe who can disturb its peace and its blessedness in the everlasting possession of the inheritance given to it by the Lord."[17]

Even more forcefully, Daniel Block commented, "Ezekiel's declaration that not a single individual will be left behind when Yahweh restores his people is without parallel in the OT. Yahweh's restoration is not only total, however, it is permanent. He promises never again to hide his face from his people."[18]

Of course, little needs to be said concerning the impossibility of Israel experiencing genuine security before the Antichrist is destroyed. Israel will only truly dwell securely after all of her enemies have been destroyed, Jesus the Messiah is present, and the Lord has poured out His Spirit on all Israel.

GOD POURS OUT HIS SPIRIT ON ISRAEL

In one of the most powerful prophetic testimonies in Scripture, the prophet Zechariah speaks of a day when, after destroying the nations that surround Jerusalem, the Lord will pour out His spirit on the surviving Jewish people.

> And on that day I will seek to destroy all the nations that come against Jerusalem. And I will pour out on the house of David and the inhabitants of Jerusalem a spirit of grace and pleas for mercy, so that, when they look on me, on him whom they have pierced, they shall mourn for him, as one mourns for an only child, and weep bitterly over him, as one weeps over a firstborn. On that day the mourning in Jerusalem will be as great as the mourning for Hadad-rimmon in the plain of Megiddo. (Zechariah 12:9–11)

According to this passage, there are three events that coincide: (1) the Lord destroys the invading nations; (2) the Jewish people come to recognize that Jesus, the one whom they (and we all) have pierced, is in fact the Messiah; and (3) the Lord pours out His Spirit upon the Jewish people. Isaiah the prophet described precisely the same day:

> "And a Redeemer will come to Zion, to those in Jacob who turn from transgression," declares the LORD. "And as for me, this is my covenant with them," says the LORD: "My Spirit that is upon you, and my words that I have put in your mouth, shall not depart out of your mouth, or out of the mouth of your offspring, or out of the mouth of your children's offspring," says the LORD, "from this time forth and forevermore." (Isaiah 59:20–21).

Thus, if the previous description in Ezekiel of Israel coming to know the Lord "from that day forward" was not sufficient to establish the conclusive nature of this event, then certainly Ezekiel's next description will seal its meaning: "And I will not hide my face anymore from them, when I pour out my Spirit upon the house of Israel, declares the Lord GOD" (Ezekiel 39:29).

Many attempt to restrict this to a very limited spiritual revival in Israel that takes place several years prior to the coming of Jesus. Bible teacher David Reagan, for instance, says of these events: "Many [Jewish people] will open their hearts to the Lord. In fact, this event could mark the occasion when the 144,000 Jews of Revelation 7:1–8 accept Yeshua as their Messiah and are sealed by the Lord for special service throughout the seven year period of the Tribulation."[19]

But it is clear that this event involves far more than a glorified gospel tent revival sweeping through town. Not only did the Lord say that not a single Jew would be left among the nations (39:28), and all of Israel would know Him "from that day forward" (39:22), but He also said that He would pour His spirit out upon them and never again hide his face from them (v. 29). In light of this undeniable evidence, most responsible commentators agree that this passage represents the final and complete turning of the Jewish people to the Lord forever.

- Daniel Block rightfully stated, "It marks the beginning of a new era, which will be characterized by Israel's recognition of Yahweh, that is, the full realization of covenant relationship."[20]

- C. F. Keil said that this verse marks the turning point in Ezekiel's prophecy, wherein "Israel will know that the Lord is, and will always continue to be, its God."[21]

- Leslie C. Allen in the *Word Biblical Commentary* says, "By the events of 'that day' the covenant relationship between them and Yahweh would be fully and finally endorsed."[22]

- Robert W. Jenson, in *The Brazos Theological Commentary on the Bible*, says, "Moreover, 'from that day forward,' from the day when the Lord openly demonstrates his deity, also the house of Israel will acknowledge 'that I am their God.' Here this outcome of the Lord's act is stated with special intensity, for the event that will compel this knowledge is the revelation of God's deity itself: Israel—like the nations—will know God precisely as God."[23]

- Iain M. Duguid in *The NIV Application Commentary* says that after Gog's destruction, "this will bring about a radical change in the hearts of his people and in the security of his presence with them, such that he will never again hide his face from them."[24]

- Matthew Henry, in speaking of this passage, said, "The indwelling of the Spirit is an infallible pledge of the continuance of God's favour. He will hide his face no more from those on whom he has poured out his Spirit."[25]

THE MESSIAH IS PRESENT

As the crowning proof that Gog is the Antichrist, Ezekiel reveals that at the conclusion of Gog's destruction, Jesus the Messiah is physically present on the ground, in the land: "For in my jealousy and in my blazing wrath I declare, on that day there shall be a great earthquake in the land of Israel. The fish of the sea and the birds of the heavens and the beasts of the field and all creeping things that creep on the ground, and all the people who are on the face of the earth, shall quake at my presence" (38:19–20).

The Lord says that throughout the earth, both people and animals will "quake at [His] presence." The word used for *presence* is the Hebrew word *panim*. *Panim* is a reference to the actual face or presence of a person. When God says that the people of the earth will quake at His *panim*, He is saying that they will be terrified because of His actual presence. Concerning the word *panim*, *The New Unger's Bible Dictionary* says, "The presence (face) of Jehovah is Jehovah in his own personal presence."[26] *The New International Encyclopedia of Bible Words* says, "In the OT, being in God's or another's presence is indicated by a preposition (l) prefixed to the Hebrew word panim ('face'). The thought is to be 'before the face of the person.'"[27]

Panim is used throughout the Old Testament to refer to the actual presence of God. Jacob, for instance, after wrestling with the Angel of the Lord, referred to seeing God face-to-face: "So Jacob called the name of the place Peniel, saying, 'For I have seen God face [*panim*] to face [*panim*], and yet my life has been delivered'" (Genesis 32:30).

It is also interesting to note that in place of the Hebrew *panim*, the Septuagint used the Greek word *prosopon*. *Prosopon* is one of two words commonly used in the New Testament to refer to actual presence. The other word is *parousia*, which is commonly associated with the Second Coming. Between *parousia* and *prosopon*, *prosopon* is the more powerful term. *Parousia* implies coming, but *prosopon* implies actual face-to-face presence. As Jesus is coming on the clouds, this is His *parousia*, but once

He has actually arrived, then the word *prosopon* is used. An excellent example of the New Testament usage of *prosopon* is a scene where the righteous are actually looking upon the face of God in the eternal city: "No longer will there be anything accursed, but the throne of God and of the Lamb will be in it, and his servants will worship him. They will see his face [*prosopon*], and his name will be on their foreheads" (Revelation 22:4).

Ezekiel's description of people quaking in fear of God's face reveals that at the conclusion of the Battle of Gog and Magog, Jesus the Messiah, God incarnate, is physically present on the earth, in the land of Israel.

THE HOLY ONE IN ISRAEL

Further evidence for the physical presence of Jesus at the conclusion of this battle is seen in Ezekiel 39:7: "And my holy name I will make known in the midst of my people Israel, and I will not let my holy name be profaned anymore. And the nations shall know that I am the LORD, the Holy One in Israel."

This is the only time that the phrase "the Holy One in Israel" is used in the Bible. It is the Hebrew *qadowsh qadowsh baYisra'el*. A similar phrase, "the Holy One *of* Israel" (*qadowsh qadowsh Yisra'el*), is used thirty-one times in Scripture (e.g., Isaiah 12:6; 43:3; 55:5; 60:9). But here, the Lord is not merely the Holy One *of* Israel; He is actually present *in* the land and on the ground! While the popular position holds that this passage concludes several years before the return of Jesus, this verse makes this an absolute impossibility.

GOD DIRECTLY DECLARES THAT GOG IS THE ANTICHRIST

But beyond all of the evidences that we have seen thus far, perhaps the clearest and most direct proof that Gog is the Antichrist is quite simply because God says so. First, the Lord calls Gog's invasion and subsequent destruction "the day of which I have spoken": "Behold, it is coming and it will be brought about, declares the Lord GOD. That is the day of which I have spoken" (Ezekiel 39:8).

Of course, "the day" that the Lord is continually speaking of throughout the prophets, the day that is the focal point of all of redemptive history, is the Day of the Lord. Then the Lord informs Gog that he is the one that the Lord has been speaking about throughout the prophets: "This is what the Sovereign LORD says: Are you not the one I spoke of in former days by my servants the prophets of Israel? At that time they prophesied for years that I would bring you against them" (Ezekiel 38:17 NIV).

The Septuagint words the passage not as a rhetorical question, but as a declaration: "Thus saith the Lord God, to Gog; Thou art he concerning whom I spoke in former times, by the hand of my servants the prophets of Israel, in those days and years, that I would bring thee up against them" (LXX).

While numerous prophetic passages written prior to Ezekiel reference an invader that would come against Israel in the last days, these are antichristic passages set within the context of the Day of the Lord. Once again, this verse is deeply problematic for those who argue that Gog is not the Antichrist or that he is from Russia. One can search and search, but throughout the prophets, there is no pre-Ezekielian prophet who references a Russian invasion of Israel.

SUMMARY

In summary, then, as a direct result of the destruction of Gog and his armies, the following things take place:

- God's name will never again be blasphemed.

- The surviving nations will come to a saving knowledge of Him.

- The captives of Israel will be delivered.

- God will pour out His Spirit on Israel.

- Israel will come to know the Lord forever.

- Israel will dwell securely in their land eternally.

And beyond these things, Jesus the Messiah will be present in the land of Israel. While many interpreters attempt to either separate these events from the destruction of Gog by several years, or to diminish their significance by claiming they do not refer to the age of the Messiah, no truly reasonable exegesis of this passage can arrive at such a position. It is abundantly clear that these things happen during the age of the Messiah and as a direct result of the destruction of Gog and his armies. Everything about the events and language in this passage indicate that this "battle" is not merely the opening act of the Great Tribulation, but rather, it is the grand conclusion of that period.

EZEKIEL 38–39:

GOG OF MAGOG: PART II

T HUS FAR IN OUR STUDY of Ezekiel 38–39, we have seen that the passage concludes with several events that can only be understood as occurring after the return of Jesus. We also saw that the text directly states that Jesus—the Holy One of Israel—is actually physically present in the land. And even beyond that, we saw that God Himself directly stated that Gog is the Antichrist, referring to him as the one of whom the prior prophets spoke. But even beyond this, there are still numerous very solid reasons to see Gog and the Antichrist as one and the same person. In this chapter, we will consider some of the commonalities shared by Ezekiel's prophecy and several other antichristic prophecies. We will also consider some problems with the popular position, and lastly, we will respond to a few common arguments frequently set forth by proponents of the popular position.

THE FEAST OF GOD

The first and most obvious commonality shared by the Battle of Gog of Magog and Armageddon is that at the conclusion of both, a call goes out to the birds of the air and the beasts of the field to partake of the flesh of the fallen soldiers. But this portion of Ezekiel's prophecy is also quoted in the book of Revelation and applied to the Antichrist's Battle of Armageddon. Consider the following side-by-side comparison of both passages:

Battle of Gog of Magog Ezekiel 39:17–20	Battle of Armageddon Revelation 19:17–18
"Assemble and come, gather from all around . . .	"Come, gather . . .
to the sacrificial feast that I am preparing for you, a great sacrificial feast on the mountains of Israel . . .	for the great supper of God . . .
"You shall eat the flesh of the mighty, and drink the blood of the princes of the earth . . . And you shall be filled at my table with horses and charioteers, with mighty men and all kinds of warriors," declares the Lord GOD.	to eat the flesh of kings, the flesh of captains, the flesh of mighty men, the flesh of horses and their riders, and the flesh of all men, both free and slave, both small and great.

As we see, Revelation takes its description of this unparalleled "feast" directly from Ezekiel's prophecy. This is not a mere similarity, but a direct citation. Consider the implications of this. In Revelation 19, we have what is no doubt the most well-known passage concerning the return of Jesus throughout Scripture. Jesus is seen bursting forth from heaven to destroy the armies of the Antichrist. Then the cry goes out to the birds and beasts to gather together to devour the enemy soldiers. But this call is taken directly from the portion of Ezekiel's prophecy where the conquered Gog and his armies are the source of feasting. Both prophecies describe the same events, although John's Revelation adds much additional information concerning the fact that it is the Messiah Himself who brings the actual destruction on Gog's armies.

In searching through several popular prophecy books that reject any connection between Gog and the Antichrist, I found that there is a stunning silence concerning John's usage of Ezekiel here. Revelation's obvious assumption of Ezekiel's material is simply ignored. This is not the case, however, among numerous other Christian commentaries.

•   Charles L. Feinberg says in *The Prophecy of Ezekiel,* "Incidentally, the figure gives a clue as to the time setting of the entire passage. It is the same scene as that of Revelation 19, the great supper of God, and the chronology is clear. The events will transpire at the end of the tribulation and just before the millennial reign of the Messiah of Israel."[1]

•   G. K. Beale and Sean McDonough, in the *Commentary on the New Testament Use of the Old Testament,* also observe the clear connection between the two passages: "The angel announces the coming destruction of the beast, false prophet, and their troops through the same imagery by which the defeat of Gog and Magog was announced . . . Rev. 19:17–18 continues this prophetic portrayal and reaffirms that it will assuredly occur."

•   Robert Jensen observes John's usage of Ezekielian imagery: "When in the Christian apocalypse the warfare of the 'Logos of God' against 'the beast' reaches its climax, Ezekiel is reprised."[3]

•   Daniel Block observes the clear connection between the two passages, seeing the beast (Antichrist) of Revelation and Ezekiel's Gog as one and the same: "The scene of the birds gathered for the great supper of God in [Rev.] 19:17–21 is clearly borrowed from Ezekiel's last frame (39:17–20) . . . Although this passage never mentions Gog by name, the beast certainly represents him. In the prophecy John fills in several details missing from Ezekiel's prophecy . . . John's use of Ezekiel's oracle against Gog represents a remarkable adaptation of an OT tradition for a Christian theme. An event whose timing in the original prophecy is only vaguely set in 'the latter days' is now the penultimate event in human history; the picture of national peace and tranquility is transformed into a portrait of universal peace; the foreign foe, becomes a satanic and diabolical force; the divine victory is placed in the hands of the Messiah. The message that had originally been presented to the Jewish exiles to bolster their sagging hopes has been transformed into a message of hope for all Christians."[4]

•   Grant R. Osborne observes, "There will be two great messianic banquets at the eschaton: The feast with the Lamb for the saints and the feast on the sinners for the carrion birds. The saints will partake of the great banquet and the sinner will be the banquet! This image [from Revelation 19] is drawn from Ezek. 39:17–20, where the judgment against Gog is punctuated by an invitation to the birds and wild animals to 'come together' for 'the great sacrifice on the mountains of Israel.'"[5]

For those who reject the notion that Gog and the Beast/Antichrist of Revelation are one and the same, who see no genuine connection between Revelation 19 and Ezekiel 39, the question must be asked, why would the Lord use a passage that describes the destruction of Gog and apply it to the destruction of the Antichrist? If the two are not the same, this would be awfully confusing, if not outright misleading. The only way John's usage of Ezekiel's imagery here can be reasonably understood is by viewing John's prophecy as an expanded retelling of Ezekiel's oracle.

BOTH ARE DESTROYED THROUGH A GREAT EARTHQUAKE

But John's borrowing of material from Ezekiel is not limited to the great feast. Revelation borrows from other portions of Ezekiel's oracle against Gog as well. Consider the following further parallels:

Battle of Gog of Magog Ezekiel 39:19–20	Battle of Armageddon Revelation 16:18–20
In the land of Israel	At the place that in Hebrew is called Armageddon
On that day there shall be a great earthquake	And a great earthquake such as there had never been since man was on the earth
And every wall shall tumble to the ground	And the cities of the nations fell
And the mountains shall be thrown down	And every island fled away, and no mountains were to be found
And I will rain upon him and his hordes and the many peoples who are with him torrential rains and hailstones, fire and sulfur.	And great hailstones, about one hundred pounds each, fell from heaven on people; and they cursed God for the plague of hail, because the plague was so severe.

So as a result of the Lord executing judgment on both Gog and the Antichrist, "the mountains" all fall down, as plagues and massive hailstones are poured out on the enemies of God. But if all of the mountains are thrown down when Gog is destroyed, how can they all be thrown down again only a few years later? Obviously, this wouldn't make any sense unless the two passages are simply telling the same story.

BOTH ARE STRICKEN WITH PLAGUES

In one of the most rarely discussed, but most powerfully visual passages portraying the return of Jesus in the Old Testament, Habakuk describes the Messiah emerging from Arabia, executing judgment on His enemies. Within this text, we find many of the same themes found in Ezekiel's oracle:

> God came from Teman [Arabia], and the Holy One from Mount Paran. His splendor covered the heavens, and the earth was full of his praise. His brightness was like the light; rays flashed from his hand; and there he veiled his power. Before him went pestilence, and plague followed at his heels. He stood and measured the earth; he looked and shook the nations; then the eternal mountains were scattered; the everlasting hills sank low. (Habakkuk 3:3–6)

Again, the theme of the "mountains" falling is repeated. But a new theme here is that of the Messiah sending forth "plague" and "pestilence" upon His enemies. In another well-known antichristic prophecy, the prophet Zechariah also spoke of the "plague" that will befall the armies of the Antichrist: "And this shall be the plague with which the LORD will strike all the peoples that wage war against Jerusalem: their flesh will rot while they are still standing on their feet, their eyes will rot in their sockets, and their tongues will rot in their mouths" (Zechariah 14:12).

It is appropriate, then, that this theme is also seen in Ezekiel's messianic prophecy: "With pestilence and bloodshed I will enter into judgment with him" (Ezekiel 38:22). Even as Jesus will send forth plagues upon the armies of the Antichrist, the Lord declared that He will personally pour them out upon Gog and his armies. The commonalities are easily explainable by acknowledging that Gog and the Antichrist are the same person.

BOTH ARMIES ATTACK EACH OTHER

As we previously discussed in our examination of Daniel 2, the final kingdom of the Antichrist is specifically defined as being "divided": "And as you saw the feet and toes, partly of potter's clay and partly of iron, it shall be a divided kingdom, but some of the firmness of iron shall be in it, just as you saw iron mixed with the soft clay" (v. 41).

Of course, this is a perfect description of the global Islamic community, which from its beginnings has been divided between the two sects of Sunni and Shi'a Muslims. It is also a perfect fulfillment of the ancient prophecy declared over Ishmael, the father of the Arab peoples, who would forever be in conflict with other men and even his own brothers: "He shall be a wild donkey of a man, his hand against everyone and everyone's hand against him, and he shall dwell over against all his kinsmen" (Genesis 16:12).

It is not surprising, then, that the armies of the Antichrist, while in the land of Israel, right up to the very last moment, are seen attacking each other, fulfilling the well-known proverb. Although they are able to temporarily suspend their endless infighting for the purpose of joining together to attack Israel, once in the land, they are unable to hold back their ancient sectarian enmity: "Each man will seize the hand of another, and they will attack each other" (Zechariah 14:13). Not surprisingly then, Ezekiel describes precisely the same dynamic occurring among the armies of Gog: "I will summon a sword against Gog on all my mountains, declares the Lord GOD. Every man's sword will be against his brother" (Ezekiel 38:21).

Thus, even as the armies of the Antichrist are seen to be killing each other while in the land of Israel, so also are Gog's armies killing one another. And once more, the common traits and actions of the armies of the Antichrist and Gog are easily explained in that both passages are describing the same events.

BOTH COALITIONS CONSIST OF THE SAME NATIONS

In Daniel 11, after conquering Egypt, we are told that the two nations of Libya and Sudan (Cush) will submit to the Antichrist: "He shall become ruler of the treasures of gold and of silver, and all the precious things of

Egypt, and the Libyans and the Cushites shall follow in his train" (v. 43).

But in Ezekiel 38, we read that these same two nations will be a part of the military coalition of Gog: "Cush [Sudan], and Libya with them; all of them with shield and helmet" (v. 5). This is a significant problem for the popular position, which separates Gog from the Antichrist. If Gog and his armies, including Libya and Sudan, are utterly destroyed, how is it that these same two nations are resurrected only a couple years later, to join the armies of the Antichrist? Logically, this would be impossible. Once more, the popular position conflicts with common sense. According to this view, we are to believe that these two radical Islamic nations will first willingly submit to a Russian leader, and after being utterly annihilated, only a couple years later, will be altogether ready to willingly submit to a European humanist dictator. Once again, it is far more reasonable to simply conclude that Gog and the Antichrist are one and the same.

BOTH INVADE ISRAEL TO TAKE SPOILS

According to Isaiah, one of the primary motivations of the Antichrist in invading the land of Israel is the seizing of loot: "Ah, Assyria, the rod of my anger; the staff in their hands is my fury! Against a godless nation I send him, and against the people of my wrath I command him, to take spoil and seize plunder, and to tread them down like the mire of the streets" (Isaiah 10:5–6).

Likewise, Zechariah describes looting by the Antichrist and his forces: "Behold, the day of the LORD is coming, And your spoil will be divided in your midst. For I will gather all the nations to battle against Jerusalem; The city shall be taken, The houses rifled, and the women ravished. Half of the city shall go into captivity, But the remnant of the people shall not be cut off from the city" (14:1–2).

Daniel also informs us that Antiochus IV Epiphanes, the most powerful individual type of the Antichrist in Scripture, also did the same: "When the richest provinces [Israel] feel secure, he will invade them and will achieve what neither his fathers nor his forefathers did. He will distribute plunder, loot and wealth among his followers" (11:24 NIV).

Finally, in Ezekiel's oracle, we are told that Gog's motivations will also be to take plunder:

> Thus says the Lord God: On that day, thoughts will come into your mind, and you will devise an evil scheme and say, "I will go up against the land of unwalled villages . . . to seize spoil and carry off plunder, to turn your hand against the waste places that are now inhabited, and the people who were gathered from the nations, who have acquired livestock and goods, who dwell at the center of the earth. . . . Have you assembled your hosts to carry off plunder, to carry away silver and gold, to take away livestock and goods, to seize great spoil?" (38:10–13)

Even as one of the Antichrist's motivations for invading Israel will be to steal booty, Gog's specified motivation is the same—because he and the Antichrist are the same.

BOTH COME FROM THE NORTH

One of the more common themes throughout the prophets is the invasion of the evil army from the north. While some of these prophecies concerned historical invasions, they all ultimately foreshadowed the final, last-days invasion of the Antichrist. The prophet Joel spoke of the end-time invasion from the north: "But I will remove the northern army far from you, and I will drive it into a parched and desolate land, and its vanguard into the eastern sea, and its rear guard into the western sea. and its stench will arise and its foul smell will come up, for it has done great things" (Joel 2:20).

The invading army from the north was also a common theme within the prophecies of Jeremiah: "Then the Lord said to me, 'Out of the north the evil will break forth on all the inhabitants of the land'" (Jeremiah 1:14 NASB). And: "Thus says the LORD: 'Behold, a people is coming from the north country, a great nation is stirring from the farthest parts of the earth'" (Jeremiah 6:22).

Thus when Ezekiel began to speak of an invasion from the great northern army, his listeners would have already been quite familiar with this theme and would have understood it to be a reference to the final, evil, end-time invasion:

> On that day when my people Israel are dwelling securely, will you not know it? You will come from your place out of the uttermost parts of

the north, you and many peoples with you . . . Behold, I am against you, O Gog, chief prince of Meshech and Tubal. And I will turn you about and drive you forward, and bring you up from the uttermost parts of the north, and lead you against the mountains of Israel. (Ezekiel 38:14–16; 39:1–3)

Even as the other prophets' descriptions of the Antichrist's last-days invasion were typified by his coming from the north, or with the "northern army," so also does Gog follow the same pattern and use precisely the same imagery.

BOTH INVADE ISRAEL WHEN SHE FEELS SECURE

According to Daniel, the Antichrist will engage in a peace treaty with the nation of Israel (9:27). Isaiah informs us that the Jewish people will actually come to trust and even rely (Hebrew: *sha`an*) on the false overtures of the Antichrist (10:20). Paul the apostle warned of the deceptive nature of this false security: "For you yourselves are fully aware that the day of the Lord will come like a thief in the night. While people are saying, 'There is peace and security,' then sudden destruction will come upon them as labor pains come upon a pregnant woman, and they will not escape" (1 Thessalonians 5:2–3).

Through the foreshadowing of Antiochus IV Epiphanes, Daniel likewise warns us concerning the Antichrist: "He will cause deceit to prosper, and he will consider himself superior. When they feel secure, he will destroy many and take his stand against the Prince of princes. Yet he will be destroyed, but not by human power" (8:25 NIV).

And later, Daniel warns again: "When the richest provinces feel secure, he will invade them" (11:24 NIV). And so, one more time, we are not surprised to find that Ezekiel describes exactly the same plans as emanating forth from Gog, who says in his heart: "I will invade a land of unwalled villages; I will attack a peaceful and unsuspecting people—all of them living without walls and without gates and bars" (38:12–13).

The reason Gog's methodology of creating and using false peace in order to destroy his enemies is precisely the same as the Antichrist's is simply because the two are one.

SUMMARY OF COMMONALITIES BETWEEN GOG AND ANTICHRIST

1.   Both are devoured at the great feast of God by birds and beasts (Ezekiel 39:17–20; Revelation 19:17–18).

2.   Both are destroyed through the greatest earthquake ever described in Scripture (Ezekiel 38:19–20; Revelation 16:18–20).

3.   Both are attacked with plagues (Ezekiel 38:22; Zechariah 14:12; Habakkuk 3:3–6).

4.   Both armies attack each other (Ezekiel 38:21; Zechariah 14:13; Daniel 2:41; Genesis 16:12).

5.   Both consist of the same nations (Ezekiel 38:5; Daniel 11:43).

6.   Both come for spoil (Ezekiel 38:10–13; Zechariah 14:1–2; Isaiah 10:5–6; Daniel 11:24).

7.   Both come from the north (Ezekiel 38:14–16; 39:1–3; Joel 2:20; Jeremiah 1:14; 6:22).

8.   Both come from the same region (Ezekiel 38:1–6; Daniel 11:40; Isaiah 7:17; 10:12; Micah 5:6).

9.   Both use false peace and invade when Israel feels secure (Ezekiel 38:12–13; Daniel 8:25; 9:27; 11:24; Isaiah 10:20; 1 Thessalonian 5:2–3).

10. Both die from the "sword" of the Lord (Ezekiel 38:21; Revelation 19:15, 21).

11. Both fall in the land of Israel (Ezekiel 36:1–6; 38:9; 39:5).

12. Both die in Israel (Ezekiel 39:5; Daniel 7:11; 9:27; 11:45; 2 Thessalonians 2:8).

13. Both are buried (Ezekiel 39:11; Isaiah 14:13–20).

14. After both of their deaths, God's name will never again be blasphemed (Ezekiel 38:23; 39:7; Revelation 20:2; 21:8).

15. After both of their deaths, the surviving nations will come to a saving knowledge of God (Ezekiel 39:6–7; Isaiah 11:9; 60:14; Psalm 22:27).

16. After both of their deaths, Israel's captives will be delivered (Ezekiel 39:25–28; Zephaniah 2:7; Joel 3:1; Zechariah 9:10–12; Isaiah 61:1–3; Psalm 102:13–16, 19–21).

17. After both of their deaths, God will pour out His Spirit on Israel (Ezekiel 39:29; Isaiah 59:20–21; Zechariah 12:9–11).

18. After both of their deaths, the survivors of Israel will come to know the Lord forevermore (Ezekiel 20:33–42; 39:22; 2 Kings 19:30–31; Joel 2:32; Micah 4:7; Jeremiah 31:34; Isaiah 10:20; John 17:3; Romans 9:27–28).

19. After both of their deaths, Israel will dwell securely in the land for eternity (Ezekiel 39:26, 28; Micah 5; Isaiah 60–66).

20. After both of their deaths, Jesus is present in Israel (Ezekiel 38:19–20; 39:7; Revelation 19–21).

Other commonalities could certainly be cited. But despite the numerous characteristics shared by Ezekiel 38–39 and other antichristic passages, many refuse to acknowledge the abundance of evidence we've just examined. In summarizing a thirty-part series on Ezekiel 38–39, Thomas Ice explained why he believes we should not see these chapters as describing the same event in Revelation 19: "There are some broad similarities between the two battles, however, it is the differences that prove decisive when it comes to evaluating whether they are the same battle."[9] But as we have just seen, there are more than "some broad similarities" here. The similarities and commonalities are outright overwhelming. Now, in the remainder of this chapter, we will examine some of these alleged differences to show that, in fact, they don't even exist.

ARGUMENTS FROM SILENCE

When attempting to show that differences exist between Ezekiel 38–39 and other antichristic prophecies, many look primarily to arguments from silence. For instance, Fruchtenbaum has stated, "In the Ezekiel invasion, there is a protest against the invasion; in the Armageddon Campaign, there is no protest."[7] In other words, because one passage contains information that the other does not, this proves that they are two different events. But this argument assumes that every passage is utterly comprehensive in its description. If this same logic were applied to the Gospels, one would conclude that they are all different stories. Say, for instance, one gospel account contained a detail that another did not; therefore they are two different events. Yet we know that any such suggestion is foolish. Throughout the prophets, numerous messianic prophecies present the reader with extremely summarized portrayals of the work of the Messiah. None of these prophecies contain a comprehensive description of Messiah's life. Simply because one prophet informs us of certain details concerning a future event and another does not, in no way does this indicate that the two were describing different events. Arguments from silence are fallacious and should carry no weight whatsoever with careful and thoughtful students of Scripture.

BOTH ARE DESTROYED ON "THE MOUNTAINS OF ISRAEL"

In attempting to show differences between Gog's invasion and the Antichrist's, Fruchtenbaum has written, "The Ezekiel invasion is destroyed on the mountains of Israel; the Armageddon Campaign is destroyed in the area between Petra and Jerusalem."[8] Although this argument is made quite frequently with genuine seriousness, with all due respect to Dr. Fruchtenbaum, and others who have repeated his claim, it is simply a silly argument that has not been thought through. First, Fruchtenbaum seems to ignore the equally prominent verse 39:5, where God informs Gog, "You shall fall in the open field, for I have spoken, declares the Lord God." Likewise, in 38:9 Gog is told, "You will advance, coming on like a storm. You will be like a cloud covering the land, you and all your hordes." So it isn't even true that Gog's armies will be somehow limited to the mountains of Israel. His armies cover the whole land, and he himself dies in an open field. But more important, the argument is simply silly because "the mountains of Israel" is simply a synecdoche for the whole land of Israel. This is clearly seen only two chapters earlier, where God calls on Ezekiel to prophesy specifically to "the mountains of Israel" but then includes, "the hills, the ravines and the valleys, the desolate wastes and the deserted cities":

> Son of man, prophesy to the mountains of Israel, and say, "O moun-
> tains of Israel . . . Thus says the Lord GOD to the mountains and the
> hills, the ravines and the valleys, the desolate wastes and the deserted
> cities, which have become a prey and derision to the rest of the nations
> all around . . . Therefore prophesy concerning the land of Israel, and
> say to the mountains and hills, to the ravines and valleys, Thus says
> the Lord GOD: Behold, I have spoken in my jealous wrath, because you
> have suffered the reproach of the nations. (Ezekiel 36:1–6)

When God referred to "the mountains of Israel," He meant the whole land of Israel. This would be similar to the phrase "all across the fruited plains" as a reference to the United States of America. "The fruited plains" is simply an allusion to the vast expanse of the United States. Likewise "mountains of Israel" clearly refers to the whole land of Israel.

BURNING THE WEAPONS

Another argument frequently made against the Gog battle concluding at the return of Jesus is that the victorious Jewish people burn the weapons of the fallen armies for seven months, which would be unnecessary during the Millennium. Nathan Jones has said, for instance, "With Jesus then present to provide everyone's needs, the curse partially lifted and the Earth reformatted by earthquakes, there would be no need for Israel to have to burn any weapons for fuel."[9]

But this claim fundamentally misunderstands the true nature of the age to come. During the Millennium, for millions of people, a very earthly life will continue. The Lord does not destroy the earth; He restores it. There is a clear continuity between this age and the next. Zechariah for instance, describes previously unbelieving survivors from among the nations that will live as believers during the Millennium: "Then everyone who survives of all the nations that have come against Jerusalem shall go up year after year to worship the King, the LORD of hosts, and to keep the Feast of Booths (14:16).

Later in Ezekiel, we read of a thriving fishing industry during the messianic age: "Fishermen will stand beside the sea. From Engedi to Eneglaim it will be a place for the spreading of nets. Its fish will be of very many kinds, like the fish of the Great Sea" (47:10).

The prophet Amos described the people of Israel rebuilding cities and planting vineyards and gardens during the millennial reign of Jesus: "I will restore the fortunes of my people Israel, and they shall rebuild the ruined cities and inhabit them; they shall plant vineyards and drink their wine, and they shall make gardens and eat their fruit" (9:14).

Even as things such as fishing and agriculture will not cease, neither will the need for fuel for cooking or light cease. Just because Jesus will be present in these days does not mean that all things will be done magically. During the Millennium, the prophets Isaiah and Micah famously foretold, the people of the earth will beat their swords into plowshares (Isaiah 2:4; Micah 4:3). This prophetic-poetic description of the conversion of military weapons into farm implements is virtually identical to Ezekiel's description of burning weapons for fuel. In each of these descriptions, weapons are transformed into tools for domestic or agricultural purposes. Any claim that weapons burning is incompatible with the nature of the Millennium is born from a misunderstanding of the Millennium as described throughout the Scriptures.[10]

GOG'S INVASION IS LIMITED, WHILE ARMAGEDDON INCLUDES ALL NATIONS

Some claim that in the Battle of Armageddon, every nation is involved, while Gog's coalition involves a limited number of nations. But this distinction is not in accord with Scripture. In chapter 3, we saw that the Antichrist's coalition is primarily composed of ten nations, with many others later joining. So, not *every* last nation of the earth will be aligned with the Antichrist. If the Antichrist ruled over *every* nation on Earth, we would have global peace—*Pax Antichristus*. Yet Daniel 9:27 reveals that the Antichrist is at war until the very end. Simply stated, war necessitates resister militaries and governments. Daniel 11 speaks of nations that will be at war with the Antichrist, and others that will "escape his hand." Any claim then that every single nation on the globe will accompany the Antichrist's coalition against Jerusalem ignores this and other relevant passages. Second, efforts to limit Gog's coalition to the nations specifically named in Ezekiel 38–39 ignore the statement right within the passage that says that "many" other nations will join those already listed.

ON THE BURIAL OF GOG/ANTICHRIST

Another argument against equating Gog with the Antichrist is the claim that Gog receives a burial, whereas the Antichrist does not. First, it is correct to say that the body of Gog will receive a burial: "On that day I will give to Gog a place for burial in Israel, the Valley of the Travelers, east of the sea. It will block the travelers, for there Gog and all his multitude will be buried. It will be called the Valley of Hamon-gog" (Ezekiel 39:11).

Concerning the Antichrist, many have misread portions of Isaiah 14 and concluded that he never receives a burial. Isaiah 14 is a poetic-prophetic dirge against the king of Babylon, a prophetic type of the Antichrist. The king/Antichrist first claims that he would make his throne on the "mount of assembly . . . in the far reaches of the north." This is a reference to the Temple Mount in Jerusalem, the location of God's throne: "You said in your heart, 'I will ascend to heaven; above the stars of God I will set my throne on high; I will sit on the mount of assembly in the far reaches of the north; I will ascend above the heights of the clouds; I will make myself like the Most High'" (vv. 13–14).

But instead, God declares that the Antichrist will find himself in the pit of hell: "But you are brought down to Sheol, to the far reaches of the pit" (v. 15). This final resting place in hell is where his soul will descend, but his physical body will be also be buried in an utterly shameful way. In ancient times, wealthy families and kings shared a family tomb or sepulchre. These were cave-like graves where bodies were given their own individual places in compartments along the sides of the tomb, much like modern mausoleums. In this passage, shame is being cast upon the Antichrist because, unlike the other kings and nobles of the earth, he will not be buried in his family or royal sepulchre, but in a mere pit, and his only clothing will be other dead bodies:

> All the kings of the nations lie in glory, each in his own tomb; but you are cast out, away from your grave, like a loathed branch, clothed with the slain, those pierced by the sword, who go down to the stones of the pit, like a dead body trampled underfoot. You will not be joined with them [the kings of the earth] in burial, because you have destroyed your land, you have slain your people. "May the offspring of evildoers nevermore be named!" (vv. 18–20).

The passage does not say that Antichrist will never be buried. Instead it is simply showing the nature of his shameful death and burial. As J. Alec Motyer, in his exceptional commentary on Isaiah, wrote, "Stripped of his royal robes, the king has nothing to clothe him but the bodies of those who died in the battle, heaped together ignominiously . . . His grave is unmarked and therefore unconsciously trampled underfoot, walked over . . . There is no-one concerned to secure a suitably royal burial for the king. His forebears were carried to the family mausoleum, but he will not join them."[11]

Instead of dying like royalty—as he has said in his heart that he will be like the Most High—he will be treated like dung with the rest of those who are slain. He is buried, not in a royal tomb, but in a common pit, a mass grave. The claim that Gog and the Antichrist must be two different individuals because one is buried and the other is not is founded upon a shallow misreading of the texts.

ON THE DEATH OF GOG/ANTICHRIST

Another similar argument against equating Gog with the Antichrist is the claim that Gog will be killed and buried, whereas the Antichrist is said to be "thrown alive into the lake of fire that burns with sulfur" (Revelation 19:20). Thus, it is argued that the two cannot be the same entity. But this argument fails to consider other relevant passages that speak about the physical death of the Antichrist. Paul the apostle tells us that the Antichrist will, in fact, be slain by Jesus: "And then the lawless one will be revealed, whom the Lord Jesus will kill with the breath of his mouth and bring to nothing by the appearance of his coming" (2 Thessalonians 2:8).

Daniel also tells us that the Antichrist will be destroyed and his body thrown into the lake of fire: "I looked then because of the sound of the great words that the horn was speaking. And as I looked, the beast was killed, and its body destroyed and given over to be burned with fire" (7:11).

Later Daniel tells us that the Antichrist will come to his end in the land of Israel: "And he shall pitch his palatial tents between the sea and the glorious holy mountain. Yet he shall come to his end, with none to help him" (11:45).

It is clear, then, that the Antichrist will die as any other man. This does not conflict with his being thrown "alive" into hell (Greek: *Hades* or Hebrew: *Sheol*). As Motyer has written concerning "life" after death in hell: "First, the dead are alive—in Sheol. In the Bible, 'death' is never 'termination' but a change of place and of state with continuity of personal identity. Sheol is the 'place' where all the dead live."[12]

Simply put, while the body of the Antichrist will be killed by Jesus, his soul will be sent to hell "alive" as it were, to experience the consciousness of eternal torment: "And the devil who had deceived them was thrown into the lake of fire and sulfur where the beast and the false prophet were, and they will be tormented day and night forever and ever" (Revelation 20:10).

The claim that Gog cannot be the Antichrist based on these passages is inaccurate and simply the result of inadequate study.

PROBLEMS WITH THE POPULAR POSITION: THE DEMOGRAPHIC PROBLEM

Beyond all that we have examined thus far, there are also some glaring problems with the popular interpretation of Ezekiel 38–39 that few have considered. This problem is simply demographics. Many Westerners believe that most of the world's Muslims live in the Middle East. The truth, however, is that close to half of all Muslims globally live in the four countries of Indonesia, Pakistan, India, and Bangladesh. (Indonesia has a Muslim population of 202 million, Pakistan 175 million, India 161 million, and Bangladesh 145 million). Ezekiel's prophecy does not include any of these nations. Most Muslims, in fact, live outside of the Middle East. Today there are more Muslims in either France (3.5 million) or Germany (4 million) than in Lebanon (2.5 million). According to the popular interpretation, the nations specified in Ezekiel's prophecy include Russia and several Middle Eastern, central Asian, and North African nations. However, even if we included every nation that has ever been suggested in even the most broad interpretation, this would still only represent less than one-third of the total Muslim world population. If every soldier in every one of these nations was destroyed, today this would represent less than 2 percent of the total 1.6 billion Muslims of the world. Even if every single one of these nations was utterly and completely destroyed—something that no one is suggesting will occur—there would still remain well over a billion Muslims worldwide. Islam would continue to be a vast and vibrant force worldwide. Any suggestion that Islam will disappear from the earth several years prior to the return of Jesus is simply an illusion. Consider the following statistics:[13]

Nation	Percentage of Global Muslim Population	Total Number of Active Military
Turkmenistan	0.3	22,000
Uzbekistan	1.7	87,000
Kyrgyzstan	0.3	20,400
Tajikistan	0.4	16,300
Turkmenistan	0.3	22,000
Azerbaijan	0.6	382,000
Turkey	4.7	1,151,200
Lebanon	0.2	175,000
Palestinians	0.1	56,000
Syria	1.3	747,000
Iraq	2	578,270
Iran	4.7	3,833,000
Jordan	0.4	175,500
Saudi Arabia	2	250,000
Kuwait	0.2	46,300
Bahrain	0.1	19,460
Oman	0.2	47,000
UAE	0.2	51,000
Egypt	5	1,345,000
Libya	0.4	116,000
Sudan	1.9	211,800
Total	**29.6%**	**31,213,730**

CONCLUSION

In considering all of the relevant texts, it has become abundantly, if not painfully clear that Antichrist and Gog are one and the same. The various arguments used against this view all fail. As has been argued throughout this book, Ezekiel 38–39 is simply yet one more retelling of the same story that all the prophets tell:

- A group of nations, led by Gog/Antichrist, attacks Israel and persecutes Christians.

- As a result, over a period of three and a half years, the nation of Israel experiences one final utter devastation with many being taken captive.

- Through the Messiah, the Lord intervenes to rescue the survivors and deliver the captives.

- The gentile nations turn to the Lord.

- Israel returns to the Lord forever.

- The Messiah rules from Jerusalem.

As Miller rightfully states: "The battle described from different perspectives in Ezekiel 38–39 and that of Daniel 11:40–45 is best constructed as occurring immediately prior to the coming of the Lord and may be referred to as the Battle of Armageddon."[14]

And finally, we must acknowledge that until Christ returns, Islam is simply not going away. Despite the great efforts, and perhaps even the great desire, of some interpreters, this notion is simply wishful thinking. The sooner the Church acknowledges that Islam is here for the long haul—representing the final and greatest challenge it will ever face—the sooner it can rise to meet the missionary challenge, instead of sitting back and awaiting a pre-messianic destruction of Islam of which the Scriptures nowhere speak. *Now* is the moment for the Church to give herself wholeheartedly in intercession, evangelism, and missions to the Islamic world!

15

EZEKIEL 38–39:

GOG OF MAGOG: PART III

Having identified the Ezekiel 38–39 invasion as simply one more retelling of the many prophecies that speak of the Antichrist and his last-days assault against Israel, we must now turn to identifying which nations the passage says will be involved. While the most popular position interprets these two chapters as pointing to a Russian-led Islamic invasion, as we will see, a far more solid case can be made for a Turkish-led Islamic invasion. This Turkey-versus-Russia debate among scholars is nothing new. As far back as 1706, Matthew Henry, in his classic Bible commentary, acknowledged the difference of opinion among scholars: "Some think they find them [Gog and Magog] afar off, in Scythia, Tartary, and Russia. Others think they find them nearer the land of Israel, in Syria, and Asia the Less [Turkey]."[1]

The purpose of this chapter is to approach the debate in a fair, reasonable, and responsible manner, as we identify the nations involved in this terrible last-days invasion of Israel and demonstrate how clearly Ezekiel's prophecy correlates and flows with the other prophecies of Scripture.

DEFINING OUR METHOD OF INTERPRETATION

It is important that before we begin, we clearly define our method of identifying the nations of Ezekiel's prophecy. There are a few important factors to consider. First, as we have previously discussed, there are two distinct methods commonly used by prophecy analysts to identify the meaning of the ancient peoples and places within various prophecies. The first method, the geographic-correlation method, simply attempts to identify the location of the ancient people or place at the time of the prophet, and matches that location to the modern nations that now occupy that territory. The ancestral-migration method, on the other hand, seeks to trace the descendants, their migrations, and their intermingling with other peoples, ultimately to modern-day peoples. One method emphasizes identifying the original historical context and understanding of the prophet, and another endeavors to accomplish the arduous task of tracing bloodlines into modern times. As we previously discussed, the ancestral-migration method is fraught with difficulties, dangers, and inconsistencies and should be avoided altogether by all who seek to responsibly interpret biblical prophecy. Using the ancestral-migration method, five different researchers can, and most often do, arrive at five different conclusions. Sad to say, a survey of many efforts to interpret Ezekiel 38–39 reveals that many otherwise excellent scholars and teachers use this method. Even Wilhelm Gesenius, the revered Hebrew scholar, attempts to identify the Rosh people, not by determining where they lived specifically during Ezekiel's day, but by trying to determine where some of their their descendants eventually dwelt more than sixteen hundred years later! Consider Gesenius's definition of "Rosh" in his classic *Hebrew and English Lexicon*: "Rosh: of a northern nation mentioned along with Tubal and Meshech, Ex. 38:2-3; 39:1 probably . . . the Russians, who are described by the Byzantine writers of the tenth century [A.D.] . . . as inhabiting the northern part of Taurus; and also by Ibn Foszlan, an Arabian writer of the same period . . . dwelling upon the river Wolga.[2]

So for Gesenius, because tenth-century Byzantine writers identified some alleged descendants of Rosh people in modern-day Russia, we should thus understand Ezekiel's prophecy to refer to Russia! But as we will see later, modern scholarship has shown that Rosh people also lived in several different parts of the world far removed from Russia. Because ancestry and migration were among Gesenius's primary standards for interpreting Ezekiel's prophecy, if he were alive today, he would have to significantly modify his position. This is simply one reason among many why this method should be entirely avoided. Ultimately, if Ezekiel's prophecy is to be properly understood, this deeply flawed yet widely utilized methodology must be rejected. Any responsible effort to understand Ezekiel's prophecy must use the historical-grammatical method, which strives to discover the biblical author's original intended meaning and understanding of the text, not some historical wild goose chase that tries to establish blood ties to people who lived more than three thousand years ago.

Another important factor that must guide our understanding and interpretation of these nations are other clues found both within the context of the immediate prophecy itself. As we examined in detail in the last chapter, God Himself spoke directly to Gog and said quite clearly that he is the one of whom so many of the previous biblical prophets had spoken. For years now, I've inquired of and even challenged numerous prophecy teachers who hold to the Russia-Gog position to show me a single verse from any of the previous prophets where they spoke of a last-days Russian-led invasion of Israel. To date, not a single verse has been offered. This point cannot be missed. In our efforts to identify the nations of Ezekiel 38–39, our conclusions cannot be limited to historical research alone, but must also consider the larger context of the passage. Because God made it clear that the Gog invasion was spoken of by the former biblical prophets, if proponents of the popular Russian-Gog theory cannot show a single verse by any of the previous prophets that speaks of a Russian-led invasion, then simply stated, they have misinterpreted the passage.

And finally, it is important that we not only attempt to identify the nations individually, but also the group of nations as a whole. Because the phrase "Gog of Magog, the prince, chief of Meshech and Tubal" identifies Magog, as the region from where Gog the leader comes, the verse also requires us to identify the regions of Meshech and Tubal. They are all obviously related. The wording of the phrase requires that it be interpreted as a whole and not merely according to each nation individually.

And so, in summary, this chapter will responsibly identify the nations of Ezekiel's prophecy by taking the original and the greater context of the passage into consideration.

Within the first six verses of Ezekiel 38, there are eight (or nine) ancient names given to identify Ezekiel's invading coalition. The leader of the invasion is called Gog:

> Son of man, set your face toward Gog, of the land of Magog, the chief prince of Meshech and Tubal, and prophesy against him and say, Thus says the Lord GOD: Behold, I am against you, O Gog, chief prince of Meshech and Tubal. And I will turn you about and put hooks into your jaws, and I will bring you out, and all your army, horses and horsemen, all of them clothed in full armor, a great host, all of them with buckler and shield, wielding swords. Persia, Cush, and Put are with them, all of them with shield and helmet; Gomer and all his hordes; Beth-togarmah from the uttermost parts of the north with all his hordes—many peoples are with you. (Ezekiel 38:2–6)

The leader of the coalition, again, is named Gog, from the land of Magog. The peoples or nations of his coalition are Meshech, Tubal, Persia, Cush, Put, Gomer, and Beth-togarmah. Some scholars also believe that the word translated as "chief" should be translated as "rosh," referring to an ancient people. We will examine this debate further on.

GOG

Attempts by scholars to identify the meaning of the word *Gog* are greatly varied. Beginning with Franz Delizsch, a nineteenth-century German theologian and Hebraist, a majority of scholars believe that "Gog" is a reference to a king who ruled Lydia, a kingdom that spanned the western half of Turkey during Ezekiel's day. The Assyrians called him *Gugu*, and the Greeks called him *Gyges*. Some scholars say that the evidence is inconclusive. Regardless, all agree that Gog is from Magog and is the prince of "Meshech and Tubal," though some would add "Rosh" to this list. Thus identifying Magog, Meshech, and Tubal (and perhaps Rosh) will do much to reveal from where the leader of this coalition will emerge. Let's begin by considering the location of Magog in Ezekiel's day.

DOES MAGOG REFER TO RUSSIA?

Ever since the release of C. I. Scofield's Reference Bible, numerous popular prophecy teachers today identify Magog with Russia or the former Soviet Central Asian nations (Kazakstan, Turkmenistan, Uzbekistan, Tajikistan, and Kyrgyzstan). The primary support for this position is found in a comment made by Flavius Josephus, a Jewish historian from the first century. What did Josephus say that has so swayed such a large segment of Christian prophecy teachers and scholars?

FLAVIUS JOSEPHUS

In discussing the various descendants of Japheth, Noah's son, Josephus wrote, "Magog founded those that from him were named Magogites, but who are by the Greeks called Scythians."[3] But there are a few fatal problems with relying on Josephus to identify Ezekiel's Magog as Russia. First, as historian K. Kristianson has written, the Scythians "were not a specific people," but rather variety of peoples, "referred to at a variety of times in history, and in several places, none of which was their original homeland."[4] In other words, referring to "Scythians" as if they all were one people is simply historically inaccurate. All historians today acknowledge that "Scythian" was a catch-all term loosely used to refer to a vast group of tribal peoples, often related by similar cultures, but not genetically. Equating Magog to all so-called Scythian peoples, as dozens upon dozens of prophecy books continue to do, is no different from saying that all "Indians" of early America were the same people. Any effort to connect Magog to all Scythians in an unqualified manner, without identifying a specific tribe or cluster of tribes is to be flatly rejected. Likewise, while it is also now increasingly common to associate Magog with the central Asian nations, apart from this fallacious and broad "Magog = Scythian" equation, there is no basis for this claim.

The second problem with Josephus's comments is that they were made in the first century. Ezekiel lived close to seven hundred years earlier than Josephus. In Josephus's identifications of the various descendants of Noah, he repeatedly spoke of those "who are now called by the Greeks" thus and such. In other words, his comments tell us nothing about how Ezekiel would have understood the term *Magog*. For these reasons and others, as we will see, a wide majority of scholars today reject the Russian-Magog position and place Magog instead in modern-day Turkey.

PHILO JUDEAUS

Some scholars are so determined to prove that Magog is Russia that they even rely on evidence that doesn't exist. Numerous popular prophecy books and articles make the claim that the Russian-Magog connection is supported by Philo of Alexandria.[5] But in all of Philo's works, no such reference exists. He never once even mentioned Magog.

HERODOTUS

Like Josephus, Herodotus is also often quoted in support of the Russian-Magog theory. But like Philo, Herodotus also never once mentioned Magog. He only spoke at length about the Scythians. But even if the people Herodotus knew as the Scythians were related to Magog, this still would not support the Russian-Magog position. After citing three conflicting theories concerning the origins of the Scythians, Herodotus expressed his preferred belief, not of a Russian origin, but of a Turkish one: "There is also another different story, now to be related, in which I am more inclined to put faith than in any other. It is that the wandering Scythian once dwelt in Asia [Turkey]." (The Greeks referred to Asia Minor simply as "Asia.") But even some of them later migrated. According to Dr. Michael Kulikowski, a historian and professor at Pennsylvania State University, the Scythians to whom Herodotus often referred "were to be found in a bit of modern Bulgaria and Romania, and across the grasslands of Moldova and Ukraine," but not in Russia.[7] So although widely cited by those seeking to establish a Russian-Magog connection, Herodotus provided no such evidence. Instead, he claimed that the Scythians originated in Turkey, and some ended up in Eastern Europe and Ukraine. But he never spoke of his Scythians as inhabiting Russia.

DOES MAGOG REFER TO TURKEY?

In conducting the research for this chapter, I consulted numerous reputable Bible atlases, encyclopedias, dictionaries, and commentaries, and compared them to a large sampling of popular Bible prophecy books. The discrepancies between these references and the prophecy books were shocking. While practically every popular prophecy book or treatment of Ezekiel places Magog in Russia, this position is almost never given serious credence in the more scholarly reference works. While some say it is not possible to know the location of Magog with any certainty, the overwhelming majority say that Magog likely refers to modern-day Turkey. Consider the following sampling of reference works and scholars who support the Turkish-Magog position. As you do, ask yourself why this view is utterly ignored in virtually every popular prophecy book on this subject:

- Old Testament scholar Daniel I. Block, in the *New International Commentary on Ezekiel*, says, "It seems best to interpret Magog as a contraction of an original *māt Gūgi*, 'land of Gog,' and to see here a reference to the territory of Lydia in western Anatolia [Turkey]."[8]

- *The Zondervan Illustrated Bible Dictionary* states, "Magog, possibly meaning 'the land of Gog,' was no doubt in Asia Minor [Turkey] and may refer to Lydia."[9]

- *The IVP Bible Background Commentary* lists Magog, Meshech, Tubal, and Togarmah as "sections or peoples in Asia Minor" [Turkey].[10]

- *The New Unger's Bible Dictionary*, under the entry for "Magog," states, "It is clear that Lydia [Turkey] is meant, and that by 'Magog,' we must understand, 'the land of Gog.'"[11]

- *The Zondervan Illustrated Bible Backgrounds Commentary* places Magog in Anatolia, or modern-day Turkey.[12]

- *The Catholic Encyclopedia* states, "It seems more probable that . . . Magog should be identified with Lydia [Turkey]. On the other hand, as Mosoch and Thubal were nations belonging to Asia Minor, it would seem from the text of Ezechiel that Magog must be in that part of the world. Finally, others with Josephus identify Magog with

Scythia, but in antiquity this name was used to designate vaguely any northern population."[13]

- *The Holman Bible Atlas* places Magog in Turkey.[14]

- *The New Moody Atlas of the Bible* also places Magog in Turkey.[15]

- *The Zondervan Atlas of the Bible* places Magog in Turkey.[16]

- *The IVP Atlas of Bible History* places Magog in Turkey.[17]

Now let's consider some of the historical sources that support this position:

MAIMONIDES

Maimonides, also known as Rambam, the revered Jewish sage, in *Hichot Terumot*, identified Magog as being in Syria on the border of Turkey.[18]

PLINY THE ELDER

Pliny the Elder was a first-century Roman military commander, author, naturalist, and philosopher. He spoke of a city called "Bambyce, otherwise called Hierapolis; but of the Syrians, Magog."[19] Ancient Heirapolis sat on the border of modern-day Turkey and Syria; thus, according to Pliny, so did Magog. Pliny's comments are easily as significant as Josephus's. Yet where Josephus's remarks have been cited dozens upon dozens of times to support the identification of Magog with Russia, Pliny's comments are cited nowhere. Pliny's view is also supported by Sir Walter Raleigh in his *History of the World*:

> Yet it is not to be denied, that the Scythians in old times coming out of the north-east, wasted the better part of Asia the Less, and possessed Coelesyria, where they built both Scythopolis and Hierapolis, which the Syrians call Magog. And that to this Magog Ezekiel had reference, it is very plain; for this city Hierapolis, or Magog, standeth due north from Judea, according to the words of Ezekiel, that from the north quarters those nations should come.[20]

HIPPOLYTUS OF ROME

Hippolytus of Rome, an early Christian theologian, in his *Chronicon*, written in the early third century, rejected Josephus's identification of Magog with the Scythians, connecting them instead to the Galatians in Asia Minor, modern-day Turkey.[21]

Why are none of these historical sources ever mentioned in most of today's popular prophecy books?

MAGOG: CONCLUSION

After all historical sources have been considered, and after considering the varied opinions of modern-day scholarship, the origins of Magog seem to have been on the border of Syria and Turkey. After planting the self-named city of Magog, also called Heirapolis in Syria, near the border of Turkey, some Magog peoples migrated to central and western Turkey and planted the kingdom of Lydia, which occupied the whole western half of Turkey, and thrived during Ezekiel's day. As previously mentioned, Lydia was the territory whose king was known as Gugu by the Assyrians and Gyges by the Greeks, and whom many Bible scholars identify with Ezekiel's Gog. Near to Ezekiel's day, some from Magog likely migrated north of the Black Sea to Moldova, the Ukraine, and Russia. These northern tribes could have been those whom Josephus and Herodotus referred to as the "Scythians." But while some from Magog likely dwelled north of the Black sea during Ezekiel's day, many others from Magog also retained a strong presence in their historical homeland of Asia Minor (Turkey). As such, far more scholars today identify Magog as the region of Turkey rather than Russia.

Ultimately however, as we have said, determining how Ezekiel would have understood the term *Magog* cannot be done by analyzing the singular term "Magog," but rather, the full phrase, "Gog of Magog, the prince, chief of Meshech and Tubal." Because Gog is from Magog and is prince over these other two principalities, it is important that we continue to study the location of these other people groups during Ezekiel's day, to understand the phrase as a whole.

ROSH

Before proceeding, we must discuss the controversial word *rosh*. Massive conflict within the scholarly community surrounds this word. Some translators feel as though the word should be understood as the adjective "chief," while others think it should be understood as the proper noun "Rosh." But beyond arguing for *Rosh* as a proper noun, many popular prophecy teachers also attempt to draw a connection to modern Russia. To support this position, four points must be proven; the first two points are grammatical, and the second two are historical: (1) The word *rosh* should be translated as a noun and not an adjective; (2) as a noun, *rosh* should be translated as the proper noun "Rosh"; (3) Rosh was a people well-known to Ezekiel; and (4) as a people, Rosh was most likely known by Ezekiel to refer to those from the region that is now Russia. To establish this argument, the same four scholars have been repeatedly cited: Wilhelm Gesenius, Carl Friedrich Keil, James Price, and Clyde Billington. But despite the many impressive points brought up by these scholars, when we consider the totality of their arguments, the case for Ezekiel's prophecy referring to Russia completely fails. Lets consider the arguments and where they fall short.

WILHELM GESENIUS

Wilhelm Gesenius is by far the most referenced scholar in support of the Russian-Rosh position. While his grammatical arguments must be considered, as we saw earlier, his effort to link Rosh to Russia relies almost entirely on the testimony of Byzantine and Arab writers who lived close to sixteen hundred years after Ezekiel's day. Gesenius's clear reliance on the ancestral-migration method should be rejected by any scholar seeking to responsibly interpret the text through the historical-grammatical method.

CARL FREDERICH KEIL

The next scholar often looked to in support of the Russian-Rosh position is Carl Friedrich Keil. But on grammatical grounds, Keil is far less dogmatic than Gesenius, admitting that the translation of *rosh* as a proper name is only "probable." Interestingly, eight years after the release of

Keil's commentary on Ezekiel, Keil's instructor in Hebrew, Ernest W.
Hengstenberg, released his own commentary on Ezekiel and quite directly
disagreed with his student:

> Gog is prince over Magog, moreover chief prince, king of the kings
> over Meshech and Tubal, the Moschi and Tibareni (ch. xxvii. 13, xxxii.
> 26), who had their own kings, but appear here as vassals of Gog. Many
> expositors render, instead of chief prince, prince of Rosh, Meshech, and
> Tubal. But the poor Russians have been here very unjustly arranged
> among the enemies of God's people. Rosh, as the name of a people,
> does not occur in all the Old Testament.[22]

On historical grounds, Keil, only follows Gesenius, also basing his
larger arguments on the testimony of those tenth-century Byzantine and
Arabic writers: "The Byzantine and Arabic writers frequently mention a
people called Rûs, dwelling in the country of the Taurus, and reckoned
among the Scythian tribes, so also there is no reason to question the
existence of a people named Rosh."[23]

Beyond this, concerning his identification of Rosh as Russia, Frederick Delitzsch, another German Hebraist and scholar who co-authored
the *Commentary on The Old Testament* with Keil also disagreed with him,
placing Magog not in Russia, but Turkey.[24]

Of course, in all of the many prophecy books that take the Russian-
Rosh position, none ever reference either Delitzsch or Hengstenberg.

JAMES PRICE

James Price is another authority frequently cited by those who take the
Russian-Rosh position. Price, a Hebrew scholar, in his article "Rosh:
An Ancient Land Known to Ezekiel," argues, like Gesenius and Keil
before him, in favor of interpreting Rosh as a place name. Again, Price's
grammatical arguments must be considered. Price also contends that
Rosh would have been known in Ezekiel's day. But that is all he claims.
Nowhere does Price ever attempt to identify where the Rosh people lived
at that time. In fact, throughout his article, he repeatedly cited other
scholars who place Rosh people in lands other than Russia. At the very
outset of his article, for example, Price cited J. Simmons, who places Rosh

squarely in Asia Minor (Turkey): "That in one or more of these texts a people of that name whose home was in Asia Minor, is indeed mentioned, is not entirely disproved but it is at any rate rendered improbable by the fact that the same name can be discerned only very doubtfully in other [Assyrian] documents."[25]

Other sources cited by Price place Rosh in either Iraq or Iran, but none in Russia.

CLYDE BILLINGTON

Clyde Billington is the fourth scholar frequently cited in support of the Russian-Rosh position. Of the four, Billington is the only one who truly attempts to tackle the historical aspects of the argument. In researching this issue, I was able to personally consult with Dr. Billington. While he is clearly an ardent supporter of the popular Russian-Rosh position, he also admits that in Ezekiel's day, the inhabitants of Rosh were a diverse and vast group of peoples, who lived in nations as far and wide as modern-day Russia, Central Asia, India, Iraq, and Turkey:

> It is likely the Ras/ Ros/ Rosh/ Rish/ Resh were a very large group of people located over a broad area north of the Caucasus Mountains. Some members of this group—[th]e "Ris"[—]moved south and con-quered India in ca. 1600 B.C. where they formed the ruling class there. Other members of this group conquered and ruled northern Mesopotamia—the Kingdom of Mitanni—for about 200 years, 1580–1350 B.C. When the Kingdom of Mitanni was destroyed by the Hittites in ca. 1350 B.C., some Ros/ Resh/ Ras peoples joined the Philistines in attacking Israel. Some also moved into Turkey, which is where some probably joined the Philistines. The Egyptians called these allies of the Philistines "Teresh." In other words, the Rosh people were widely dispersed.[26]

Billington even mentioned some "Rosh" peoples during Ezekiel's day who lived in China: "Some Rosh peoples penetrated as far east as the borders of northeast China in ca. 500 BC, where blonds were found buried in the permafrost."[27]

But there is another important factor that causes the identification of the Rosh people to extend far beyond even China and India. According to Billington (and numerous others who have followed him on this point), the word "Rosh" is simply a variant of "Tiras": "The Rosh name is probably derived from the name Tiras in Genesis 10:2 . . . Both Tiras and Rosh, and variations of these two names, were used for centuries for the Rosh people.[28]

Yet during Ezekiel's day, Tiras-Rosh peoples lived in regions far removed from Russia. In Josephus's *Antiquities of the Jews*, only a few lines beyond the well-cited comment regarding Magog and the Scythians, he also said, "Thiras [Tiras] called those whom he ruled over Thirasians; but the Greeks changed the name into Thracians."[29]

Thrace was located in modern-day Turkey, Bulgaria, and Greece. Tiras is also said to have founded a colony called Miletus in western Turkey in the sixth century BC.[30]

Other historical evidence indicates that the descendants of Tiras were the Etrucscans (called by the Greeks "Tyrsenoi") of Asia Minor, who later came to occupy Italy. For this reason, both the *Macmillan Bible Atlas* and the *Zondervan Atlas of the Bible* place Tiras in either Greece or Italy. Interestingly, the ancient Etruscans called themselves the Ras-enna. Billington believes this is due to a clear connection to the Ras/Ros/Rosh peoples.

In other words, (1) even if we do accept the translation of Rosh as a noun and (2) understand it to be a place name, (3) in no way does this point solely to Russia. In fact, most scholarly works place Tiras on the west coast of Turkey or the greater region of the Aegean Sea on the west coast of Turkey.

Because various Rosh peoples lived in numerous locations during Ezekiel's day, any effort to identify Rosh solely with Russia, while ignoring the other Rosh peoples of Turkey, Iraq, Italy, India, or China, is simply not an honest approach. When teachers cherry-pick the historical data to support their prophetic positions, they do a great disservice to their students. Yet unfortunately, in considering a majority of popular prophecy books today, this is precisely what many teachers do in their ongoing effort to point to Russia as the leader of Ezekiel's prophesied last-days invasion.

DO "ALL" REALLY AGREE?

Authors of today's top prophecy books that support the Russian-Rosh position frequently use superlatives to create the impression that no legitimate scholar would reject the translation of *rosh* as a place name and its identification with Russia. Concerning the fact that Russia will head an alliance against Israel, "all agree," says Scofield. But the picture some of these authors paint can at times border on dishonesty. Consider the following sampling of other equally qualified scholars who do, in fact, disagree with the Russian-Rosh position:

- Daniel I. Block argues that "the popular identification of Rosh with Russia is impossibly anachronistic, and based on a faulty etymology, the assonantal similarities between Rosh and Russia being purely coincidental . . . Ezekiel's point is that Gog is not just one of many Anatolian [from the region of modern Turkey] princely figures, but the leader over several tribal/national groups."[31]

- Charles Ryrie, in his *Ryrie Study Bible*, disagrees with the Russian-Rosh interpretation and states that "the prince of Rosh" should be translated as "the chief prince."[32]

- Dr. Merril F. Unger, admits that "linguistic evidence for the equation [Rosh as Russia] is confessedly only presumptive."[33]

- Edwin Yaumauchi argues that the word *rosh* "can have nothing to do with modern 'Russia.' This would be a gross anachronism, for the modern name is based upon the name Rus, which was brought into the region from Kiev, north of the Black Sea, by the Vikings only in the Middle Ages." Yamauchi goes on to claim that associating Ezekiel's *rosh* with Russia to be "groundless," and having "unfortunately gained widespread currency in the evangelical world through many channels."[34]

- A. R. Millard endorses Yaumauchi's claims: "Some commentators have tried to interpret the prophecies as applying literally to to Russia . . . Although these views have spread widely and convinced many, Yaumauchi shows why they are wrong and should be avoided by careful Bible students."[35]

- Ralph H. Alexander in *Expositors Bible Commentary on Ezekiel* states of *rosh*, "The accentual system and syntactical construction of the Hebrew language strongly indicate an appositional relationship between the words 'prince' and 'chief.' Both terms are related equally, then, to the two geographical words Meshech and Tubal. Grammatically, it would seem best to render the phrase, 'the prince, the chief, of Meshech and Tubal.'"[36]

- A. B. Davidson, in his commentary *The Book of the Prophet Ezekiel*, wrote, "Of course, any connexion between the name [rosh] and Russia is to be rejected."[37]

- J. W. Weavers, in *The New Century Bible Commentary on Ezekiel*, says, "The word for *head* is misunderstood as a proper name, [Ros] leading to a bizarre identification by the misinformed with Russia!"[38]

- Walther Zimmerli, in *A Commentary on the Book of the Prophet Ezekiel Chapters 25–48*, states, "Certainly Rosh 'Chief' is to be connected with 'Prince' and is not to be interpreted as a geographical indication."[39]

- Charles Feinberg, author of *The Prophecy of Ezekiel: The Glory of the Lord*, wrote, "There have been many writers who connected the name Rosh with the Russians, but this is not generally accepted today."[40]

- D. R. W. Wood in *The New Bible Dictionary*, said, "The popular identification of Rosh with Russia . . . has nothing to commend it from the standpoint of hermeneutics."[41]

- John Bright, author of *The Kingdom of God*, said, "In Ezekiel 38–39, we have a prophecy which some (quite wrongly!) believe will be fulfilled by present-day Soviet Russia."[42]

So it is clear that despite the many statements to the contrary, numerous very well-qualified scholars reject the popular Russian-Rosh position.

ASSESSING THE ARGUMENT

Now let's revisit the first two elements of the Russian-Rosh argument to assess if these two points hold up to scrutiny. As previously mentioned, the first two points are grammatical: (1) the word *rosh* should be translated as a noun, not an adjective; and (2) as a noun, *rosh* should be translated as the proper noun "Rosh."

Our brief review of the division among scholars on this issue shows that both sides raise legitimate points. One side argues that the construction of the phrase demands that *rosh* be interpreted as a noun. The other side argues that (1) rosh as a name is nowhere used in Scripture, and (2) its relationship to the other words in the passage demands that it be translated as simply "head" or "chief." For years, the two sides have been unable to resolve this conflict. But in more recent years, having the advantage of being able to consider all sides of this centuries-old debate, as well as the modern advances in scholarship, Daniel I. Block, has very ably offered a solution, satisfying the issues raised by both sides. Block acknowledges the need to translate *rosh* as a noun, but also recognizes that it should be translated according to its normal usage throughout the Bible as a reference to "chief," as well as its appositional relationship to the other names in the text. Block's translation reads as follows: "Set your face toward Gog, of the land of Magog, the prince, chief of Meshech and Tubal" (Ezekiel 38:3). For a fuller technical explanation of Block's translation, see Block's commentary on Ezekiel,[43] referred to by *The Commentary and Reference Survey: A Comprehensive Guide to Biblical and Theological Resources* as "the best commentary on any book of the Old Testament."[44]

And so, of the first two grammatical arguments, we see that while the first point seems to be valid (*rosh* should be translated here as a noun), as Block demonstrates, it does not follow that it should translated as a *proper* noun. While Block's translation is now widely accepted by a vast majority of scholars, most prophecy teachers are not aware of this, and still clinging to the outdated view.

But what about the two historical arguments necessary to prove the Russian-Rosh position? Of these two, the first point, that Rosh was a people well-known to Ezekiel, seems to have been proven fairly substantially by Billington and other historians. On the final point, however—

namely, that Rosh was most likely known by Ezekiel as a people from the region of modern Russia—Billington and all others fail to establish their case. Because of the wide range of Rosh peoples (and all of their variants) that were well known by the kings and cititzens of the region in those days, any effort to point solely to Russia is futile.

ROSH: CONCLUSION

In the end, then, two of the four points necessary to show that Ezekiel's rosh is a reference to Russia succeed, and two fail. After having considered all of the information—even if Ezekiel understood Rosh to be a proper name—there are far more reasons to see Rosh as pointing to Turkey than Russia. Even Billington, who is the leading champion of the Russian-Rosh position, admits, "There are scholars who do associate Rosh, Meshech, Tubal with Asia Minor, and certainly all three peoples were there in Ezekiel's day."[45] But once more, because our efforts are to understand how Ezekiel would have holistically understood the full phrase "Gog of Magog, the prince, chief of Meshech and Tubal," we must continue in our study to determine the location of the final two areas (Meshech and Tubal). Thankfully, identifying both of these names is far simpler than either Magog or Rosh.

MESHECH AND TUBAL

In keeping with its Russian-centric interpretation of Ezekiel 38, the Scofield Study Bible identifies Meshech as the city of Moscow, and Tubal as Tobolsk, a city in central Russia. This position was followed by numerous prophecy books for many years, but because of the complete lack of any historical support for this position, today it has been abandoned by virtually all. Following is a partial list of reference works that place both Meshech and Tubal in the region of modern-day Turkey:

- *Holman Bible Atlas*[46]

- *Oxford Bible Atlas*[47]

- *IVP New Bible Atlas*[48]

- *The IVP Atlas of Bible History*[49]

- *New Moody Atlas of the Bible*[50]

- *Zondervan Atlas of the Bible*[51]

- *Zondervan Illustrated Bible Backgrounds Commentary*[52]

- *The Macmillan Bible Atlas*[53]

- *Baker Bible Atlas*[54]

It is important to note that today, nearly all scholars identify both Meshech and Tubal as relating to modern-day Turkey. As we have stated throughout our study, to properly identify Magog, the homeland of Gog, we must first identify both Meshech and Tubal. Because both of these areas would have been understood by Ezekiel to be found in the region of modern Turkey, we can also deduce that Magog is also a reference to Turkey. Simply stated, if Magog refers to Russia, then the wording of the phrase simply doesn't make any sense. How could Gog, a leader from Russia, be referred to as the prince or leader of Turkey (Meshech and Tubal)? The Russian-Gog position understands Ezekiel's statement to be saying, "Gog of Magog [Russia], prince of Rosh [Russia], Meshech [Turkey] and Tubal [Turkey]." This would be similar to saying something like, "Obama of America, president of Washington, Moscow, and Beijing." This simply wouldn't make any sense. Neither does Ezekiel 38:3 as it is understood from the Russian-Gog position. But if we simply follow the leaning of most scholars, who place Magog in Turkey, then it makes complete sense both grammatically and geographically that Gog would be the prince of Meshech and Tubal, which are also in Turkey. As Daniel I. Block has written, "The order of Ezekiel's triad of names reflects an awareness of geographic and recent political realities in Anatolia. Gog (Lydia), situated farthest west, is at the head of an alliance with Meshech on her eastern border, and Tubal east of Meshech."[55]

Beyond making sense of the passage grammatically and geographically, the Turkish-Gog position also flows harmoniously with all the other prophecies that we've previously examined. As was discussed at the onset of this chapter, one of the primary factors that should determine our understanding of this passage is God's declaration to Gog that he and his hordes are the ones who have been repeatedly referenced in previous prophetic Scriptures. While this statement of God has been an insurmountable problem for those who seek to paint this passage as a Russian invasion, it only serves to establish the case for a Turkish-led, Islamic invasion of Israel. Whether we are speaking of the prophet Joel's invading army from the north, Zechariah's invasion of Israel, Daniel's desolating "king of the North," or several other key end-time texts, Ezekiel 38–39 is simply one more retelling of the story all the prophets penned.

PERSIA, CUSH, AND PUT

Before concluding our discussion, it is important that we identify the final five nations involved in the Gog invasion. Scholars, historians, and even most popular prophecy books generally all agree on the identities of Persia, Cush, and Put. Persia refers to modern-day Iran. Ancient Cush, often translated as Ethiopia, is actually a reference to the region immediately south of Egypt: northern Sudan. Put refers to Libya, and could possibly include other portions of Northern Africa.

GOMER AND TOGARMAH

The last two nations, Gomer and Togarmah, once again refer to modern-day Turkey. In the earlier part of the last century, it was common for prophecy teachers to tie Gomer to Germany. But today, this view has been rejected by virtually all reputable Bible scholars and prophecy teachers. Almost every Bible atlas will place both Gomer in Turkey and Togarmah in eastern Turkey, among them:

- *Holman Bible Atlas*[56]

- *Oxford Bible Atlas*[57]

- *The IVP Atlas of Bible History*[58]

- *New Bible Atlas*[59]

- *The Macmillan Bible Atlas*[60]

- *Zondervan Atlas of the Bible*[61]

- *Zondervan Illustrated Bible Backgrounds Commentary*[62]

- *New Moody Atlas of the Bible*[63]

- *Baker Bible Atlas*[64]

THE REMOTE PARTS OF THE NORTH

It is important to briefly discuss an argument frequently used by Russian-Gog theorists concerning the phrase "the uttermost parts of the north."

Ezekiel 38:14–15 says, "Therefore, son of man, prophesy, and say to Gog, Thus says the Lord God: On that day when my people Israel are dwelling securely, will you not know it? You will come from your place out of the uttermost parts of the north." Because Gog is said to come from "the uttermost parts of the north" (Hebrew: *yerekah yerekah tsaphown*), many say that this can only mean Russia. Prophecy teacher David Reagan, for example, has written: "Ezekiel 38 clearly states that the invasion will be led by the Prince of Rosh coming from 'the remote parts of the north' (Ezekiel 38:15). There is no way that Turkey could be considered a nation located in "the remote parts of the north.""[65]

Clyde Billington also argues that this phrase cannot be referring to Turkey: "Note again that Ezekiel refers to this coalition as coming from 'the remotest parts of the north.' This cannot be Asia Minor."[66]

Joel C. Rosenberg follows the same line of reasoning, drawing some dramatic conclusions: "Ezekiel 38:15 says that Gog 'will come from your place out of the remote parts of the north' . . . The country that is farthest to the north in relation to Israel is Russia. Thus, we can determine that a Russian dictator will build a diplomatic and military coalition to surround and attack the State of Israel in the End-Times."[67]

But this argument is not thought through, for within the same chapter in Ezekiel, the very same phrase (Hebrew: *yerekah yerekah tsaphown*) is used of Togarmah (v. 6), and virtually all scholars agree that Togarmah was located in eastern Turkey or in neighboring Armenia. As such, any argument that says, "There is no way that Turkey could be considered a nation located in 'the remote parts of the north'" falls flat on its face. If Togarmah in Turkey is referred to as being in "the remote parts of the north," then there is absolutely no basis to use precisely the same phrase to argue for a Russian identification of Gog. In fact, because we know that the phrase "remote parts of the north" is used elsewhere in Ezekiel to refer to Turkey, it would also only stand to reason that the same phrase applied to Gog would establish him as coming from Turkey. In a slightly more technical explanation of the weakness of this argument, J. Paul Tanner has explained:

> Those who often equate the Ezekiel passage with Russia point out that Gog and its allies do not simply come from "the north" but from the "remote parts of the north" (Ezek 38:6, 15; 39:2). In fact the NASB reads "the remotest part of the north" in Ezek 39:2. In the NT, however, the three phrases are essentially the same: *yrkty spwn*. Hence there is no reason to translate Ezek 39:2 differently than the previous two references. The noun *yrkh* has the basic idea of "extreme portion," "extremity." But other occurrences of the word when used geographically reveal that the term does not have to mean the farthest point away. The expression *myrkty-rs* ("from the remote parts of the earth") occurs four times in Jeremiah. In Jer 6:22 we read: "Behold, a people is coming from the north land, and a great nation will be aroused from the remote parts of the earth." There is general agreement that this refers to Babylon in this context. Jeremiah 50:41 reads: "Behold, a people is coming from the north, and a great nation and many kings will be aroused from the remote parts of the earth." The context is dealing with God's judgment upon Babylon and the enemies that he will bring upon Babylon. Although the invaders are not clearly specified, there is mention of the "kings of the Medes" in the general context (51:11; cf. 51:27, 28). In two other verses (25:32; 31:8) God is depicted as stirring up nations from the remote parts of the earth, but the reference is quite vague. Outside of Ezekiel 38–39 *yrkh* is used in a geographical sense of nations from the Middle East, thereby demonstrating that the expression need not be taken to mean the farthest point possible.[68]

CONCLUSION CONCERNING THE NATIONS INVOLVED:

In conclusion, then, after having considered all of the many arguments concerning the identity of Gog and his coalition, we can confidently say that the invading coalition of Ezekiel 38–39 refers to the following nations:

Ancient Name	Modern Nation
Magog	Turkey
Rosh (if a nation)	Turkey
Meshech	Turkey
Tubal	Turkey
Persia	Iran
Cush	Sudan
Put	Libya
Gomer	Turkey
Togarmah	Turkey, Armenia

Of course, this list is not exhaustive. Many scholars see Ezekiel's list as detailing only one major nation from each corner of the compass as indicating that Ezekiel's list is a non-comprehensive summary. In fact, the text specifically says that many other nations will be included in this invasion (Ezekiel 38:6). Is it possible that Russia will participate in the last-days invasion? Yes, but nowhere is this ever expressly prophesied in Scripture. To discuss this possibility would be nothing more than speculation. As we have said from the beginning of this book, as students of the Scriptures, our end-time perspective should emphasize that which the Scriptures emphasize, and where they are silent, we should remain silent or use extreme caution. Because this prophecy so clearly emphasizes Turkey as the head of the coming Antichrist's invasion of Israel, it would seem quite reasonable for Bible students to watch Turkey very carefully. Of course, in light of the great debate and wide range of opinion that has surrounded this passage for thousands of years, in our watchfulness, we must also remain humble and cautious. As always, it is God who knows best.

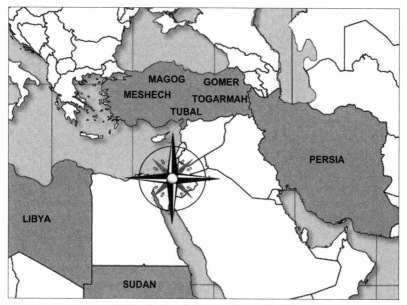

Distribution of the nations in Gog's coalition, according to Ezekiel[69]

1 6

PSALM 83

THE PURPOSE OF THIS CHAPTER is to address what has in recent years become a very widely held theory regarding Psalm 83. This theory, popularized by Bill Salus in his book *Isralestine*, holds that the Bible predicts at least three specific future invasions of the nation of Israel. The first of these invasions, it is taught, is described in Psalm 83. The second invasion is most commonly referred to as "the Battle of Gog of Magog." We have already dealt with this invasion in great detail. After these two invasions, some believe that we will see yet a third massive invasion of Israel, led by the Antichrist and his armies. This last of the three invasions most refer to as the Battle of Armageddon. So in summary, this growing popular theory holds that three distinct invasions of Israel will occur in the following order:

1.   The Psalm 83 invasion of Israel

2.   The Gog of Magog invasion of Israel (Ezekiel 38–39)

3.   The Antichrist's invasion of Israel (Revelation 16, 19)

But there are at least six fatal problems with this emerging popular theory. The first is that most scholars reject the idea that Psalm 83 is even an actual prophecy, but is simply "a national prayer of lament." Second, this interpretation approaches biblical prophecy from a mixture of the historicist approach and the futurist approach, rather than a consistent futurist approach. We will elaborate on what this means. Third, the primary reasoning behind the theory is rooted in poor logic and reasoning. Fourth, even if Psalm 83 is considered to be a prophecy, then the proponents of this theory have dramatically failed to properly identify all of the nations and peoples involved. Fifth, this theory's advocates ignore the numerous similarities between Ezekiel 38–39 and Psalm 83 contained within these passages. And sixth, the Bible is clear that several of the nations in Psalm 83 are judged, not several years prior, but specifically at the Battle of Armageddon and the Day of the Lord. We will discuss each of these problems in order.

PROBLEM #1: PSALM 83 IS NOT A PROPHECY
ABOUT AN INVASION

The first problem with the Psalm 83, multiple-invasion theory is that most conservative scholars reject the idea that this chapter even contains a prophecy concerning an invasion. Instead, as Marvin Tate states, "Ps 83 is generally accepted as a national lament, manifesting several characteristics of this form."[1] Dr. Thomas Ice has taken particular theological umbrage with the growing popular view that Psalm 83 is predicting a soon-coming invasion of Israel. Dr. Ice is correct that most of the nations mentioned in Psalm 83 are specifically revealed to be judged at the Day of the Lord:

> There is absolutely no doubt that Psalm 83 is 100% inspired by God, just like all the rest of Scripture. However, there is no prophecy in this Psalm, simply a petition to God by Asaph to judge those enemies that are against Israel. *I challenge anyone to show me a prophetic portion or statement in Psalm 83!* The Psalm is a detailed request by Asaph to judge the enemies surrounding Israel. God does not answer Asaph in Psalm 83. I believe that God will one day judge these enemies mentioned in Psalm 83, but I do not believe that based upon this Psalm.[2]

Author and teacher Mark Hitchcock agrees with Ice:

We have to remember that the Psalms were written long before the prophets began to write and give specific prophecies concerning the nations. The prophets are where we look to find specific prophecies concerning the nations and end time events. There are certainly messianic prophecies in the Psalms, but I'm not aware of other specific prophecies in the Psalms concerning the Gentile nations in the end times. It may be that constructing a separate end time war out of Psalm 83 is reading too much into a text that is simply saying that Israel has been and always will be surrounded by enemies and that some day the Lord will finally deal with them. It could be that this national lament during the Davidic reign is raising the ubiquitous question for Israel—why does everyone hate us? When will it ever end? God's reassuring answer is, "don't worry; I will come some day to destroy them and make it right." God is bolstering and encouraging the nation at the very beginning of the Davidic kingship that He will ultimately prevail over His enemies and will protect His people from extinction.[3]

While it is certainly possible that Psalm 83 contains shades of a last-days prophecy, Ice and Hitchcock are correct when they emphasize that it should be viewed in a general nature and not as pointing to some specific and distinct "Psalm 83 war," as many students of prophecy have now named it. Instead, as we will discuss further, all of the nations listed in Psalm 83 will be judged at the Battle of Armageddon and the Day of the Lord.

PROBLEM #2: INCONSISTENT METHODOLOGY

The first principle that I think many who hold to the multiple-invasion theory miss is the fact that all biblical prophecy is ultimately Messiah-centric and Day of the Lord–centric. The primary focus and prophetic burden of all of the prophets is the return of the Messiah and the events that surround His coming. In easy-to-understand terms, all of the biblical prophets, though each one spoke through the diverse circumstances and events of his day, were ultimately prophesying and pointing us to the Day of the Lord and the messianic kingdom that follows. This belief is a central feature of what is known as the *futurist* method of interpretation. Alternately, the approach that looks to the Bible as a pan-historical prophecy sourcebook is called *historicism.* But this is not the nature of biblical prophecy. While some may look to the Bible to find things such as the assassination of President Kennedy or the World Trade Center attacks, these things are not the focus of the prophets. Many read the Bible in the same way that they read the prophecies of Nostradamus. This historicist method of interpretation is today rejected by most conservative students of prophecy. The problem with the view that places Psalm 83 prior to the beginning of the final seven-year tribulation is that it represents an inconsistent mixture of the historicist and futurist positions. Dr. Thomas Ice has well articulated this problem:

> Further evidence of a futurist retreat toward historicism within some otherwise futurist circles, can be seen by those who insist that Psalm 83 is a war that will take place before the rapture, during the current church age and not in association with the tribulation. Historicists believe that Old Testament prophetic passages can be fulfilled during the current church age. Consistent futurists believe that future Old Testament prophecy will start to be fulfilled after the rapture of the Church, except the prophecy of the rapture itself. Bill Salus champions this view in his book entitled *Israelestine* . . . Salus teaches that before the tribulation, before the Battle of Gog and Magog, which will take place before the tribulation, and even before the rapture, toward the end of the current church age, Israel will be invaded by all the nations surrounding her . . . My contention is that Salus, who would consider himself a futurist, has put forth a historicist interpretative approach of Psalm 83, along with other exegetical errors. Salus contends that Psalm 83 teaches an Israeli war with her surrounding neighbors before the rapture takes place that will set the stage for post-rapture events like the Gog & Magog war and the tribulation. I believe that such a view is simply a product of Salus' fertile imagination and has no basis in the biblical text (1 Tim. 1:4; 2 Tim. 4:3–5) . . . Such a view is blatant historicism, which was proved defective at least a hundred and fifty years ago.[4]

PROBLEM #3: FLAWED REASONING

The most significant reason that so many believe this theory is because each of these various passages contain certain details that the other passages do not. For instance, among the invading nations, Psalm 83 lists a few that are not mentioned in Ezekiel 38–39. Thus it is reasoned, these two passages must be speaking of two separate invasions.

In my opinion, the reasoning that forms the very foundation of this theory is deeply flawed. Consider, for example, if this method of interpretation were applied to the four gospels where various retellings of the same events often contain different, and sometimes even seemingly contradictory, details. Of course, the details are not genuinely contradictory, but in some cases, on the surface they may appear to be so. If we applied the same reasoning used by the proponents of the "Psalm 83 war" theory to the Gospels, our understanding of the ministry of Jesus would be pure chaos. Thoughtful students of Scripture should reject the idea that just because one prophetic passage contains some information that another does not, it proves that we are dealing with two distinct battles.

PROBLEM #4: IMPROPER IDENTIFICATION OF THE NATIONS OF PSALM 83

The fourth problem with the multiple-invasion theory is that it fails to properly identify the nations involved. Let's look at the actual nations delineated in Psalm 83: "For they conspire with one accord; against you they make a covenant—the tents of Edom and the Ishmaelites, Moab and the Hagrites, Gebal and Ammon and Amalek, Philistia with the inhabitants of Tyre; Asshur also has joined them; they are the strong arm of the children of Lot" (vv. 5–8).

According to Bill Salus, author of *Israelestine*,

> The modern equivalents of the Psalm 83 confederates are: tents of Edom (Palestinian Refugees and Southern Jordanians), Ishmaelites (Saudi Arabians), Moab (Palestinian Refugees and Central Jordanians), Hagrites (Egyptians), Gebal (Northern Lebanese), Ammon (Palestinian Refugees and Northern Jordanians), Amalek (Arabs South of Israel), Philistia (Palestinian Refugees and Hamas of the Gaza Strip), inhabitants of Tyre (Hezbollah and Southern Lebanese), Assyria (Syrians and perhaps Northern Iraqis), and the children of Lot (Moab and Ammon above).[5]

I would largely agree with most of Salus's identifications, however, I would add that beyond these nations and groups, a few others are also included.

ASSYRIA

While Salus claims that the mention of Assur (Assyria) points only to modern-day Syria and Iraq, such an identification is too limiting. The capital of ancient Assyria was Nineveh, which is in modern-day northern Iraq, near the city of Mosul, but far from speaking only to the region of northern Iraq, Assyria included a much larger region. Because modern conservative scholarship holds that Psalm 83 was written sometime close to 950 BC during the reign of King David, we should consider the whole region that was part of the Assyrian Empire during this time. Throughout this period, beyond Iraq and Syria, Assyria also included a substantial portion of what is now the nation of Turkey. As such, Turkey should be included in Psalm 83's list of nations.

See the following map of Assyria:

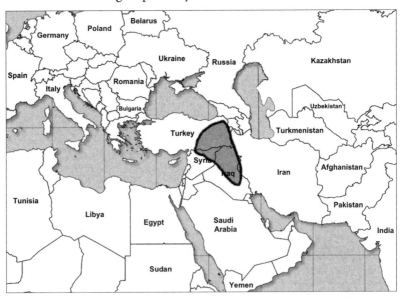

The Assyrian Empire (c. 950 B.C. during the reign of King David)[6]

THE ISHMAELITES

Beyond Assyria, there is another very important name listed among the invaders: the Ishmaelites. Because the Ishmaelites as a people have remained fairly consistent throughout the centuries, if Psalm 83 is to be understood prophetically, then we would understand its use of the term "Ishmaelites" to be a general reference to the greater Arab peoples. This vast growth and dispersal of the Ishmaelites was even prophesied in various passages in Genesis:

> The angel of the LORD also said to her, "I will surely multiply your offspring so that they cannot be numbered for multitude." (16:10)

> As for Ishmael, I have heard you; behold, I have blessed him and will make him fruitful and multiply him greatly. He shall father twelve princes, and I will make him into a great nation. (17:20)

> Up! Lift up the boy, and hold him fast with your hand, for I will make him into a great nation. (21:18)

When Psalm 83 was written, the Ishmaelites would have lived throughout the greater region of the Arabian Peninsula and portions of Egypt, Jordan, and Iraq. Today, of course, this would be expanded to include Lebanon, Syria, and most of North Africa.

The point is that if we consider this expanded interpretation of Assyria and the Ishmaelites, the nations and peoples mentioned in Psalm 83 point us to a region far more substantial than the countries that immediately surround Israel. Instead we would be looking at the modern countries shown on the following map:

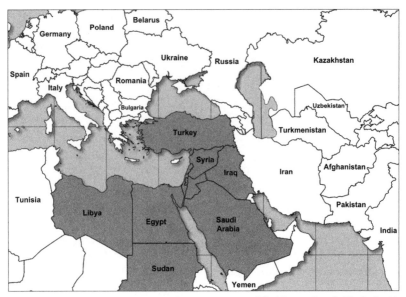

The Nations Specified by Psalm 83

PROBLEM #5: FAILURE TO ACKNOWLEDGE THE SIMILARITIES OF EZEKIEL 38–39 AND PSALM 83

Although Psalm 83 and Ezekiel 38–39 do contain differences, they also contain some dramatic similarities. Though one passage may emphasize some nations over others, in the final analysis, both passages are speaking of the same general region. Several nations are not included in both prophecies, but more of them are. Beyond this, the open-ended phrase in Ezekiel "and many nations with you" leaves the door wide-open for the involvement of any of the nations mentioned in Psalm 83.

Ezekiel 38–39	Psalm 83
Turkey	Turkey
Syria	Syria
Libya and Northern Sudan	Northern Africa
Iran	Arabia
"And many nations with you"	Jordan
	Egypt
	Iraq
	Arabs of West Bank and Gaza

Ultimately the distinctions between the two passages are easily accounted for by the differing emphasis of each passage. While Psalm 83 emphasizes a list of nations that immediately surround Israel, as we have already seen, Ezekiel only lists the leader of the invasion as well as one nation from each of the four corners of the compass. By highlighting a single nation from each corner of the compass, Ezekiel was emphasizing that beyond the nations mentioned, other nations from all corners of the compass would be involved. See the following map of Ezekiel's invasion.

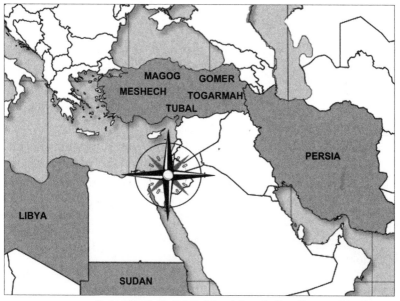

Ezekiel 38–39: Turkish-Led Attack from the Four Corners of the Compass

Because the primary basis for the multiple-invasion theory is founded on the alleged drastic differences between these two passages, after having examined these passages in further detail, I believe it is inaccurate to claim that they point to drastically distinct nations. If indeed Psalm 83 is even a prophecy, then it would make far more sense to simply see it as another telling of the same invasion described in Ezekiel 38–39.

PROBLEM #6: THE PSALM 83 NATIONS ARE JUDGED AT THE DAY
OF THE LORD

The final and perhaps most fatal flaw in the Psalm 83 multiple-invasion
theory is that several of the nations specified in the psalm are specifically
mentioned in numerous other passages as being reserved for judgment on
the Day of the Lord and the Battle of Armageddon. We addressed a few
of these passages in chapter 2. There we saw that most of the nations and
peoples listed in Psalm 83 will specifically be judged on the Day of the
Lord. These include Edom (Numbers 24, Obadiah, Ezekiel 25, Isaiah 34,
63), Moab (Numbers 24, Isaiah 25), Egypt (Habakkuk 3, Zephaniah 2,
Isaiah 19), Arabia (Ezekiel 25, 30), Philistia (Joel 3, Zephaniah 2, Ezekiel
25,) Lebanon (Joel 3), and Assyria (Micah 5, Zephaniah 2).

Concerning the destruction of Edom, the prophet Obadiah was clear
that it will take place in the context of the Day of the Lord. Yet Salus uses
the phrase "The Day of the Lord is near" to argue that it happens well
prior to the actual Day of the Lord. But this represents a fundamental
misunderstanding of this commonly used expression. When a prophet
declares that the Day of the Lord is near, it is a call to repent in light of
the impending judgments of that day. Thus when Obadiah wrote, "The
Day of the LORD is near," he was warning his readers to repent in light of
the judgments that will take place on that day, including the destruction
of Edom. As Dr. Ice observes:

> When will Obadiah's prophecy be fulfilled? Verse 15 says, "For the day
> of the LORD draws near on all the nations. As you have done, it will be
> done to you. Your dealings will return on your own head." The passage
> clearly says it will be fulfilled when "the day of the LORD draws near
> on all the nations." Such an event is clearly scheduled to occur at the
> same time when Isaiah, Jeremiah, Ezekiel, Amos, and others indicate
> that the nations will be judged at the end of the tribulation, during
> the Campaign of Armageddon.[7]

Dr. Ice is absolutely correct. But of course, his observations could
equally be applied to the many other Islamic nations that make up the
Ezekiel 38–39 alliance. All of the Islamic world that comes against Israel
will be judged at the Day of the Lord and the Battle of Armageddon.

DANGERS OF THE PSALM 83 WAR THEORY

From a pastoral perspective, I believe that "the Psalm 83 war theory" represents a great danger to the body of Christ. Because this theory holds that after the Psalm 83 confederacy is defeated, Israel as a nation will literally occupy all of the nations that now surround her, it adheres to a certain Israeli triumphalism that is simply not taught in Scripture. As Salus has explained, "Because of this Israeli conquest over the inner circle of the core surrounding Arab populations of Palestinians, Syrians, Saudi Arabians, Egyptians, Lebanese, and Jordanians, Israel's borders are enlarged, prosperity increases, and national stature is enhanced."[8] After Israel has defeated the nations that surround her, Salus has claimed that Israel will experience

> a condition of regional superiority, which enables it to dwell securely in an otherwise insecure neighborhood. The Jews still dispersed throughout the world at that time will flow back into their safe haven of Israel. With this influx of Jewish population, the Jews will exploit the resources of the conquered Arab territories and the people will be set to experience the "restoration of their fortunes." At that time Israel will become one of the wealthiest nations in the world, perhaps the wealthiest of them all.[9]

My personal concern with such a view, first, is that it stands in direct conflict with what the Bible says lies ahead for Israel. What Salus has done is taken the many promises of God to Israel that will be fulfilled during the millennial kingdom of the Messiah and placed them in the very near future, prior to the return of Jesus. He has taken the victory that will be accomplished by Jesus and given the Israeli Defense Forces the credit. But when one surveys the many prophecies throughout the Scriptures concerning Israel, it is obvious that very dark days lie ahead. The Church must be prepared to stand with Israel and the Jewish people during these times. On a personal note, I would like to say that I consider Bill Salus a good brother who has always been a gentleman and represented Jesus well. My desire and purpose here is not to criticize Bill personally. However, I genuinely believe that the Psalm 83 multiple-invasion theory is demonstrably unscriptural, and instead of preparing believers for the days ahead, it has the potential to inspire passivity and set many up for a big letdown and great disillusionment.

1 7

ISAIAH AND MICAH 5:
THE ASSYRIAN

NOTHER ESSENTIAL BIBLICAL MOTIF related to the Antichrist is "the Assyrian." The theme of the Assyrian is found primarily in the books of Isaiah and Micah. Both of these prophets prophesied in great detail concerning both Jesus the Messiah and the Antichrist. As we will see, the theme that runs through the prophecies of both Isaiah and Micah is the final conflict between Jesus the Messiah and the Antichrist, who throughout these prophecies is referred to again and again as "the Assyrian."

THE CONTEXT OF THE BOOK OF ISAIAH

Briefly, the historical context of Isaiah relates to conflict in the prophet's day between the two Hebrew kingdoms: the Northern Kingdom, often referred to as Israel or Ephraim, and the Southern Kingdom, referred to as Judah. Israel had allied itself with Aram-Damascus against the looming threat from Assyria. The threat of an Assyrian invasion was ever pressing. God's call on his people was to trust in Him rather than in military alliances with surrounding pagan kingdoms. God's promise was that a military leader would be born from the line of David who would deliver all of God's people from "the Assyrian." The problem, however, is that this never occurred in history. The Assyrians decimated the northern kingdom of Israel and took most of its inhabitants away into exile. But as for the promised Messiah who would defeat the Assyrian in a military battle, this is entirely prophetic; it has yet to come. Many Bible scholars have concluded that the term "the Assyrian," while used historically to refer to the various kings of Assyria, is also a clear reference to the Antichrist, who will be defeated by Jesus when He returns. Then, in Isaiah 13–23, after prophesying the coming judgment against the Antichrist, we are given a list of many of the nations that will be destroyed or judged with him when the Messiah comes to bring the promised victory to His people. This, then, is the background and context of the book of Isaiah, which we will examine in this chapter.

THE ASSYRIAN IN ISAIAH

Many are surprised to find out that the fuller context of some of the most famous messianic prophecies in all of Scripture revolve around the theme of the conflict between Jesus and the Antichrist. Consider, for instance, the following passage in Isaiah. Untold thousands of Christmas cards, plays, sermons, and narratives have centered around this verse: "Therefore the Lord himself will give you a sign. Behold, the virgin shall conceive and bear a son, and shall call his name Immanuel" (Isaiah 7:14).

But rarely does anyone continue reading the passage to discover its original context. If they did, they would soon learn that this prophecy actually refers to an event that occurred in Isaiah's day when a young girl bore a child and named him Immanuel. This child was to be a prophetic sign concerning the looming invasion of the northern kingdom of Israel by the Assyrian armies. Of course, this prophecy actually has two fulfillments; one in Isaiah's day and another through Mary and Jesus. You see, the word used in this prophecy that is most often translated as "virgin" doesn't always necessarily mean a maiden who has never had sexual relations. Rather, the Hebrew word used here (*alma*) most literally refers to a very young girl who was most often not yet married and was thus a virgin. In Mary's case, of course, she was truly a virgin, but in the case of the first *alma*, she both conceived and gave birth through entirely natural means. After this young girl gave birth to her Immanuel, Isaiah explained what signs would follow:

He shall eat curds and honey when he knows how to refuse the evil and choose the good. For before the boy knows how to refuse the evil and choose the good, the land whose two kings you dread will be deserted. The LORD will bring upon you and upon your people and upon your father's house such days as have not come since the day that Ephraim departed from Judah—the king of Assyria. In that day the LORD will whistle for the fly that is at the end of the streams of Egypt, and for the bee that is in the land of Assyria. And they will all come and settle in the steep ravines, and in the clefts of the rocks, and on all the thornbushes, and on all the pastures. In that day the Lord will shave with a razor that is hired beyond the River—with the king of Assyria—the head and the hair of the feet, and it will sweep away the beard also. (Isaiah 7:15–20)

Isaiah says that before the child grows up, the king of Assyria would invade the northern kingdom of Israel. The graphic descriptions of the shaving of the head, beards, and legs of the Israelites is an indication of the abasement, the complete humbling, and ultimately the enslavement that God was bringing to the northern tribes through the Assyrians. The point in citing this passage is to show that as soon as the famous messianic Immanuel prophecy is introduced, the Assyrian, or the king of Assyria, is also brought into the picture. Again, the events described in this passage refer to real historical events that occurred in Isaiah's day. Yet the historical king of Assyria was merely a type of the Antichrist—the ultimate prophetic invader of Israel. Throughout Isaiah's prophecy, we will see this same Messiah-versus-Assyrian theme repeated several times. Nearly all of chapter 8 centers around the coming invasion of Israel by the Assyrian: "The Lord is bringing up against them the waters of the River, mighty and many, the king of Assyria and all his glory. And it will rise over all its channels and go over all its banks, and it will sweep on into Judah, it will overflow and pass on, reaching even to the neck, and its outspread wings will fill the breadth of your land" (vv. 7–8).

But then in chapter 9, once again, we are informed of God's ultimate solution. There Isaiah gave us what is unarguably the most famous messianic prophecy in the Old Testament:

But there will be no gloom for her who was in anguish. In the former time he brought into contempt the land of Zebulun and the land of Naphtali, but in the latter time he has made glorious the way of the sea, the land beyond the Jordan, Galilee of the nations. The people who walked in darkness have seen a great light; those who dwelt in a land of deep darkness, on them has light shined . . . For the yoke of his burden, and the staff for his shoulder, the rod of his oppressor, you have broken as on the day of Midian. For every boot of the tramping warrior in battle tumult and every garment rolled in blood will be burned as fuel for the fire. For to us a child is born, to us a son is given; and the government shall be upon his shoulder, and his name shall be called Wonderful Counselor, Mighty God, Everlasting Father, Prince of Peace. Of the increase of his government and of peace there will be no end, on the throne of David and over his kingdom, to establish it and to uphold it with justice and with righteousness from this time forth and forevermore. The zeal of the LORD of hosts will do this. (vv. 1–7)

This passage declares that the Messiah will deliver Israel from the Assyrian in the same manner that Gideon in Judges 8 delivered Israel from the Midianite armies. There is a fascinating connection here to the last-days Islamic armies. A bit of history is necessary. After having defeated the Midianites, Gideon's men implored him to rule over them. But Gideon refused this position, as it belongs to the Lord alone. Then Gideon made a request of his own. He asked the Israelites to give him the gold jewelry belonging to the defeated armies: "And Gideon said to them, 'Let me make a request of you: every one of you give me the earrings from his spoil.' For they had golden earrings, because they were Ishmaelites" (Judges 8:22–24).

But what is so fascinating is that the "ornaments" of these Ishmaelites and their camels (v. 21) were shaped like crescent moons:

And they answered, "We will willingly give them." And they spread a cloak, and every man threw in it the earrings of his spoil. And the weight of the golden earrings that he requested was 1,700 shekels of gold, besides the crescent ornaments and the pendants and the purple garments worn by the kings of Midian, and besides the collars that were around the necks of their camels. (vv. 25–26)

So we are told that the Messiah's final victory over the Assyrians would be similar to Gideon's historical victory over the Ishmaelites. Then when we examine this victory, we see that Gideon, a type of the Messiah, is seen stripping crescent moon ornaments off of the kings. The crescent moon, of course, is the symbol of Islam, featured prominently on most Muslim flags as well as on top of virtually every mosque throughout the earth. When Jesus returns and defeats the invading and persecuting Islamic armies of the Antichrist, He will likewise remove the symbols of Islam and idolatry from among the nations.

A second interesting connection here is seen in the word used for crescent ornaments, the Hebrew *śa·hă·rō·nîm*. This word is closely related to *śā·har*, which is used later in Isaiah 14, a passage wherein the Lord refers to Satan as Lucifer, son of the morning star (*śā·har*) (v. 13). Then only a few verses later, we see that He "will crush the Assyrian in my land; on my mountains I will trample him down." This is also precisely the same picture as is painted in the book of Revelation, where Jesus is portrayed as crushing the Antichrist and his armies outside Jerusalem, also referred to as the "the great winepress of the wrath of God" (Rev. 14:19, 19:15). In other words, the picture painted is of God gathering the armies of the Assyrian into one location, where He will squish them like grapes.

So despite the numerous references throughout Isaiah to the Messiah destroying the king of Assyria in the land of Israel, historically this deliverance never occurred. Instead, Sennacherib, the king of Assyria, took numerous cities in Judah, and laid siege to Jerusalem. According to 2 Kings 18–19 and parallel passages in 2 Chronicles 32:1–23, the angel of the Lord did kill a great number of the Assyrian soldiers, but this cannot be that which of which Isaiah so frequently spoke, because: (1) Sennacherib, the "king of Assyria" was not killed in the land; (2) the victory was not carried out by the Messiah; and (3) ultimately, Assyria's chipping away of Israel and Judah was eventually followed by Nebuchadnezzar, who left Judah virtually desolate. In Sennacherib's day, the prophesied deliverer did not come; the "yoke" was not shattered. And thus, scholars agree that Isaiah's theme of the coming Messiah who would destroy the Assyrian is a reference to the future, when Jesus the Messiah will deliver the Israelites from the invading armies of "the Assyrian."

ISRAEL'S MISPLACED TRUST

Throughout Isaiah's prophecy, God is repeatedly calling on His people not to place their trust in natural political alliances, but rather to simply trust in Him. Like ancient Israel, the Israel of the future will also rely on political alliances, treaties, and false promises of peace. She will accept the covenant made with the Antichrist: "And he shall make a strong covenant with many for one week, and for half of the week he shall put an end to sacrifice and offering. And on the wing of abominations shall come one who makes desolate, until the decreed end is poured out on the desolator" (Daniel 9:27).

But then the Antichrist will renege on his agreements and will invade the land "that has recovered from war, whose people were gathered from many nations to the mountains of Israel" (Ezekiel 38:8). The Lord, through Isaiah, rebukes Israel severely for making this treaty, which He calls a "covenant with death." Rather than trusting in the Messiah, "the tested corner stone," Israel will instead trust in the peace agreement. The result will be their being invaded and beaten down by the Assyrian:

> Therefore hear the word of the LORD, you scoffers, who rule this people in Jerusalem! Because you have said, "We have made a covenant with death, and with Sheol we have an agreement, when the overwhelming whip passes through it will not come to us, for we have made lies our refuge, and in falsehood we have taken shelter"; therefore thus says the Lord GOD, "Behold, I am the one who has laid as a foundation in Zion, a stone, a tested stone, a precious cornerstone, of a sure foundation: 'Whoever believes will not be in haste.' . . . Then your covenant with death will be annulled, and your agreement with Sheol will not stand; when the overwhelming scourge passes through, you will be beaten down by it." (Isaiah 28:14–18)

Then after the Lord has finished with His redeeming work of chastisement toward His people, He will punish the Assyrian: "When the Lord has finished all his work against Mount Zion and Jerusalem, he will say, 'I will punish the king of Assyria for the willful pride of his heart and the haughty look in his eyes'" (Isaiah 10:12).

After this work is complete, and the surviving remnant of Israel has returned to the Lord and repented of their reliance on the Antichrist and his false promises, "the remnant of Israel, the survivors of the house of

Jacob, will no longer rely on him who struck them down but will truly rely on the LORD, the Holy One of Israel. A remnant will return, a remnant of Jacob will return to the Mighty God. Though your people, O Israel, be like the sand by the sea, only a remnant will return" (vv. 20–22).

In conclusion, then, as we have seen, whether it be the prophecy of Immanuel (God with us) to come in Isaiah 7, or the Prince of Peace in Isaiah 9, in both of these passages, the fuller context is the coming of the Messiah to break the Assyrian. But despite this clear and repeated theme throughout Isaiah, nowhere is the conflict between Jesus and the Assyrian described more clearly and more concisely than in the prophecy of Micah.

MICAH 5

Now let's consider the prophecies concerning the coming of the Messiah as found in Micah 5. The following verse begins with another famous messianic prophecy, concerning the Messiah's place of birth: "But you, O Bethlehem Ephrathah, who are too little to be among the clans of Judah, from you shall come forth for me one who is to be ruler in Israel, whose coming forth is from of old, from ancient days" (v. 2).

The Gospels record that the chief priests and scribes consulted this very verse when King Herod gathered them together to inquire as to where the Messiah was to be born. Their answer was unequivocal; He would be born in Bethlehem of Judea (Matthew 2:4–5). Why did the Jews of Jesus' day so look forward to this passage? "Therefore he shall give them up until the time when she who is in labor has given birth; then the rest of his brothers shall return to the people of Israel" (Micah 5:3). This coming Messiah was to be a sign to the Israelites that an epoch had ended. No longer would they be abandoned by God. They would live securely under the leadership of the Messiah: "And he shall stand and shepherd his flock in the strength of the LORD, in the majesty of the name of the LORD his God. And they shall dwell secure, for now he shall be great to the ends of the earth" (Micah 5:4).

The wording is clear. Israel would no longer have to fear their enemies. The greatness of this Messiah would reach to the ends of the earth. But it is the next verse that is so essential to consider, for there we are told that this very Messiah will deliver Israel from the invading Antichrist, whom the passage refers to as "the Assyrian": "And he shall be their peace. When the Assyrian comes into our land and treads in our palaces, then we will raise against him seven shepherds and eight princes of men; they shall shepherd the land of Assyria with the sword, and the land of Nimrod at its entrances; and he shall deliver us from the Assyrian when he comes into our land and treads within our border" (vv. 5–6).

When the "Assyrian" invaded the land of Israel, then it would be the Messiah who would be their peace, protection, and deliverance. Scholars see this passage as referring to the day when Jesus would deliver Israel from the invasion of the imperial "Assyrian" forces:

- Frederich Delitzsch has written, "The Messiah is called the Prince of peace in Isa. 9:5 . . . But in what manner? . . . By defending Israel against the attacks of the imperial power. The Messiah will prove Himself to be peace to His people . . . by the fact that He protects and saves it from the attacks of the imperial power represented by Asshur."[1]

- Leslie C. Allen wrote, "The coming of this royal hero is presented as the eventual antidote to the threat and fact of the Assyrian invasion. Eventual, because this birth lies still in the future and so his saving activity is to be later still. There will be no immediate end to Assyrian domination. The attacking imperialist will be allowed his fling for a time, but is doomed to meet his match in the person of the victorious king of Israel. In this respect Micah agrees with this promised king as the answer to the menace of Assyria."[2]

- D. A. Carson wrote, "Micah refers to future attacks against the Messiah's kingdom as being carried out by the Assyrians, who were destroyed in 612 BC, centuries before Christ's advent. Prophets did not see the centuries that separated them from the fulfillment of their predictions but saw future happenings as imminent events on a flat tableau."[3]

- And beyond modern scholars, the early church also understood the term "the Assyrian" to be a reference to the Antichrist: Hippolytus of Rome (c.170–c. 236), one of the early church's most important theologians, in the second century said, "That these things, then, are said of no one else but that tyrant, and shameless one, and adversary of God, we shall show in what follows. But Isaiah also speaks thus: 'And it shall come to pass, that when the Lord has performed His whole work upon Mount Zion and on Jerusalem, He will punish (visit) the stout mind, the king of Assyria, and the greatness (height) of the glory of his eyes.'"[4] Elsewhere, when referring to the many prophecies about the "Assyrian" found in Micah and Isaiah, Hippolytus stated quite directly that "the Assyrian is another name for the Antichrist."[5]

- Victorinus, bishop of Pettau (c. 280), who was martyred for his faith in Christ, in what is the most ancient complete commentary on the book of Revelation in our possession, stated that "the Assyrian" mentioned in Micah 5:5 is the Antichrist: "There shall be peace for our land . . . and they shall encircle Assyria—that is antichrist."[6]

- Lactantius (c. 307), yet another early church writer from the third century, stated that the Antichrist would come from precisely the same region: "A king shall arise out of Syria, born from an evil spirit, the over-thrower and destroyer of the human race, who shall destroy that which is left by the former evil, together with himself . . . But that king will not only be most disgraceful in himself, but he will also be a prophet of lies . . . and power will be given to him to do signs and wonders, by the sight of which he may entice men to adore him . . . Then he will attempt to destroy the temple of God and persecute the righteous people."[7]

Now, while it shouldn't need to be said, Assyria is not in Europe. Yet the Antichrist is clearly referred to as "the Assyrian." He will invade a "land" with "borders." This is not a passage that can be spiritualized or allegorized away. The Messiah will deliver the nation of Israel from the invasion of "the Assyrian," after which Israel will rule over the land of Assyria. Obviously, this has never happened in history. As such, this passage is impossible for *preterists* (those who view most or all biblical prophecy as past) to explain in any way that is even slightly satisfactory. In this passage, we are clearly looking at a yet-future event when a leader from the former region of the Assyrian Empire will invade the land of Israel.

ASSYRIA

In concluding, then, we see that once again, Scripture uses a historical king from the ancient Assyrian Empire as a type of the coming Antichrist. This is not insignificant, as whichever nation one may point to within the former Assyrian Empire, today they are all Muslim majority. Beyond this, we also see that the Antichrist's title, "the Assyrian," confirms the general locations that we have seen repeated in previous passages. Ezekiel's "Gog" was a ruler from the region of Turkey and Syria. Isaiah's "Assyrian" controlled much of eastern Turkey, as well as parts of Syria and Iraq. Likewise, Daniel's "king of the North" ruled over the territory of the former Seleucid Empire, which also included Turkey, Syria, and Iraq. Whether Ezekiel's "Gog," Isaiah's "Assyrian," or Daniel's "king of the North," these different terms all point to the same man, from the same region, with the same motivations. These are all references to the Antichrist. With such a repeated and clear emphasis on these geographical areas, then, how can so many continue to look to Europe for the coming end-time dictator? Once again, all of the prophets were retelling the same story. By the grace of God, through His repeated emphasis on the same portion of the world, in the same story retold again and again, His people will get the message.

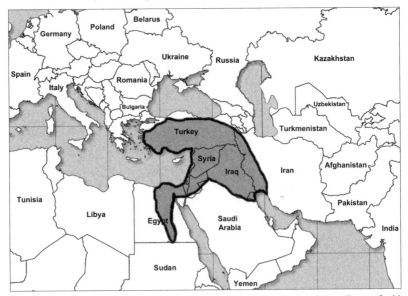

Map of Ancient Assyria (c. 650 B.C.). Region from which the Antichrist will come forth[8]

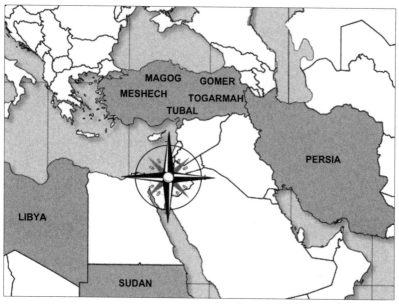

Invading nations according to Ezekiel 38–39

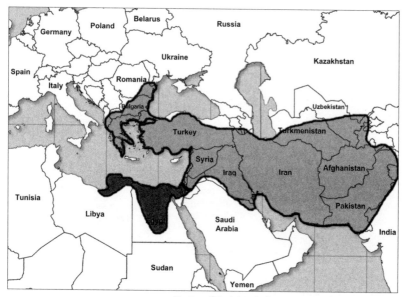

Region of Antichrist's dominion according to Daniel 11

1 8

LOVING MUSLIMS

I N WRITING THIS BOOK, I am acutely aware of the danger that some who read it will use the information to solidify their view that Muslims are "the enemy," who should be hated or feared. Of course, this is precisely the opposite response that Jesus would have His followers take. And thus, it is imperative that we take this chapter to help us see Muslims through His eyes, in such a way that encourages and empowers outreach.

Ultimately the unfolding of the ancient conflict between Muslims, Jews, and Christians began with the story of Abram and Sarai, whom the Lord would later rename Abraham and Sarah. And so it is in the book of Genesis that we find the origin of this historic clash. The Lord had promised Abram and Sarai that the day would come when they would have a child, through whom all the nations of the earth would be blessed. But the promise had been a long time in coming, and they both became impatient and began to take things into their own hands. Sarai's terrible idea is contained at the beginning of chapter 16:

> Now Sarai, Abram's wife, had borne him no children. She had a female Egyptian servant whose name was Hagar. And Sarai said to Abram, "Behold now, the LORD has prevented me from bearing children. Go in to my servant; it may be that I shall obtain children by her." And Abram listened to the voice of Sarai. So, after Abram had lived ten years in the land of Canaan, Sarai, Abram's wife, took Hagar the Egyptian,

her servant, and gave her to Abram her husband as a wife. And he went in to Hagar . . . (vv. 1–4)

Regrettably, Sarai's awful idea of having her husband sleep with her maidservant was matched by Abram's equally foolish agreement to do so. And not surprisingly, we immediately begin to see the snowballing effect of their poor choices: ". . . and she conceived. And when she saw that she had conceived, she looked with contempt on her mistress. And Sarai said to Abram, 'May the wrong done to me be on you! I gave my servant to your embrace, and when she saw that she had conceived, she looked on me with contempt. May the LORD judge between you and me!'" (vv. 4–5).

Abram's response was to shirk any responsibility for his own actions. Instead, he gave Sarai permission to do whatever she desired to Hagar: "But Abram said to Sarai, 'Behold, your servant is in your power; do to her as you please.' Then Sarai dealt harshly with her, and she fled from her" (v. 6).

Hagar ended up in the desert, and there she was encountered by the Lord, who promised her that her offspring would be so greatly multiplied, they would be beyond counting:

The angel of the LORD found her by a spring of water in the wilderness, the spring on the way to Shur. And he said, "Hagar, servant of Sarai, where have you come from and where are you going?" She said, "I am fleeing from my mistress Sarai." The angel of the LORD said to her, "Return to your mistress and submit to her." The angel of the LORD also said to her, "I will surely multiply your offspring so that they cannot be numbered for multitude." (vv. 7–10)

Then came one of the pivotal moments of the story. God Himself named Hagar's child: "And the angel of the LORD said to her, "Behold, you are pregnant and shall bear a son. You shall call his name Ishmael, because the LORD has listened to your affliction. He shall be a wild donkey of a man, his hand against everyone and everyone's hand against him, and he shall dwell over against all his kinsmen" (vv. 11–12).

A couple of important points should be considered here. First, the name Ishmael means "God hears." There are very few people in Scripture that were named by God before birth, but Ishmael is one of them. The Lord imparted a prophetic promise to Ishmael through his name: God would hear him. Second, we see that Ishmael would be a "wild donkey of a man" who would be at war with everyone, and everyone would likewise be in conflict with him. Today Arab Muslims, many of whom trace their ancestry back to Ishmael, often look to this verse and accuse the Jews of having long ago inserted this prophecy into the Scriptures to insult the Arab people.

The chapter concludes with Hagar returning to the camp.

> So she called the name of the LORD who spoke to her, "You are a God of seeing," for she said, "Truly here I have seen him who looks after me." Therefore the well was called Beer-lahai-roi; it lies between Kadesh and Bered. And Hagar bore Abram a son, and Abram called the name of his son, whom Hagar bore, Ishmael. Abram was eighty-six years old when Hagar bore Ishmael to Abram. (vv. 13–16).

Now we skip forward fourteen years to chapter 21. Abram and Sarai are now Abraham and Sarah. Here, the Lord's promise of a child born to them finally comes to pass:

> The LORD visited Sarah as he had said, and the LORD did to Sarah as he had promised. And Sarah conceived and bore Abraham a son in his old age at the time of which God had spoken to him. Abraham called the name of his son who was born to him, whom Sarah bore him, Isaac. And Abraham circumcised his son Isaac when he was eight days old, as God had commanded him. Abraham was a hundred years old when his son Isaac was born to him. And Sarah said, "God has made laughter for me; everyone who hears will laugh over me." And she said, "Who would have said to Abraham that Sarah would nurse children? Yet I have borne him a son in his old age." (vv. 1– 7)

Now, sad to say, we see the cycle of sin and poor choices continue to come back to bite Abraham and Sarah: "And the child grew and was weaned. And Abraham made a great feast on the day that Isaac was weaned. But Sarah saw the son of Hagar the Egyptian, whom she had borne to Abraham, laughing. So she said to Abraham, 'Cast out this slave woman with her son, for the son of this slave woman shall not be heir with my son Isaac'" (vv. 8–10).

Notice that when Sarai wanted to give Hagar to Abram, she referred to her as his "wife," but now in her bitterness, she referred to Hagar as "that slave woman." Sarah demanded that Abraham cast both Hagar and Ishmael out of the camp, out of the family, into the desert.

Understandably, Abraham was very upset: "And the thing was very displeasing to Abraham on account of his son. But God said to Abraham, 'Be not displeased because of the boy and because of your slave woman. Whatever Sarah says to you, do as she tells you, for through Isaac shall your offspring be named. And I will make a nation of the son of the slave woman also, because he is your offspring'" (vv. 11–13).

This command of the Lord to cast Ishmael out may seem harsh to many. But essentially what God was saying is that it would be through Isaac's lineage that the Lord's grand plan of redemption would be carried out. The salvation of all of God's creation was at stake. And as harsh as it may sound, Ishmael's happiness would need to be sacrificed for the greater good. Ultimately, it was Abraham's refusal to trust in the Lord's promise that was now bearing its painful fruit.

> So Abraham rose early in the morning and took bread and a skin of water and gave it to Hagar, putting it on her shoulder, along with the child, and sent her away. And she departed and wandered in the wilderness of Beersheba. When the water in the skin was gone, she put the child under one of the bushes. Then she went and sat down opposite him a good way off, about the distance of a bowshot, for she said, "Let me not look on the death of the child." And as she sat opposite him, she lifted up her voice and wept. (vv. 14–16)

So in a single day, Ishmael lost his home, his father, and his family. And if this were not bad enough, now even his mother had abandoned him, leaving him to die of dehydration.

Then the Lord intervened.

GOD HEARS THE CRY OF ISHMAEL

What happened next is a beautiful example of the character and nature of the God of the Bible. His loving actions fulfilled the prophetic name He had Himself given to Ishmael: "And God heard the voice of the boy, and the angel of God called to Hagar from heaven and said to her, 'What troubles you, Hagar? Fear not, for God has heard the voice of the boy where he is. Up! Lift up the boy, and hold him fast with your hand, for I will make him into a great nation'" (Genesis 21:17–18).

Once more, the Lord promised that He would make Ishmael into a great nation. The passage concludes with the Lord providing for Ishmael: "Then God opened her eyes, and she saw a well of water. And she went and filled the skin with water and gave the boy a drink. And God was with the boy, and he grew up. He lived in the wilderness and became an expert with the bow. He lived in the wilderness of Paran, and his mother took a wife for him from the land of Egypt" (vv. 19–21).

Now, it is easy to hear such stories and casually pass over them as simple Sunday School tales. But the fact of the matter is that this is a true story. This very traumatic event actually happened to a fourteen-year-old-boy. Try to imagine the shock that Ishmael went through. In a single day, he went from being a happy child with a family, a mother, a father, and an inheritance, to being alone in the desert, with no family, no father, no inheritance, and even abandoned by his mother, to die. He was utterly alone. Meanwhile, in Ishmael's mind, his baby brother was to blame; Isaac had stolen *everything*. He had usurped his father, his home, his birthright—his very life!

THE BIRTH OF ISLAM

I can't say that I fully understand the power of generational patterns of sin and bondage. I do know that the presence or absence of a father's blessing in a child's life is a powerful factor in his or her overall well-being. But if I were to guess how deeply these things impact a person, I would tend to think they only affect a few generations. But here in the story of Ishmael and his descendants, we have an amazing example of just how deep the wounds, the trauma, and the brokenness of one man can go. For approximately twenty-six hundred years after Ishmael's life and death, a direct descendant of his, named Muhammad, rose to become the "prophet" of a new religion called Islam. And what does the religion of Islam declare? Among its most central doctrines are the following:

- God is not a Father!

- God has no Son!

- Ishmael, not Isaac, is the heir of the Abrahamic promises!

It is easy to see the generational bitterness of Ishmael being channeled through Muhammad's teachings. Not surprisingly, Muhammad himself was also an orphan, having lost a few of his closest caregivers during his upbringing. So in Muhammad, Ishmael's resentment found a perfect conduit. From a spiritual sense, then, we may view Islam as the broken and bitter cry of Ishmael, the fatherless, the orphan, memorialized and canonized as a religion—the greatest antichristic religion the world has ever known.

THE DOCTRINES OF ISLAM: THE DOCTRINES OF ANTICHRIST

I understand that this is a very strong statement to make, to refer to another religion as espousing "the doctrines of *Antichrist*." But from the biblical definition of this term, this is entirely accurate. John the apostle defined the spirit of the Antichrist this way: "Who is the liar? It is the man who denies that Jesus is the Christ. Such a man is the antichrist–he denies the Father and the Son. No one who denies the Son has the Father; whoever acknowledges the Son has the Father also" (1 John 2:22–23).

Now, some people may say that Islam does not deny that Jesus is the Messiah/Christ, but this objection misses the point. While Islam does apply the title of Messiah (Arabic: *Masih*) to Jesus (the Qur'an mistakenly calls him "Isa"), it strips this term of all of its biblical meaning. According to Islamic belief, the term *Messiah* simply refers to one in a long line of prophets. The only factor that distinguishes Isa from other Muslim prophets is that he was born of a virgin. But as far as the messianic role as the divine deliverer, king, and savior of all who place their faith in Him, Islam absolutely denies all of these things. As missiologist Jeff Morton says, "Words are boxes that contain meanings." Simply because Islam gives Jesus the title Messiah doesn't mean that it affirms Him as *the* Messiah according to its biblical and accurate meaning. So it is entirely appropriate to say that in the truest sense, Islam denies that Jesus is the Messiah. But beyond this, Islam also clearly denies both the Father and the Son. Let's briefly consider what this means.

ISLAM DENIES THE FATHERHOOD OF GOD

According to Islamic doctrine, if Allah is compared to anything on the earth, this belittles him. As such, the Qur'an teaches that Allah is not a father (one who begetteth) and is certainly not a son (one who is begotten): "Say: He is Allah, the One! Allah, the eternally Besought of all! He begetteth not nor was begotten. And there is none comparable unto Him" (Surah 112:1–4).

Islam actually misunderstands the terms *father* and *son* with respect to Christian doctrine. The Bible doesn't use the term *begotten, father,* or *son* in a way that infers sexual reproduction; rather, each suggests special relationship. Thus, when the apostle John spoke of Jesus as "the only begotten of the Father" (John 1:14), he was conveying the unique deity of Jesus. Likewise, when the apostle Paul referred to Jesus as "the firstborn over all creation" (Col. 1:15), he was emphasizing the Messiah's preeminence or prime position as the Creator of all things. Although Islam fundamentally misunderstands what the Bible actually teaches concerning the fatherhood of God and the sonship of Jesus, in denying these things, Islam denies the most foundational and core doctrines of the Christian faith and affirms what John the apostle referred to as the doctrines of the Antichrist. This fact is undeniable. But beyond denying the fatherhood of God, Islam also very directly, and quite aggressively, denies that Jesus the Messiah is God's Son.

ISLAM DENIES THE SONSHIP OF JESUS THE MESSIAH

Following are two passages from the Qur'an that specifically deny the son-ship of Jesus. In this first passage, Christians are attacked as blasphemers: "They said, 'The Most Gracious has begotten a son'! You have uttered a gross blasphemy! The heavens are about to shatter, the earth is about to tear asunder, and the mountains are about to crumble because they claim that the Most Gracious has begotten a son. It is not befitting the Most Gracious that He should beget a son!" (Surah 19:88–92).

Next, we are equated to the pagans, upon whom Allah's curse rests: "The Christians call Christ the son of Allah. That is a saying from their mouth; in this they but imitate what the unbelievers of old used to say. Allah's curse be on them: how they are deluded away from the Truth!" (Surah 9:30).

It couldn't be any clearer. The Qur'an directly attacks the most foundational and most essential doctrines of biblical faith. In fact, it is even fair to say that the creed of Islam, known as the *shahada*, is the most antichristic creed known to mankind.

THE SHAHADA: THE CREED OF ANTICHRIST

If someone desires to convert to Islam, he recites the shahada. Throughout the Islamic world, the shahada, or Islam's creed, is declared regularly among Muslims. It is also the first pronouncement that every Muslim baby hears as the father whispers these words into his child's ears. In Arabic, the Shahada is transliterated as, "*La ilah ha il Allah, Muhammadan Rasul-Allah.*" The translation is "There is no god but Allah, and Muhammad is his final messenger." The first component of the creed states that the Allah of Islam is the only One True Supreme God. Not Yahweh, the name that every prophet throughout the Bible knew and used, but Allah, the god of Islam. The second component is that Muhammad, not Jesus, is the final messenger, or sent one, of Allah. Thus, in one very succinct declaration, Islam has managed to formulate a perfect antichristic confession.

ISLAM FORBIDS ADOPTION

In the midst of Islam's perfect manifestation of Ishmael's bitterness, its antichristic spirit, it is also not surprising that Islam forbids adoption. Muslims may raise another's child; in fact, they are even encouraged to do so if one has lost his or her parents, but the Qur'an specifically forbids Muslims from actually adopting any child. While Muslims may take another child under their roof, the child may never take on the family name. The Qur'anic proscription against adoption reads: "Nor has He made your adopted sons your [biological] sons. Such is only the manner of speech by your mouths. But Allah tells the Truth, and He shows the right Way. Call them by [the names of] their fathers; that is juster in the sight of Allah. But if you know not their father's names, call them your brothers in faith, or your trustees" (Surah 33:4–5).

According to Islamic doctrine, a child who is brought into a home can later grow up to marry the other children in the home, but he or she would never share in the family name or inheritance.

THE GOSPEL IS ADOPTION

This issue is particularly pressing to me personally, as my wife and I are deeply committed to the cause of adoption. This past year, we adopted a son and at the time of this writing are in the process of adopting another child. The experience has been truly miraculous and among the greatest blessings of our lives. In the overwhelming love that we feel for our son, we have also been able to catch a glimpse of the Father's love for us. But the beauty of my own personal relationship with God, whom I know as a Father, also saddens me when I consider that Muslims only look to Allah as a slave to a master. The distinction is captured eloquently by the apostle Paul: "For you did not receive the spirit of slavery to fall back into fear, but you have received the Spirit of adoption as sons, by whom we cry, 'Abba! Father!'" (Romans 8:15).

Before Jesus ascended to the Father, He promised His disciples that He would always be with them through the Holy Spirit, and would not leave them as orphans: "And I will ask the Father, and he will give you another Helper, to be with you forever, even the Spirit of truth, whom the world cannot receive, because it neither sees him nor knows him. You know him, for he dwells with you and will be in you. I will not leave you as orphans; I will come to you" (John 14:16–18).

The point here is essential to grasp. Throughout the earth there are more than 18.3 million orphans. When I see images of orphans sitting on the side of the road, say, in Uganda or Sudan, I think of my son. I think of his giant smile and his hilarious and high-energy personality. I imagine how I would feel if my son were alone, perhaps two or three years old, with no one in the world to go to for comfort, no one to turn to, no one to champion his cause. If my son were in this position, I would tear the world apart to get to him and rescue him. I wouldn't care how much money it cost. I would give away everything I own to rescue him. And if I couldn't get to him myself, I would tell all of my friends that if they were truly my friends, they would go in my place immediately. And yet I know that this is only a shadow of the kind of love that the Father has for every single, last orphan of the earth; all 18 million. The Father is burning with compassion, pleading with His people throughout the earth to go and save as many as we can. Of course, preaching this message to the Church is easy, because it involves innocent little defenseless children and adorable babies. It is easy for people to be moved by compassion for these little lost ones. But as much as the Lord is calling His people to go save the physical orphans of the earth, He is also burning for His people to go save Muslims, who in so many ways are the earth's spiritual orphans. Muslims are largely a people who are God-seekers. But they have been sold a false bill of goods. Their made-up god is a distant and absentee slave master who demands everything but gives nothing in return other than an eternity in hell. Muslims are "god-seekers," but they are utterly lost. They deny the Son and do not have the Father. And on top of all that, Muslims are the largest and most unreached people group in the world. The Lord is calling His people to give everything up in order to save the lost children of Ishmael.

OUR CHRISTIAN DUTY TOWARD MUSLIMS

In light of the understanding that we have gained by looking at part of Ishmael's story, I want to briefly list a few things that believers must do in their efforts to reach Muslims. The first is to speak the truth with boldness. Everything in this world is pushing believers to keep their opinions to themselves, to shut up. But if Islam results in multiple millions of Muslims being lost to hellfire, then it must forever be our enemy. Yes, God does have a Son. His name is Jesus, and "blessed are all who take refuge in Him" (Psalm 2:12). We can make no apologies for boldly speaking the truth. Love demands that we do so.

Second, believers must demonstrate the Father's amazing, unrelenting love to Muslims. The Islamic world is not a culture of the cross. As such, when the Church truly lives as the body of Messiah crucified, Muslims will be touched. And many will be changed forever.

Third, the praying Church must seize upon the prophetic promise that the Father has placed within Ishmael's name and cry out, "Father, once more, hear the cry of Ishmael! Do for his offspring what you have done for us. Open their eyes. Remove their blindness and reveal Jesus to them as the Son of God. Save a multitude of Muslims, O Father!"

And finally, love God's people the Jews. A sad but true reality is that many Muslims, even after becoming Christians, continue to maintain their anti-Semitism. The reason is simply because many churches espouse replacement theology[1] and various other theological ideas that reinforce anti-Semitism. I am going to be bold enough to say that if you find yourself in such a church, then go somewhere else. The Lord will not simply wink at such systemic anti-Semitism. And so, after having led Muslims to love the Father and to embrace Jesus as the divine Son of God, we must also make every effort in the discipleship process to teach them to become lovers of their brother, Isaac. Then and only then will the reconciliation process be complete and Abraham's family be restored.

I 9

THE MERCY OF THE LORD:

HOPE FOR INTERCESSORS

THROUGHOUT THIS BOOK, we've examined the numerous passages that show the Islamic nations surrounding Israel to be the primary nations that will fill the role of the coming Antichrist's empire. We also discussed how the widely held belief that the kingdom of the Antichrist will be completely universal does not square with Scripture. We learned, for instance, that some nations will escape the Antichrist's control. Other nations will be at war with the him until Jesus returns. By assessing all of the biblical data, we can conclude that the nations that will come under the most severe judgment on the Day of the Lord are the Islamic nations that surround the land of Israel. While there is no doubt that every last nation throughout the earth will undergo God's judgment, the nations that will be judged the most severely by the Messiah are those that are emphatically marked for judgment throughout the Scriptures. When people ask me which nations will join the Antichrist's alliance, I try to comment in a way that reflects the emphasis of Scripture. I simply say that "the head of the spear" of the coming antichristic empire will be the Islamic nations that surround Israel. Which nations will comprise the "shaft of the spear" is yet to be seen. It is unknown because beyond a list of nations from the Middle East and North Africa, the Bible does not tell us which nations will follow the Antichrist.

While this book's position is admittedly nontraditional, consider the widely held alternative, which sees every last nation on Earth following the Antichrist. This begs the question, when Jesus returns and executes judgment on the nations that are specified throughout the prophetic Scriptures, does He actually completely annihilate *everybody*? Does Jesus literally kill every man, woman, and child in all of the nations that He will judge? Although there are certain passages that seem to paint such a bleak picture, a fuller reading of Scriptures tells us otherwise. Jesus will execute judgment on the guilty, but He will clearly spare many from among the nations that He judges. Let's consider a few passages where this is seen.

ZECHARIAH 14

The prophet Zechariah wrote of "survivors" from among the nations that came against Jerusalem. These are nations that will follow the Antichrist in his assault against Israel. Yet during the millennial kingdom of the Messiah, survivors from among these very nations will go to Jerusalem to worship the Lord: "And it shall come to pass, that every one that is left of all the nations which came against Jerusalem shall even go up from year to year to worship the King, the LORD of hosts, and to keep the feast of tabernacles" (14:16).

ZEPHANIAH 3

In the prophecy of Zephaniah, the Lord calls out to the nations to repent of their idolatry and rejection of Him. Because of their unwillingness to repent, He will bring them to Jerusalem on the Day of the Lord, and pour out His wrath in order to humble them and lead them to repentance: "For my decision is to gather nations, to assemble kingdoms, to pour out upon them my indignation, all my burning anger; for in the fire of my jealousy all the earth shall be consumed. For at that time I will change the speech of the peoples to a pure speech, that all of them may call upon the name of the LORD and serve him with one accord" (3:8–9).

We must always remember that the ultimate purpose behind the Lord's harsh wrath against nations and people is to purify them and lead them to repentance. Here we see that even among the enemy nations that come against Jerusalem, the Lord deeply desires their repentance. In the end, they will become His worshippers, serving the Lord together with His people Israel.

ISAIAH 19

Isaiah 19, while expressed initially as a prophesy *against* Egypt, ends with some wonderful promises for the remnant of Egyptians who live during the messianic reign of Jesus. Verse 1 begins with the Messiah riding into Egypt to execute judgment: "The burden against Egypt. Behold, the LORD rides on a swift cloud, and will come into Egypt; the idols of Egypt will totter at His presence, and the heart of Egypt will melt in its midst."

From verses 2 to 21, we read of the many difficulties that will come to Egypt, from domination by a "cruel master" to a civil war to drought, famine, and economic collapse. But as the chapter concludes, we see that despite the Lord's harsh judgments against Egypt, during the messianic age Egypt will be considered one with Israel, His people.

> Then the LORD will be known to Egypt, and the Egyptians will know the LORD in that day, and will make sacrifice and offering; yes, they will make a vow to the LORD and perform it. And the LORD will strike Egypt, He will strike and heal it; they will return to the LORD, and He will be entreated by them and heal them. In that day there will be a highway from Egypt to Assyria, and the Assyrian will come into Egypt and the Egyptian into Assyria, and the Egyptians will serve with the Assyrians. In that day Israel will be one of three with Egypt and Assyria—a blessing in the midst of the land, whom the LORD of hosts shall bless, saying, "Blessed is Egypt My people, and Assyria the work of My hands, and Israel My inheritance." (vv. 22–25)

Despite the fact that the Lord will clearly "strike" Egypt, He will also "heal" it. These are promises that those who love Egypt can pray into today! Although the Lord's coming judgments against Egypt are sure, so also is His great mercy. As we consider the coming judgment against the greater Islamic world, believers must be very careful never to forget the Lord's burning desire to save a remnant from among the Muslim people for Himself and His glory. While we must acknowledge the repeated emphasis on the Islamic world for judgment throughout the Scriptures, our response to these things must not be to give ourselves over to passive fatalism. We must also never forget the Christian communities within these Islamic nations. The Church's response must be intercession! We must cry out for mercy, and give ourselves in prayer for the Islamic world, that the Lord would do for Muslims what He has done for us. We must pray that the grace we have been shown will likewise be revealed to Muslims, that their hearts will be softened, their eyes opened, and that there will be a great harvest from among the Muslims of the earth. I would even argue that this is one of the premier mandates of the Church today.

ISAIAH 60

Perhaps the most beautiful chapter in the Bible that speaks of the kingdom of the Messiah is Isaiah 60. In this chapter we find some very clear references to the people of the earth who will come and serve the Jewish people and their King in Israel.

The passage begins "Arise, shine; For your light has come! And the glory of the LORD is risen upon you. For behold, the darkness shall cover the earth, and deep darkness the people" (v. 1).

But then we see that the nations and foreign kings will be turned toward Israel, bringing their wealth as a peace offering: "But the LORD will arise over you, and His glory will be seen upon you. The Gentiles shall come to your light, and kings to the brightness of your rising . . . Then you shall see and become radiant, and your heart shall swell with joy; because the abundance of the sea shall be turned to you, the wealth of the Gentiles shall come to you" (vv. 2–5)

Then we are told specifically which nations will come:

> The multitude of camels shall cover your land, the dromedaries of Midian and Ephah; all those from Sheba shall come; they shall bring gold and incense, And they shall proclaim the praises of the LORD. All the flocks of Kedar shall be gathered together to you, The rams of Nebaioth shall minister to you; they shall ascend with acceptance on My altar, and I will glorify the house of My glory. (vv. 6–7).

The names Midian, Sheba, and Kedar point us to the modern-day region of Saudi Arabia all the way south to Yemen. Look at what the inhabitants of these nations will do: "Surely the coastlands shall wait for

Me; and the ships of Tarshish will come first, to bring your sons from afar, their silver and their gold with them, to the name of the LORD your God, and to the Holy One of Israel, because He has glorified you" (vv. 8–9).

The next verse could not be clearer regarding the rebuilding of Israel by foreign nations and their contribution to the beauty of Israel: "The sons of foreigners shall build up your walls, and their kings shall minister to you; for in My wrath I struck you, but in My favor I have had mercy on you" (v. 10).

The gates of Israel are specifically left open so the wealth and offerings of the surrounding nations can be brought into Jerusalem to honor both the Jewish people and their King, Jesus: "Therefore your gates shall be open continually; They shall not be shut day or night, that men may bring to you the wealth of the Gentiles, and their kings in procession. For the nation and kingdom which will not serve you shall perish, and those nations shall be utterly ruined" (vv. 11–12).

Earlier we examined Joel 3, which speaks of Tyre and Sidon, corresponding to modern-day Lebanon, being judged by Jesus on the Day of the Lord. But here we see that Lebanon will be among the nations that come to Israel, bringing gifts: "The glory of Lebanon shall come to you, the cypress, the pine, and the box tree together, to beautify the place of My sanctuary; and I will make the place of My feet glorious" (v. 13).

Despite the frequent language in many of the various Day of the Lord passages that at times seem to speak of total annihilation of the various surrounding nations, we see that many from these nations will clearly be spared, remaining alive and serving the Jewish people during the messianic kingdom:

> Also the sons of those who afflicted you shall come bowing to you, and *all those who despised you shall fall prostrate at the soles of your feet*; and they shall call you The City of the LORD, Zion of the Holy One of Israel. Whereas you have been forsaken and hated, so that no one went through you, I will make you an eternal excellence, a joy of many generations. You shall drink the milk of the Gentiles, and milk the breast of kings; you shall know that I, the LORD, am your Savior and your Redeemer, the Mighty One of Jacob. (vv. 14–16; emphasis added)

This prophetic promise is beautiful not only for the Jewish people, but also for the Muslim nations! Despite their abundant and relentless hatred toward His people, the Lord is kind enough to spare and deliver many Muslims and make them His own. One is reminded of the words of the apostle Paul, "Therefore consider the goodness and severity of God" (Romans 11:22).

In conclusion, then, on one hand, this book has emphasized that Jesus' most severe judgments will be leveled against a limited number of nations and only a certain number of people from these nations. To even some from among those who despise and attack Israel, mercy will be shown. On the other hand, the popular position held by many prophecy teachers sees Jesus returning to a world divided strictly between followers of Jesus and followers of the Antichrist. They also claim that when Jesus returns, every unbeliever will be immediately annihilated. As David Reagan says, at the return of Jesus, "He will proceed to judge all those still living, both Gentiles and Jews . . . The Saved will be allowed to enter the Millennium in the flesh. The Unsaved will be consigned to death and Hades."[1] Nathan Jones mirrors this sentiment. Speaking of what takes place immediately after Jesus' return, Jones says, "Satan will be cast into a pit, the Antichrist and False Prophet and most likely the demons will be sent to Hell, and the unbelievers to Torments [sic] in Hades."[2] Such a starkly pessimistic position, in my opinion, belittles the mercy of Jesus and is not in accordance with the Scriptures. We know that a multitude of unbelieving Jews will come to know Him after He returns (Ezekiel 39:22; Zechariah 12:10; Romans 11:26). The Scriptures are clear that gentile unbelievers will also come to know Him after He returns (Isaiah 60; Zechariah 14:16).

CONCLUSION

Upon whom, then, will Jesus have mercy? Whomever He chooses, but one thing is sure: we can trust His judgment. At the end of this age, the saints in heaven will sing of His justice and righteousness (Revelation 15:3), not His excessive severity or unfairness. While some prophecy teachers infer that the Scriptures give us every detail of every future event in a crystal clear fashion, this is far from true. But there is actually a beauty to the lack of clarity. While this may frustrate some who desire to possess absolute foreknowledge of the future, it is liberating to the intercessor who seeks only to cry out for a good, just, and perhaps even a surprising conclusion to many of these matters: "For He is gracious and merciful, slow to anger, and of great kindness; and He relents from doing harm. Who knows if He will turn and relent, and leave a blessing behind Him?" (Joel 3:13–14).

As the end of the age draws near, for those who love both Israel and the Muslim people, the cry on our lips must be in accordance with the prophet Habakkuk, who himself cried out, "O Lord, I have heard Your speech and was afraid; O Lord, revive Your work in the midst of the years! In the midst of the years make it known; in wrath remember mercy" (Habakkuk 3:2).

Amen and Amen.

RECOMMENDED RESOURCES

Block, Daniel L. *The Book of Ezekiel, Chapters 25–48 (New International Commentary on the Old Testament)*. Grand Rapids: Wm. B. Eerdmans, 1998.

Dershowitz Alan. *The Case Against Israel's Enemies: Exposing Jimmy Carter and Others Who Stand in the Way of Peace*. N.p.: Wiley, 2008.

———. *The Case for Israel*. N.p.: Wiley, 2003.

Gaebelein, Frank E., and Gleason L. Archer Jr., *The Expositor's Bible Commentary*, vol. 7: *Daniel and the Minor Prophets*. Grand Rapids: Zondervan, 1985.

Holman Bible Atlas: A Complete Guide to the Expansive Geography of Biblical History. Nashville: Holman, 1999.

Kaiser, Walter C., Jr. *Messiah in the Old Testament*. Grand Rapids: Zondervan, 1995.

Lifsey, Dalton. *The Controversy of Zion and the Time of Jacob's Trouble: The Final Suffering and Salvation of the Jewish People*. Tauranga, New Zealand: Maskilim Publishing, 2011.

Lingel, Joshua, Jeff Morton, and Bill Nikides. *Chrislam: How Missionaries Are Promoting an Islamized Gospel*. N.p.: I2Ministries, 2011.

Longman, Tremper, III, et al. *Jeremiah–Ezekiel (The Expositor's Bible Commentary)*. Grand Rapids: Zondervan, 2010.

Miller, Steven. *The New American Commentary*, vol. 18, *Daniel*. Nashville: Holman Reference, 1994.

Moody Atlas of the Bible. Chicago: Moody, 2009.

Motyer, J. Alec. *The Prophecy of Isaiah: An Introduction and Commentary*. Downers Grove, IL: IVP Academic, 1998.

Pawson, David. *The Challenge of Islam to Christians*. (London, Hodder & Stoughton, 2003).

———. *Come with Me through Isaiah*. N.p.: True Potential Publishing, 2011.

———. *Come with Me through Revelation*. N.p.: True Potential Publishing, 2008.

———. *Defending Christian Zionism*. N.p.: True Potential Publishing, 2008.

———. *Israel in the New Testament*, N.p.: rue Potential Publishing, 2009.

———. *When Jesus Returns*. London: Hodder & Stoughton, 2003.

Pentecost, J. Dwight. *Things to Come: A Study in Biblical Eschatology*. Grand Rapids: Zondervan, 1965.

Sliker, David. *End-Times Simplified: Preparing Your Heart for the Coming Storm*. Kansas City: Forerunner, 2005.

Steyn, Mark. *America Alone: The End of the World as We Know It*. Washington, D.C.: Regnery, 2008.

NOTES

CHAPTER 2

1. James E. Smith, *What the Bible Teaches about the Promised Messiah* (Nashville: Thomas Nelson, 1993), 38; Walter C. Kaiser Jr., *The Messiah in the Old Testament* (Grand Rapids: Zondervan, 1995) 38.
2. Robert Jamieson, Andrew Robert Fausset, and David Brown, commentary on Numbers 24, in *A Commentary, Critical and Explanatory, on the Old and New Testaments*, vol. 1 (Hartford: S. S. Scranton & Co., 1871), 113.
3. William Smith, *Dictionary of the Bible: Comprising Its Antiquities, Biography, Geography and Natural History*, vol. 4 (New York: Hurd and Houghton, 1870), 2991.
4. Jerome, commenting on Isaiah 25, in Jamieson, Fausset, and Brown, *A Commentary*.
5. Chuck Smith, "Obadiah & Jonah," The Word for Today, *Blue Letter Bible* (1 June 2005, 2011).
6. Thomas Ice, "Consistent Biblical Futurism Part 13," Pre-Trib Research Center, http://www.pre-trib.org/articles/view/consistent-biblical-futurism-part-13.
7. Ralph L. Smith, *Word Biblical Commentary*, vol. 32, *Micah–Malachi* (Waco: Word Books, 1984), 135.
8. Evangelical Statement on Israel/Palestine, in David Neff, "Evangelical Leaders Reiterate Call for Two-State Solution for Israel and Palestine," *Christianity Today*, November 28, 2007, http://www.christianitytoday.com/ct/2007/novemberweb-only/148-33.0.html.

CHAPTER 3

1. Thomas Ice, Kosovo and the Preparation of Europe, http://digitalcommons.liberty.edu/pre-trib_arch/73/.
2. David R. Reagan, "The Gentiles in Prophecy, Spent Glory or Future Empire?" http://www.lamblion.com/articles/articles_issues1.php.
3. John Walvoord, *Every Prophecy of the Bible* (Colorado Springs: Chariot Victor Publishing,1999), 274.

4. Finis Jennings Dake, *Revelation Expounded* (Lawrenceville, GA: 300, 303).

5. Abraham Mitrie Rihbany, *The Syrian Christ* (Boston and New York: Houghton Mifflin, 1916), 127.

6. Gleason L. Archer Jr. *The Expositors Bible Commentary*, vol. 7, *Daniel—Minor Prophets* (Grand Rapids: Zondervan, 1985), 93.

CHAPTER 4

1. Archer, *The Expositors Bible Commentary*, 147.

2. Smith, "Obadiah & Jonah."

CHAPTER 5

1. Stephen R. Miller, *Daniel: The New American Commentary: An Exegetical and Theological Exposition of Scripture* (Nashville: Broadman and Holman, 1994), 96.

2. John Walvoord, *Daniel: The Key to Prophetic Revelation* (Chicago: Moody, 1989), 68–69.

3. *Makor Rishon*, May 22, 1998.

4. "Jews Have No Connection to Jerusalem," Palestinian Media Watch, June 9, 2009, http://www.palwatch.org/main.aspx?fi=636&fld_id=636&doc_id=1105.

5. Martin Asser, "Israeli Anger Over Holy Site Work," BBC News, August 28, 2007, http://news.bbc.co.uk/2/hi/middle_east/6967457.stm; Hillel Fendel, "Archaeologists Issue Urgent Warnings against Temple Mountain Dig," August 30, 2007, http://www.freerepublic.com/focus/f-news/1889037/posts.

6. George Rawlinson, *Parthia* (New York: Cosimo, 2007), 313–14.

7. David R. Reagan, "The Muslim Antichrist Theory: An Evaluation," http://lamblion.com/articles/articles_islam6.php.

8. Walvoord, *Daniel*, 71–72.

9. *Moody Atlas of the Bible* (Chicago: Moody, 2009), 197.

10. Ibid., 204–5.

11. Ibid., 208.

12. *The Historical Atlas of Ancient Rome* (London: Mercury Books, 2005), 96–97.

CHAPTER 6

1. *Ancient Christian Commentary on the Scriptures*, vol. 13 (Downers Grove, IL: InterVarsity Press, 2008), 223, commentary on Daniel 7:4.

2. Walvoord, *Daniel*, 153.

3. *Ancient Christian Commentary*, 222, commentary on Daniel 7:4.

4. Ibid., 224, commentary on Daniel 7:5.

5. Archer, *Expositors Bible Commentary*, 93.

6. ArtScroll Tanach Series: *Ezekiel, a Commentary Anthologized from Talmudic, Midrashic and Rabbinic Sources* (Brooklyn, NY: Mesorah Publications, 1989), 582.

CHAPTER 7

1. Ron Rhodes, in an interview with Dr. David Reagan and Nathan Jones on their blog: http://www.lamblion.com/files/publications/blog/blog_QuickQA-Will-the-Antichrist-Come-From-the-Ottoman-Empire.pdf.
2. Tacitus, *The History*, New Ed ed., bk. 5.1, ed. Moses Hadas; transs. Alfred Church and William Brodribb (New York: Modern Library, 2003).
3. Flavius Josephus, *The Complete Works of Josephus, The Wars of the Jews or The History of the Destruction of Jerusalem*, bk. 3, chap. 1, par. 3.
4. Ibid., chap. 4, par. 2.
5. Lawrence J. F. Keppie, *Legions and Veterans: Roman Army Papers 1971–2000* (Franz Steiner Verlag, 2000), 116.
6. Antonio Santuosso, *Storming the Heavens: Soldiers, Emperors, and Civilians in the Roman Empire* (Westview Press, 2001), 97–98.
7. Sara Elise Phang, *Roman Military Service: Ideologies of Discipline in the Late Republic and Early Principate* (Cambridge: Cambridge University Press, 2008), 19.
8. Ibid., 57–58.
9. Ibid., 44.
10. Nigel Pollard, *Soldiers, Cities, and Civilians in Roman Syria* (University of Michigan Press, 2000), 114.
11. Ibid., 115.
12. Josephus, *Wars*, bk. 2, chap. 4, par. 2.
13. Pollard, *Soldiers*, 116.
14. Josephus, *Wars*, bk. 2, chap. 13, par. 7.
15. David R. Reagan, "Antichrist a Muslim? God's War on Terror," *Christ in Prophecy Journal*, January 12, 2009, http://www.lamblion.us/2009/01/antichrist-muslim-gods-war-on-terror.html.
16. http://eschatologytoday.blogspot.com/2010/02/another-nail-in-islamic-antichristal.html.
17. Radio interview with Bill Salus, author of *Israelestine: The Ancient Blueprints of the Future Middle East* (Crane, MO: Highway, 2008).
18. Josephus, *Wars*, bk. 6, chap. 4.
19. Ibid.
20. Ibid., bk. 5, chap. 13.

CHAPTER 8

1. Walvoord, *Daniel*, 182.
2. *Moody Atlas of the Bible*, 208–9.
3. Steven R. Miller, *Daniel, The New American Commentary: An Exegetical and Theological Exposition of Scripture* (Nashville: Broadman & Holman, 1994), 224.
4. *Ancient Christian Commentary on the Bible*, vol. 13, *Daniel and Ezekiel* (Westmont, IL: InterVarsity, 2009), 251.
5. Walvoord, *Every Prophecy of the Bible* (Colorado Springs: Cook Communications, 2004), 242.
6. Tim Lahaye and Ed Hindson, *The Popular Bible Prophecy Commentary* (Eugene, OR: Harvest House, 2007), 239.
7. H. C. Leupold, *Exposition of Daniel* (Grand Rapids: Baker, 1969), 361.
8. Archer, *The Expositors Bible Commentary*, 96.
9. Lahaye and Hindson, *The Popular Bible Prophecy Commentary*, 239.
10. Miller, 237.
11. Ibid., 242.

CHAPTER 9

1. *Ancient Christian Commentary on the Scriptures*, vol.13 (Downers Grove, 2008), 278.
2. Archer, *Expositors Bible Commentary*, 125.
3. Lahaye and Hindson, *The Popular Bible Prophecy Commentary*, 258.
4. Walvoord, *Daniel*, 248.
5. Steven R. Miller, *Daniel, The New American Commentary: An Exegetical and Theological Exposition of Scripture* (Nashville: Broadman & Holman, 1994), 286–87.
6. John C. Whitcomb, *Everyman's Bible Commentary* (Chicago: Moody Press, 1985), 148.
7. *Ancient Christian Commentary on the Scriptures*, vol.13 (Downers Grove, 2008), 298.
8. Walvoord, *Daniel*, 270.
9. Robert D. Culver, *Daniel and the Latter Days* (Chicago, Moody Press, 1977), 176.
10. Thomas Ice, "Ezekiel 38 and 39 Part XXVII," http://www.pre-trib.org/data/pdf/Ice-Ezekiel-3839Part271.pdf.
11. As quoted in Larry D. Harper, *The Antichrist* (Mequite, TX, Elijah Project, 1992), 35.
12. Lactantius, *Divine Institutes* 7:17, AD 307.
13. *Ancient Christian Commentary on the Scriptures*, vol.13 (Downers Grove, 2008), 301.
14. Archer, *Expositors Bible Commentary*, 147.
15. G. H. Lang, *The Histories and Prophecies of Daniel* (London: Paternoster, 1930), 158.
16. Edward J. Young, *The Prophecy of Daniel* (Grand Rapids: Wm. B. Eerdmans, 1949), 251.
17. Miller, *Daniel*, 309.
18. Geoffrey R. King, *Daniel: A Detailed Explanation of the Book* (Ilford UK: Midnight Cry, 1966), 235.
19. C. F. Keil, *Commentary on the Old Testament*, vol.9, *The Book of Daniel* (Peabody, MA: Hendrickson, 2006), 808.
20. Britt Gillette, "The Nationality of the Antichrist," *Rapture Ready* (blog), http://www.raptureready.com/featured/gillette/ac2.html.
21. Leon Wood, *A Commentary on Daniel* (Grand Rapids: Zondervan, 1963), 280–315.
22. Lahaye and Hindson, *The Popular Bible Prophecy Commentary*, 262.
23. John C. Whitcomb, *Everyman's*, 155.
24. Robert Duncan Culver, *Daniel and the Latter Days* (Chicago: Moody Press, 1977), 180.
25. Lahaye and Hindson, *The Popular Bible Prophecy Commentary*, 262.
26. J. Paul Tanner, "Daniel's 'King of the North': Do We Owe Russia an Apology?" *Journal of the Evangelical Theological Society* 35, no. 3 (September 1992): 315–28, http://www.etsjets.org/files/JETS-PDFs/35/35-3/JETS_35-3_315-328_Tanner.pdf.
27. Wood, *A Commentary on Daniel*, 308–9.
28. Hippolytus, *Treatise*, 25.
29. *Ancient Christian Commentary on the Scriptures*, vol.13 (Downers Grove, 2008), 301.
30. *Moody Atlas of the Bible*, 208–9.

CHAPTER 10

1. Arno Clemens Gaebelein, *The Prophet Daniel: A Key to the Visions and Prophecies of the Book of Daniel* (New York: Our Hope, 1911), 188.
2. Nathan Jones, "Quick Q&A: Will the Antichrist Come from the Ottoman Empire?" *Christ in Prophecy Journal*, http://www.lamblion.us/2010/08/quick-q-will-antichrist-come-from.html.
3. Max Blumenthal, "Pastor Hagee: The Antichrist Is Gay, 'Partially Jewish, as Was Adolph Hitler' (Paging Joe Lieberman!)," *Huffington Post*, June 2, 2008, http://www.huffingtonpost.com/max-blumenthal/pastor-hagee-the-antichri_b_104608.html.

4. Gaebelein, *The Prophet Daniel*, 188.

5. Walvoord, *Daniel*, 274.

6. Miller, *Daniel*, 307.

7. Philip Mauro, *The Seventy Weeks and the Great Tribulation* (Choteau, MT: Old Paths Publishing), 145.

8. Walvoord, *Daniel*, 276.

9. Lahaye and Hindson, *The Popular Bible Prophecy Commentary*, 261.

10. Walvoord, *Daniel*, 276.

11. *Theological Dictionary of the New Testament Abridged in One Volume* (Grand Rapids: W. B. Eerdmans, 2000), 948.

12. Fathi Yakan, "To Be a Muslim," http://www.youngmuslims.ca/online_library/books/to_be_a_muslim/part2/vii.htm.

13. Ibid.

CHAPTER 11

1. Jerome's Commentary on Daniel 7:8, translated by Gleason Archer (Grand Rapids: Baker Book House, 1958).

2. Young, *The Prophecy of Daniel*, 274.

3. Lahaye and Hindson, *The Popular Bible Prophecy Commentary*, 266

4. Steven R. Miller, *Daniel*, 320.

5. Chuck Smith, C2000 Commentary Series, Daniel 12.

6. Walvoord, *Daniel*, 294.

7. Matthew Henry, *Matthew Henry's Complete Commentary,* Daniel 12:9.

8. Lang, *The Histories and Prophecies of Daniel*, 181.

9. David Guzik, Study Guide for Daniel 12 Enduring Word.

10. *Books of Daniel, Ezra Nehemiah, A New Translation of the Text, Rashi and a Commentary Digest* (Judaica Press, 1980), 111.

CHAPTER 12

1. Robert L. Thomas, *Revelation 8–22 An Exegetical Commentary* (Chicago: Moody Press, 1995), 296.

2. Reagan, "The Muslim Antichrist Theory."

CHAPTER 13

1. John F. Walvoord, *The Return of the Lord* (Grand Rapids: Zondervan, 1979), 139–40.

2. Grant R. Jeffrey, *Armageddon: Appointment with Destiny* (Random House Digital), 1997.

3. Reagan, "The Muslim Antichrist Theory."

4. Hitchcock, *Who Is the Antichrist? Answering the Question Everyone Is Asking* (Eugene, OR: Harvest House, 2010), 87.

5. Jones, "Quick Q&A,"

6. Ibid.

7. Reagan, "The Muslim Antichrist Theory."

8. Ibid.

9. ArtScroll Tanach Series: *Ezekiel*, 578.

10. Targum of Pseudo-Jonathan on Numbers 11:26, in Samon H. Levey, *The Messiah; An Aramaic Interpretation: The Messianic Exegesis of the Targum* (New York: Ktav Publishing House, 1974), 17–18.

11. Fragment Targum, as quoted in Levey, *Messiah*, 16.

12. Mark Hitchcock, *The Coming Islamic Invasion of Israel* (Sister, OR: Multnomah Publishers, 2002), 87.

13. Ron Rhodes, *Northern Storm Rising* (Eugene, OR: Harvest House, 2008), 182–90.

14. This principle is articulated well by Angus and Green in J. Dwight Pentecost's classic work *Things to Come* (Grand Rapids, Zondervan, 1958): "When the precise timing of individual events was not revealed, the prophets describe them as continuous. They saw the future rather in space than in time; the whole therefore, appears foreshortened . . . They seem often to speak of future things as a common observer would describe the stars, grouping them as they appear, and not according to their true positions" (p. 46).

15. Ralph Alexander, *The Expositor's Bible Commentary, Jeremiah–Ezekiel* (Grand Rapids: Zondervan, 2010), 864.

16. Burton Coffman, *Commentaries on the Old and New Testament*, Ezekiel 38.

17. Keil, *Commentary on the Old Testament*, *Ezekiel*, 341.

18. Daniel Block, *The Book of Ezekiel, Chapters 25–48 (New International Commentary on the Old Testament)* (Grand Rapids: Wm. B. Eerdmans, 1998), 487.

19. David Reagan, "End-Time Wars – #2 The First War of Gog-Magog."

20. Block, *The Book of Ezekiel*, 482.

21. Keil, *Commentary on the Old Testament*, *Ezekiel*, 340.

22. Leslie C. Allen, *Word Biblical Commentary*, vol. 29, *Ezekiel 20–48* (Nashville: Thomas Nelson, 1990), 208.

23. Robert W. Jenson, *The Brazos Theological Commentary on the Bible: Ezekiel* (Grand Rapids: Brazos Press, 2009), 297.

24. Iain M. Duguid, *The NIV Application Commentary Ezekiel* (Grand Rapids: Zondervan, 1999), 462.

25. Matthew Henry, Commentary on Ezekiel 39.

26. *The New Unger's Bible Dictionary* (Chicago: Moody, 1988), 1028.

27. *The New International Encyclopedia of Bible Words* (Grand Rapids: Zondervan, 1999), 502.

CHAPTER 14

1. Charles Lee Feinberg, *The Prophecy of Ezekiel* (Chicago: Moody, 1984), 230–31.

2. G. K. Beale and Sean McDonough, *Commentary on the New Testament Use of the Old Testament: Revelation* (Grand Rapids: Baker, 2007), 1144.

3. Jenson, *The Brazos Theological Commentary on the Bible: Ezekiel*, 295.

4. Block, *The Book of Ezekiel*, 491–93.

5. Grant R. Osborne, *Baker Exegetical Commentary on The New Testament: Revelation* (Grand Rapids: Baker Academic, 2002), 687.

6. Thomas Ice, "Ezekiel 38 & 39, Part 28," http://www.pre-trib.org/articles/view/ezekiel-38-39-part-28. No longer accessible.

7. Arnold G. Fruchtenbaum, *The Footsteps of the Messiah: A Study of the Sequence of Prophetic Events*, rev. ed. (Tustin, CA: Ariel Ministries, 2003), 119.

8. Ibid.

9. Nathan E. Jones, "Timing Gog-Magog: When will Ezekiel 38–39 Be Fulfilled?" http://www.lamblion.com/articles/articles_tribulation2.php.

10. Some point to 2 Peter 3:7–10 as proof that the heavens and earth will be destroyed. These verses, however, do not speak of a literal destruction of creation, but rather it uses the language of destruction to point to the destruction of ungodliness in the age to come.

11. J. Alec Motyer, *Isaiah: The Prophecy of Isaiah: An Introduction & Commentary* (Downers Grove, IL:, InterVarsity Press, 1998), 145.

12. Ibid., 143.

13. Tracy Miller, ed., "Mapping the Global Muslim Population: A Report on the Size and Distribution of the World's Muslim Population," Pew Research Center, October 2009.

14. Stephen R. Miller, *Daniel: The New American Commentary Series* (Nashville: Broadman and Holman, 1994), 310–11.

CHAPTER 15

1. Henry, *Matthew Henry's Complete Commentary*, Ezekiel 38.

2. Wilhelm Gesenius, *A Hebrew and English Lexicon of the Old Testament, Including the Biblical Chaldee*, 955.

3. Flavius Josephus, *Antiquities of the Jews*, bk. 6, chap. 1.

4. K. Kristiansen, *Europe before History* (Cambridge: Cambridge University Press, 1998), 193.

5. Thomas Ice, "Ezekiel 38 and 39, part V," http://tinyurl.com/3qrcf93.

6. Herodotus 4.11, trans., G. Rawlinson.

7. Michael Kulikowski, author of *Rome's Gothic Wars from the Third Century to Alaric*, (Cambridge, Cambridge University Press, 2006) in an e-mail conversation with the author 10/25/2011.

8. Daniel I. Block, *The New International Commentary on the Old Testament: The Book of Ezekiel: Chapters 25–48*, vol. 2, (Grand Rapids: Wm. B. Eerdmans, 1998), 434.

9. *Zondervan Illustrated Bible Dictionary* (Grand Rapids: Zondervan, 2011), s.v., "Gog."

10. *The IVP Bible Background Commentary: Old Testament* (Downers Grove, IL: IVP Academic, 2000), 40, 723.

11. *The New Unger's Bible Dictionary*, rev. ed. (Chicago: Moody, 2006), 804.

12. *The Zondervan Illustrated Bible Backgrounds Commentary*, vol. 4 (Grand Rapids: Zondervan, 2009), 484.

13. *The Catholic Encyclopedia: An International Work of Reference on the Constitution, Doctrine, Discipline, and History of the Catholic Church* (New York: Robert Appleton, 1909), 628.

14. *Holman Bible Atlas: A Complete Guide to the Expansive Geography of Biblical History* (Nashville: Holman, 1999), 16.

15. *New Moody Atlas of the Bible* (Chicago: Moody, 2009), 91, 94.

16. Carl G. Rasmussen, *Zondervan Bible Atlas* (Grand Rapids: Zondervan, 2010), 83.

17. *The IVP Atlas of Bible History* (Downers Grove, IL: IVP Academic, 2006), 18.

18. Maimonides, *Hilchot Terumot*, chapter. 1. sect. 9.

19. Pliny, *Natural History*, chap. 23.

20. Sir Walter Raleigh, *The Works of Sir Walter Ralegh, The History of the World*, vol. 2, bk. 3 (Oxford: Oxford University Press, 1829), 264.

21. Hippolytus, *The Chronicon*, "The Sons of Japheth."

22. Ernst Wilhelm Hengstenberg, *The Prophecies of the Prophet Ezekiel* (Edinburgh: T & T Clark, 1869), 333.

23. Keil, *Commentary on the Old Testament*, vol. 9, 330.

24. Frederick Delitzsch, *Wo Lag Das Paradies, Eine Biblisch-Assyriologische Studie: Mit Zahlreichen Assyriologischen Beiträgen Zur Biblischen Länder- Und Völkerkunde Und Einer Karte Babyloniens* (Leipzig, J. C. Hnrichs'Sche Buchandleung, 1881), 256–57.

25. J. Simons, *The Geographical and Topographical Texts of the Old Testament* (Leiden: E. J. Brill, 1959), 81.

26. Clyde Billington, in e-mail conversation with the author, 10/28/2011.

27. Ibid.

28. Clyde Billington, "The Rosh People in Prophecy and History," *Michigan Theological Journal* 3, no. 2 (Fall 1992): 166–67.

29. Josephus, *Antiquities of the Jews*, bk. 1, chap. 6.

30. Vanessa B. Gorman, *Miletos, the Ornament of Ionia: History of the City to 400 BCE* (University of Michigan Press, 2001), 123.

31. Block, *The New International Commentary on the Old Testament*, 434–35.

32. Charles C. Ryrie, *The Ryrie Study Bible* (Chicago: Moody Press, 1978), 1285.

33. Dr. Merrill Unger, *Beyond the Crystal Ball* (Chicago: Moody Press, 1974), 81.

34. Edwin Yaumauchi, *Foes from the Northern Frontier* (Grand Rapids: Baker Book House, 1982), 243; "Meshech, Tubal, and Company: A Review Article," *Journal of the Evangelical Theological Society* 19 (1976).

35. Yaumauchi, *Foes*; "Meshech, Tubal and Company."

36. Alexander, *Expositors Bible Commentary on Ezekiel*, 854.

37. A. B. Davidson, *The Book of the Prophet Ezekiel* (Cambridge: Cambridge University Press, 1892), 275.

38. J. W. Weavers, *The New Century Bible Commentary on Ezekiel* (Grand Rapids: Eerdmans, 1982), 202.

39. Walther Zimmerli, *A Commentary on the Book of the Prophet Ezekiel Chapters 25–48* (Philadelphia: Fortress Press, 1969), 305.

40. Feinberg, *The Prophecy of Ezekiel*, 220.

41. D. R. W. Wood et al., eds., *New Bible Dictionary* (Downers Grove: Intervarsity Press, 1996), 434.

42. John Bright, *The Kingdom of God* (Nashville: Abingdon-Cokesbury Press, 1980), 164.

43. Block, *The New International Commentary on the Old Testament*, 434–35.

44. John Glynn, *Commentary and Reference Survey: A Comprehensive Guide to Biblical and Theological Resources* (Grand Rapids: Kregel, 2003), 167.

45. Billington, e-mail conversation with author.

46. *Holman Bible Atlas*, 36.

47. Adrian Curtis, *Oxford Bible Atlas* (Oxford University Press, 2009), 110–11.

48. *IVP New Bible Atlas* (Downers Grove, IL: IVP Academic, 1993), 84.

49. *The IVP Atlas of Bible History*, 18.

50. *New Moody Atlas of the Bible*, 92–93.

51. *Zondervan Atlas of the Bible*, 83.

52. *Zondervan Illustrated Bible Backgrounds Commentary: Isaiah, Jeremiah, Lamentations, Ezekiel, Daniel* (Grand Rapids: Zondervan, 2009), 464.

53. *The Macmillan Bible Atlas* (London, Websters New World, 1993), 15.

54. Charles Pfeifer, *Baker Bible Atlas* (Ada, MI: Baker Books, 2003), 36.

55. Block, *The New International Commentary on the Old Testament*, 436.

56. *Holman Bible Atlas*, 36.

57. *Oxford Bible Atlas*, 110–11.

58. *The IVP Atlas of Bible History*, 18.

59. *IVP New Bible Atlas*, 84.

60. *Macmillan Bible Atlas*, 15.

61. *Zondervan Atlas of the Bible*, 160.

62. *Zondervan Illustrated Bible Backgrounds Commentary*, 464, 484.

63. *New Moody Atlas of the Bible*, 92–93.

64. *Baker Bible Atlas*.

65. David R. Reagan, "*The Antichrist: Will He Be a Muslim?*" www.tinyurl.com/76kjq2; http://www.lamblion.com/articles/articles_islam4.php.

66. Billington, e-mail.
67. Joel Rosenberg, "What Is the War of Gog and Magog?" www.tinyurl.com/3q783jo; http://flashtrafficblog.wordpress.com/2011/05/09/what-is-the-war-of-gog-and-magog-part-one/.
68. Tanner, "Daniel's 'King of the North.'"
69. *Moody Atlas of the Bible*, 93.

CHAPTER 16

1. Marvin E. Tate, *Word Biblical Commentary: Psalms 51–100, vol. 20* (Dallas: Word Publishing, 2002), 345.
2. Ice, "Consistent Biblical Futurism."
3. Mark Hitchcock, *Middle East Burning* (Eugene, OR: Harvest House, 2012).
4. Ice, "Consistent Biblical Futurism."
5. Salus, *Israelestine*, 20.
6. *New Moody Atlas of the Bible*, 184.
7. Ice, "Consistent Biblical Futurism."
8. Salus, *Israelestine*, 6.
9. Ibid.

CHAPTER 17

1. F. Delitzsch, *Commentary on the Old Testament: Volume 7, The Book of Isaiah* (Peabody, MA: Hendrickson, 2006), 329–30.
2. Leslie C. Allen, *The New International Commentary on the Old Testament: The Books of Joel, Obadiah, Jonah, and Micah* (Grand Rapids: W. B. Eerdmans, 1976), 349.
3. *New Bible Commentary* (Downer's Grove, IVP Academic, 1994), 829.
4. Hippolytus, *On Christ and Antichrist,* 16.
5. Ibid., 57.
6. Victorinus, *Commentary on the Apocalypse,* chap. 7.
7. Lactantius, *Divine Institutes* 7:17, 307.
8. *Moody Atlas of the Bible*, 850.

CHAPTER 18

1. Replacement theology, simply defined, is the belief that God has replaced Israel (the Jews) as His chosen people with the body of Christ (the Church). The promises that once belonged to Israel, adherents say, are now the Church's, and theirs alone, since God has "divorced" Israel (another faulty theology, based on an out-of-context reading of Jeremiah 3:8).

CHAPTER 19

1. David Reagan, "The Promise of Victory," http://www.crosspointechurch.co/the-promise-of-victory.
2. Nathan Jones, "*The Battle of Gog and Magog—Unfolding,*" *Christ in Prophecy Journal*, April 27, 2010, www.lamblion.us/2010/04/gog-magog-battle-unfolding.html.

ABOUT THE AUTHOR

JOEL RICHARDSON is a husband, father, and an internationally recognized speaker. Joel has a long history of outreach to the Muslim community. He is the *New York Times* bestselling author of *The Islamic Antichrist*, coeditor of the pro–human rights collection *Why We Left Islam: Former Muslims Speak Out*, and coauthor of *God's War on Terror: Islam, Prophecy and the Bible*. Joel has been featured on or has written for numerous radio, television, and news outlets, including the *Glenn Beck Show*, the *G. Gordon Liddy Show*, the *Dennis Miller Show*, Chicago Public Radio, the *Steve Malzberg Show*, *Sid Roth's It's Supernatural*, *Jewish Voice Today*, the *New York Daily News*, WND, *FrontPage Magazine*, and many others.

INDEX

H

I

J

K

In *The Islamic Antichrist*, Richardson exposes Western readers to the traditions of Islam and predicts that the end times may not be far away. His book will stun readers unaware of the similarities between the Antichrist and the "Islamic Jesus." This is *the* book to read on the world's fastest growing religion and the future of the world.

"*A fascinating and provocative work. Bravo!*"
—ROBERT SPENCER, director of Jihadwatch

THE

ISLAMIC

ANTIC☾HRIST

The Shocking Truth about the Real Nature of the Beast

JOEL RICHARDSON

 WND BOOKS

WND Books • a WND Company • Washington, DC • www.wndbooks.com

Bestselling author Hal Lindsey explains how, on September 11, an ancient fight-to-the-death conflict exploded on the shores of the U.S. Though most Americans didn't realize it, we were already involved in this struggle. A struggle driven by a hatred that goes back over 4000 years.

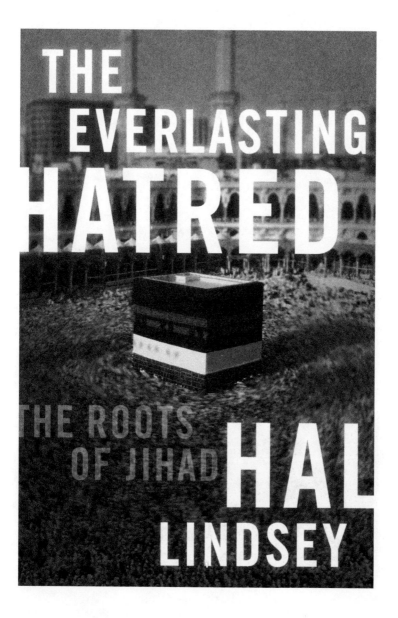

WND Books • a WND Company • Washington, DC • www.wndbooks.com

Written by an original thinker and innovative, tested, successful activist, *Stop Islamization of America* is a much-needed wake-up call about a sinister, subversive agenda that could do nothing less than destroy the United States - with unique instructions about how we can, and must, fight back now to defend our nation and our civilization.

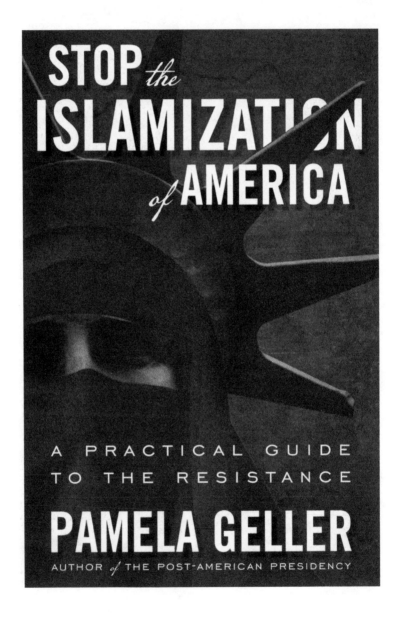

WND Books • a WND Company • Washington, DC • www.wndbooks.com

Follow intern Chris Gaubatz as he courageously gains the trust of CAIR's inner sanctum, working undercover as a devoted convert to Islam, and blows the whistle on the entire factory fueling the wave of homegrown terrorism now plaguing America.

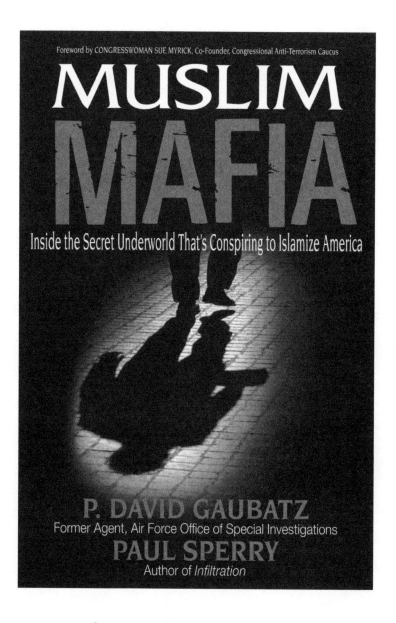

Foreword by CONGRESSWOMAN SUE MYRICK, Co-Founder, Congressional Anti-Terrorism Caucus

MUSLIM MAFIA

Inside the Secret Underworld That's Conspiring to Islamize America

P. DAVID GAUBATZ
Former Agent, Air Force Office of Special Investigations
PAUL SPERRY
Author of *Infiltration*

WND BOOKS

WND Books   •   a WND Company   •   Washington, DC   •   www.wndbooks.com